THE
PRE-ISLAMIC
MIDDLE EAST

THE
PRE-ISLAMIC
MIDDLE EAST

Martin Sicker

PRAEGER

Westport, Connecticut
London

Library of Congress Cataloging-in-Publication Data

Sicker, Martin.
   The pre-Islamic Middle East / Martin Sicker.
      p.   cm.
   Includes bibliographical references and index.
   ISBN 0–275–96890–1 (alk. paper)
      1. Middle East—History—To 622.   I. Title.
   DS62.2.S54 2000
   939′.4—dc21   99–054421

British Library Cataloguing in Publication Data is available.

Library of Congress Catalog Card Number: 99–054421
ISBN: 0–275–96890–1

First published in 2000

Praeger Publishers, 88 Post Road West, Westport, CT 06881
An imprint of Greenwood Publishing Group, Inc.
www.praeger.com

Printed in the United States of America

The paper used in this book complies with the
Permanent Paper Standard issued by the National
Information Standards Organization (Z39.48–1984).

10 9 8 7 6 5 4 3 2 1

Contents

Introduction

Throughout the second half of the twentieth century, our attention has been drawn repeatedly to the tumultuous events taking place in various parts of what has become known as the Middle East. The term, which clearly reflects a Eurocentric perspective, was coined at the beginning of the century by the American naval historian Alfred Thayer Mahan to designate the region centering on the Persian Gulf and stretching from Arabia to India. The area originally encompassed by the term reflected Mahan's particular strategic interest, one that was not necessarily shared by other writers on the history and foreign affairs of that part of the world, who assigned to the term a different content. As a result, there is no consensus regarding the precise delimitation of the territories that are included in the Middle East.

In this work, I consider the Middle East to consist of a core area surrounded by a peripheral region of intrinsic geopolitical and historical importance. The core area is composed of Iran, the Persian Gulf littoral, and the Fertile Crescent. Historian James Breasted coined the latter term early in the twentieth century to describe the arc of territory stretching from the Persian Gulf to Egypt. The crescent arches northward, encompassing the territory between the Tigris and Euphrates Rivers and circumscribing the perimeter of the Arabian Desert along the coastal region of the eastern Mediterranean, where it finally stretches south to Egypt. The Fertile Crescent thus includes the modern states of Iraq, Syria, Lebanon, Jordan, and Israel. In the east, the peripheral region includes Afghanistan and Transcaspia as far as the Syr Darya River; in the west, the Aegean and southern Balkan regions; in the north, Turkey, the southern littoral of the Black Sea, and the Caucasus region; and in the south, the Arabian Peninsula and the Horn of Africa.

Over the past several decades, the Middle East has become one of the most politically and economically important regions of the globe. Principally because of the rich petroleum resources it contains, although far from evenly distributed throughout the region, it has served until most recently as an arena for the clash of superpower interests and remains an area of primary economic importance for much of the industrialized world. Aside from its place on the global stage of international affairs, the region itself appears to be plagued with chronic internal instabilities and conflicts. It is widely acknowledged to be a veritable powder keg that is capable of erupting with great explosive force, as is amply demonstrated by the many wars that have taken place there since the end of World War II. Moreover, in terms of conventional non-nuclear weaponry, the Middle East is unquestionably the most heavily armed region in the entire world on a per capita basis.

The last two decades of the twentieth century have witnessed a seemingly endless series of conflicts in the region. A nine-year war between Iraq and Iran over domination of the Persian Gulf region was brought to an inconclusive end. This was followed by Iraq's unsuccessful attempt to assert its claim to hegemony in the Arab world with the invasion and conquest of Kuwait. Iraq also suppressed once more the age-old Kurdish yearning for national self-determination, this time by the use of internationally outlawed chemical weapons. The former Soviet Union withdrew its armies from Afghanistan after a prolonged bloody but indecisive attempt to impose its will on the country, leaving in its wake a civil war that is still ongoing at this writing. The decades long Greek-Turkish confrontation over Cyprus remains unresolved. Lebanon has recently come under the effective hegemony of Syria, which not only has its own expansionist ambitions there but also uses the country as an instrument in its ongoing low-level conflict with Israel. In the Caucasus, Armenian, Georgian, and other long-suppressed nationalisms have reemerged following the disintegration of the Soviet Union and are now testing the cohesion and stability of several states in the region. The current unresolved conflict between Armenia and Azerbaijan over control of the Nagorno-Karabakh area has the potential for involving Russia, Turkey, and Iran in a wider struggle, evoking recollections of the nineteenth-century conflicts in that volatile area. The disintegration of Yugoslavia and the struggle over the dismemberment of Bosnia threaten to trigger a series of Balkan wars that may draw in Turkey, Greece, Albania, Bulgaria, and possibly other countries, seriously undermining any potential for security and stability in the eastern Mediterranean.

Given this incomplete but nonetheless rather extensive list of current and prospective conflicts in the Middle East, it seems reasonable to ask whether these are idiosyncratic or endemic to the region. Are we witnessing an unrelated series of crises coincidentally taking place simultaneously in the Middle East, or are these events and circumstances consistent with a historic pattern that has characterized the area for centuries if not millennia? One of the tasks of this work is to provide some historical background for a reasonable response to this question.

It is a truism of modern thought that man, through the intelligent application of his rational faculty, is capable of imposing his will on many aspects of his environment. In the study of politics and international affairs, this notion is reflected in the appealing thesis that virtually every intranational or international conflict can be resolved peacefully by the conscious application of man's will and reason. What those inclined to accept the validity of this premise frequently ignore is the fact that a nation's control over its environment is at best a qualified one. It may be constrained by factors over which its leaders have little or no control, which in turn may limit the practicable options available to them. Indeed, such factors may effectively predispose their probable choices, and there is no assurance that objective reason will carry the day under any given set of circumstances.

The central thesis of this work is that there are a number of relatively constant environmental factors that have helped *condition*—not determine—the course of Middle Eastern political history from ancient times to the present. These factors, which are primarily but by no means exclusively geographic and topographic in nature, have contributed heavily to establishing the patterns of state development and interstate relations in the Middle East that have remained remarkably consistent throughout the troubled history of the region.

For example, this discussion of the region in antiquity will suggest that it was primarily because of fundamental geopolitical considerations that Egypt emerged as a unitary state dominating the Nile Valley, while the region in which Mesopotamian civilization flourished remained fragmented. Moreover, the very fact that Egypt, an African state, played a critical role in the history of the Middle East is also primarily the consequence of geopolitical factors that apply with the same force today as they did in remote antiquity.

Although a political map of the country will indicate that Egypt encompasses a substantial swath of territory, its sheer physical size has never constituted a significant component of its national power. This is because the commercial, political, and population centers of the country have always been concentrated in the relatively small Nile delta region. As a consequence, Egypt's leaders have perennially been challenged by the fact that, notwithstanding its apparent size, the country actually possesses little strategic depth in which to repel a land invasion from the northeast before the heart of the country is overrun. As will be amply demonstrated, Egypt has always been highly vulnerable to attack from Asia and has therefore consistently linked its security to its ability to dominate or at least control the territory of the African-Asian land bridge, that is, Palestine and Syria. Because of this perceived need, Egypt has been compelled to play a major role in Middle Eastern affairs throughout its long history.

When viewed geopolitically, it becomes evident that many of the contemporary political boundaries separating states in the Middle East often bear little relation to the geographical and topographical realities that have traditionally conditioned interstate relations in the region. For example, the drawing of Arabia's northern border across the peninsula from the Gulf of Aqaba to the Persian Gulf has little real geopolitical relevance because it is but an artificial line that was drawn by modern Western cartographers for particular extra-regional political purposes. The geopolitical reality is that the Arabian Desert extends northward into Syria almost as far as Aleppo. It is this fact that has made the Fertile Crescent, the arc of settlement that skirts the desert between Egypt and Mesopotamia, the primary stage on which the history of the core part of the Middle East has unfolded.

Another geopolitical factor of great importance in conditioning the political history of the region has been the location of the major trade routes that traversed it, which also constituted the primary military routes. Because much of the region is composed of either mountain or inhospitable desert, the number of such overland routes linking the Mediterranean and Black Seas to the interior of Asia was quite limited. Accordingly, much of the history of the Middle East concerns the struggle for control over those routes or the critical topographic bottlenecks through which they passed. Indeed, many of today's military and commercial highways and pipelines follow these same routes. The turbulent history of ancient Israel, as known to us from the Bible and other contemporary sources, may be understood in large measure as a direct consequence of its unfortunate geostrategic position. It straddled both the Via Maris and the King's Highway, the two major land routes linking Egypt and South Arabia to Syria and the rest of the Middle East. Moreover, until the advent of the revolutionary transportation technology of the twentieth century, a good part of Middle Eastern history revolved around possession of places little known today. The Cilician Gates, the Caucasian Gates, and the Caspian Gates, mountain passes that constituted the major gateways to the core and from the core to the periphery of the region, were of utmost geopolitical importance in earlier times.

In addition to geography and topography, religion has also played a major role in conditioning the pattern of Middle Eastern history. The ancient Greeks first introduced the politicization of religious belief into the region in the form of pan-Hellenism, which essentially sought to impose Greek forms of popular religion and culture on the indigenous peoples of the region as a means of solidifying Greek political control. This ultimately led to the institution of religious persecution as a state policy under the Seleucid king Antiochus IV, precipitating the first war of national-religious liberation under the leadership of the Hasmoneans in Palestine. Subsequently, the Persian Sassanid Empire adopted Zoroastrianism as the state religion, making it an instrument of state policy designed to unify the diverse peoples that lived within the imperial frontiers. Later, when Armenia adopted Christianity as the state religion, to be followed in this by the Roman Empire, religion became a fundamental ingredient in regional politics and has remained such ever since. But it was with the emergence of Islam that the conflation of geopolitics and religion reached its most extreme form and became the context for war and peace in the Middle East for more than a millennium.

It is my contention that such factors helped condition the circumstances of Middle Eastern history in the past and that they continue to do so today. Nonetheless, this book is not an argument for geopolitical, religious, or any other variety of historical determinism that would insist that the history of the region and its constituent elements could not have followed a different course. Politicians and generals can also be statesmen. But it would be naive to fail to recognize that the geopolitical and other factors conditioning political decision-making in the Middle East have usually tended to promote military solutions to political problems, and this remains true, for the most part, to this very day. This is not to suggest that future armed conflicts in the Middle East are inevitable. Indeed, it is within the realm of possibility that some of the current conflicts in the region may ultimately be resolved without further recourse to arms. However, a careful review of the political history of the region provides scant evidence of the sort that would encourage much optimism in this regard. Tragically, conflict resolution through war has always been the norm in the Middle East, with the peaceful settlement of disputes a welcome but rarely encountered exception. In other words, as is the case in other regions of the world as well, a decision in favor of war has most often represented the path of least political resistance, a decision for peace often encumbering far greater political risks for the decision-makers involved. This work will show that the political history of the pre-Islamic Middle East provides ample evidence of this. In any case, it is not the burden of this work to project the future but to recall and assess the past.

One of the serious difficulties encountered in the preparation of a book dealing with the geopolitics of any region in antiquity is the relative paucity of relevant reliable information, a problem that increases the farther back one attempts to go. Such ancient records as do exist generally contribute little to an understanding of why particular foreign affairs decisions were made, and are usually of far greater relevance to a history of the ancient world's internal political, economic, and cultural development, matters that are not the principal concern of this work.

The problem is particularly acute when examining the relations of certain ancient states because what information is available derives primarily from sources of dubious reliability. The histories of ancient Persia and Parthia are known to us almost entirely from Greek and Roman writers, while the history of Sassanid Persia must be constructed from a variety of not very sympathetic sources, some of which are obviously biased in their presentations. In other instances, the historical records are too meager to permit reasonable certainty with regard to the unfolding of events. Accordingly, parts of this book will necessarily involve some, hopefully, informed speculation on the part of the author as to the motive forces behind various political and strategic decisions.

In reconstructing the political history of the Middle East over a course of more than two millennia, I have attempted to convey to the reader a sense of the interaction of events taking place simultaneously throughout the region. In my view, this is crucial to a realistic appraisal of why certain critical decisions were made. For example, it is important to understand that Middle Eastern states throughout history have suffered from a chronic inability, with rare and occasionally notable exceptions, to conduct effective military campaigns on more than one front at a time. This is true, of course, for countries in many other parts of the world as well. However, that does not negate it as a factor of recurrent significance in the history of the region under examination here. The relative intensity of the Roman-Parthian or Roman-Sassanid confrontations, which took place over a period of more than 500 years in the region west of the Tigris River, can often be directly correlated to the prevailing security situation along the Persian frontier far to the northeast in Central Asia. When the Persian armies were preoccupied in the east, the likelihood of flare-ups along the Persian-Roman frontier increased significantly, even though it is not clear how information about the disposition of forces over a such a wide area was gathered and transmitted in time to be of practical use.

I have also tried to present the geopolitical history of the region in a manner that suggests the continual flow and interaction of events and circumstances, rather than in sharply differentiated segments which suggest that major historical thresholds had been crossed. In fact, few such milestones ever existed and I have found no evidence that those involved in the events thought otherwise.

In dealing with the long period of history covered in this book, it has been necessary to introduce the names of a large number of political leaders, many of whom may not be familiar to the nonspecialist. Wherever possible, the dates of their office have been included to assist the reader in maintaining a grasp on the time frame in which the events that they are concerned with took place. It should be noted, however, that there is considerable disagreement among scholars regarding the specific dates of events in ancient and early medieval times, in addition to numerous differences of opinion with regard to the correct names of persons and places. The secondary literature on the region also reflects wide variances in the transliteration of Egyptian, Mesopotamian, Persian, and Arabic names. As a result, some inconsistencies in the spelling of such names may be reflected in the pages that follow.

Reflecting on the motto "Past is Prologue," engraved in stone at the entrance of the National Archives in Washington, D.C., it is my hope that this volume will contribute to an appreciation of the contemporary significance of the long and complex geopolitical history of the Middle East.

1

The Middle East in Early Antiquity

The political history of the Middle East in antiquity is principally the story of the continuing struggle for control of the Fertile Crescent, the arching swath of territory circumscribing the Arabian Desert between Egypt and the lands of the Tigris and Euphrates Rivers that the Roman emperor Trajan named Mesopotamia. Over the centuries, the primary antagonists in this struggle were the rulers of Egypt and Mesopotamia. The prize for which they contended, for the most part, was domination of the trade routes of the eastern littoral of the Mediterranean Sea. These routes passed through the relatively narrow strip of territory stretching from the Egyptian frontier in the Sinai desert to the northern reaches of the Euphrates River in Asia Minor that constituted the land bridge between Africa and Asia. The histories of the lands contained within that geopolitical arena, which today are host to the states of Israel, Jordan, Lebanon, and Syria, were conditioned to a large extent by the prevailing state of the Egyptian-Mesopotamian struggle for regional supremacy.

As a consequence of its geopolitical role as a buffer zone between the major powers of antiquity, the people that settled along the narrow strip of territory were never permitted to evolve into a major political power in their own right. It was always in the interest of Egypt and Mesopotamia to keep the territory divided into numerous small states that would be dependent on one or the other of the major powers for their political survival. And, indeed, it was only during periods of stalemate between or internal disarray in Egypt and Mesopotamia that any formidable states arose in the land-bridge region, only to be suppressed or destroyed once the struggle between the major powers resumed. Because of this, the political history of the core region of the ancient Middle East can best be understood in terms of the political histories of Egypt and Mesopotamia, their relations with the peoples, nations, and states on their peripheries, and the competition between them for regional supremacy.

The patterns of political development in Egypt and Mesopotamia differed in significant ways. The Egyptians built their monumental civilization in the Nile Valley in relative isolation from the seemingly constant turmoil that characterized the region beyond the northern frontier. In Egypt, the circumstances of geography and climate effectively confined settlement to the banks of the Nile. Without significant rainfall, its agricultural economy was critically dependent on the regular annual flooding of the river. Beyond the Nile, Egypt was surrounded, and to a large extent protected, by desert on three sides. For most of its history, the country was organized and ruled as a single geopolitical unit, its urban centers playing a relatively minor political role. The capital was moved from one location to another according to the needs or wishes of the ruler at any particular time.

In Mesopotamia, by contrast, geography and topography conspired to create a rather different political environment. Without any significant natural barriers that could serve as defensible frontiers, the region was open to waves of migration and conquest from all directions. This was especially so with regard to the north, from where the mountain tribes and steppe-dwellers of Central Asia and Anatolia repeatedly poured across the Caucasus and Taurus Mountains to take advantage of the fertile lands to the south. As a consequence of these continuing challenges to the security of its lands and peoples, Mesopotamian civilization emerged and developed in and around fortified cities and towns that often became independent power centers, that is, city-states.

There were compelling military reasons for integrating the numerous city-states into a single powerful entity. Although the fortified cities could cope more or less well with the raids and incursions that plagued them, they were virtually helpless when confronted by the large-scale invasions that occurred every few centuries. Moreover, the individual cities were unable to assure the security of the trade routes upon which much of their commercial wealth depended. From remote antiquity onward, leaders arose in the region that recognized that it was fruitless for the individual cities to attempt to defend themselves from invasion by superior forces. Success in this regard required that the aggressor be confronted and defeated in the borderlands, not in the heart of the country. However, domination of the borderlands required a unified and centralized state that could muster the resources necessary to pursue such an expansionist policy, which was the only way the security of the interior could be assured. The cities of Mesopotamia thus clearly had need of strong central government, a need that was only rarely satisfied. The idea of local separatism and autonomy was so pervasive and entrenched that even in the case where a powerful ruler enforced unification, it would last only as long as his power lasted.

This kept the region perpetually embroiled in conflict, internally as well as with external forces.

This is not to suggest that Egypt was entirely free of such problems. It too had to confront challenges from the south and west, although rarely of the scope and intensity of those that afflicted Mesopotamia. Nonetheless, the rulers of Egypt were always quite concerned about maintaining the integrity of their frontiers against those peoples on its periphery who would have liked to share in the bounty of the rich lower Nile Valley. Accordingly, Egypt's early orientation toward Africa tended to keep it somewhat divorced from events transpiring elsewhere in the broader region beyond its northern frontier. There was, however, an ancient and important trade relationship between Egypt and the principalities of the eastern Mediterranean littoral that brought various woods and other materials to the country that would otherwise have been unavailable to it. Moreover, since its earliest days, Egypt had maintained maritime links with the states of southern Mesopotamia and the Persian Gulf region through the Wadi Hammamat. This dry river bed passage across eastern Egypt provided a practical link between the Nile Valley and the Red Sea, and thereby afforded access to the sea route to the Indian Ocean. This was perhaps the route originally followed by the prehistoric settlers of Upper Egypt who subsequently drove north down the Nile valley to conquer and fuse with Lower Egypt.

ARCHAIC EGYPT

The history of what has been called by scholars Archaic Egypt is, as one would expect, rather murky. It appears that during the early part of the fourth millennium B.C.E., the region known as Lower Egypt, that is, the Nile Delta and adjacent areas, was populated by a melange of peoples of diverse Mediterranean and Semitic-Libyan origin. These were organized in a kingdom the center of which was located at Buto in the delta. Upper Egypt, the region that begins immediately south of the First Cataract of the Nile, which was populated by Nubians and other people who may have originated from the Horn of Africa, was dominated by a kingdom centered at Hierakonpolis, between Luxor and Aswan. It was at about this time that Narmer-Menes (c. 3150–3125), pharaoh or king of Upper Egypt, succeeded in conquering the north or Lower Egypt. He fused the two regions into a single political entity, and inaugurated the First Dynasty (c. 3150–2925) of the unified state.[1] However, it was not until the sixth ruler of the dynasty, Den (c. 3050–2995), that the pharaoh assumed the title of *Insibiya*, king of Upper and Lower Egypt. It appears that it took a long time before northern Egypt reconciled itself to being dominated by the southerners, and there is evidence of civil conflict in the country over the next several centuries. Nonetheless, it was not until the close of the Second Dynasty that the capital was moved from Upper Egypt to Memphis, just south of the Nile Delta, to facilitate control of Lower Egypt.

From the beginning of the Archaic period, the rulers of Egypt relied heavily on the desert peoples of Nubia to the south to provide them with much of the conscript labor needed for their monumental construction projects. Nubians were also employed in the security forces used to maintain order in the country. Moreover, Egypt sought to maintain control over Nubia itself, which represented a major economic asset, having gold deposits in various locations in the desert as well as diorite quarries in the vicinity of Abu Simbel. As a result, from earliest times, Nubia was subjected to incursions and depredations that were the direct consequences of Egyptian self-aggrandizement. A similar desire to exploit the copper, turquoise, and malachite deposits in the western Sinai Peninsula led to repeated Egyptian expeditions into that region, engendering long-standing conflicts with the indigenous Bedouin tribes.

The centralized state founded by Narmer-Menes lasted until the latter part of the Fifth Dynasty (c. 2510–2460), when it seems to have disintegrated. Although it is virtually impossible to say with any confidence why this happened, at least one underlying cause appears to have its roots in the way the Egyptian state was organized. The country had been subdivided into a system of *nomes* or provinces administered by nomarchs or governors appointed by the pharaoh, to whom the land in its entirety was deemed to belong since he was considered the personification of the creator of the universe and therefore its rightful lord. The pharaoh of Egypt was in effect an autocrat upon whom the provincial officials were completely dependent for their office and perquisites. However, for reasons that are not known to us, during the Fifth Dynasty period the nomarchies were permitted to become hereditary. This not only weakened the direct link between the provincial governors and the pharaoh; it also eroded the allegiance to central authority that was essential for the nomarchs under the earlier arrangement. As a result, it was only a matter of time before the nomarchs achieved the degree of autonomy that enabled them to begin to challenge the authority of the pharaonic state. The erosion of central authority continued unabated and, during the reign of Djedkare-Isesi (c. 2470), for all practical purposes Egypt became transformed from a unitary into a feudatory state, with the traditional powers of the king increasingly being arrogated by the provincial nobles. This situation prevailed for the next several centuries, during which the central government became progressively weakened until it was virtually powerless beyond the confines of the capital.

This decline in power of the pharaonic state appears to have coincided with a brief period during the twenty-second century when the delta region was penetrated by an unidentified group of Asiatics. It is unclear, however, which of these two factors was cause and which effect. In either case, although the pharaohs of the period continued to reign at Memphis, their authority did not extend much beyond the city itself. The resulting power vacuum in the country was soon filled by the princes of Herakleopolis, the capital of a wealthy nomarchy in Middle Egypt, which established an independent kingdom there under the leadership of Akhtoy and his house. The Herakleopolite kings of the Ninth and Tenth Dynasties, who ruled much of Egypt for more than a century (c. 2160–2040), were eventually challenged by the princes of Thebes. Their competition for dominance in the country triggered a series of bloody civil wars that involved a number of the other nomarchs who aligned themselves with the principal contenders. The Thebans ultimately emerged victorious from the struggle and reconstituted a centralized Egyptian state (the "Middle Kingdom") under Mentuhotpe I (c. 2040–2009).

THE BEGINNINGS OF EGYPTIAN EXPANSIONISM

Since remote antiquity, Egypt had engaged in trade with virtually all the lands and peoples on its periphery. Its rulers do not appear to have harbored any serious imperial designs, although they were periodically engaged in military campaigns on all of Egypt's frontiers. As early as the Fifth Dynasty, expeditions were being sent across the Sinai into the territory that would later be called Palestine by the Romans, and during the Sixth Dynasty (c. 2460–2200) there is evidence of punitive campaigns being mounted against the "Sand-Dwellers" of the Isthmus of Suez. During this period, however, there were no attempts by the Egyptian rulers to establish a permanent presence in Palestine; the military expeditions to the area were primarily reprisals for raids mounted from Palestine against the delta region of the Nile. A similar situation prevailed along Egypt's western frontier with the peoples of the Libyan coast who continually sought to gain access to the wealth of the delta. As a result, there were sporadic wars over Libyan incursions as early as the Third Dynasty (c. 2700–2625).

Egypt's principal foreign interests during this early period lay to its south, where it sought to impose a sphere of influence over Nubia and the other lands of the upper Nile region, which were important to it from the standpoints of both trade and security. It is recorded that in the period of the Eleventh Dynasty (c. 2040–1991), a major expedition was undertaken to the Land of Punt on the Somali coast. It is noteworthy that instead of following the usual route to Punt, which was to proceed up the Nubian Nile valley and then cross over through Ethiopia, this expedition took the Wadi Hammamat route across the desert to the Red Sea coast. There the expedition boarded ships for the remainder of the trip. This suggests that, notwithstanding nominal Egyptian control over the country, it was no longer safe for caravans to use the land route through Nubia. Egypt's Nubian problem continued to plague its rulers over the centuries and, under the Twelfth Dynasty (c. 1991–1785), a more calculated imperialist policy began to take shape.

Although the principal motive for the decision to seek to extend permanent direct control over northern Nubia most probably was to be able to better regulate the flow of the Nile, on which Egypt's economy was critically dependent, there was also another consideration. The kings of Egypt had long had their eyes on the large quantities of gold that were to be found in the mines of the Nubian Desert. Starting with Ammenemes I (c. 1991–1962), and continuing with his successors, the pharaohs had great need for additional income to invest in renewal of the country's economic and cultural infrastructure, as well as in the organization and maintenance of a loyal standing army to supplement the traditional militias and troop levies. The dispatching of gold-seeking expeditions into Nubia became commonplace, and direct Egyptian control over parts of the country became a reality.

Under Sesostris I (c. 1962–1928), the area of the Third Cataract north of Dongola was brought under effective Egyptian control. But it was not until the reign of Sesostris III (c. 1878–1842) that northern Nubia was completely conquered and annexed to Egypt. Sesostris commemorated the event in a large stela that he had erected at the frontier fortress of Semneh, north of the Second Cataract. On it he declared: "Every son of mine who shall have preserved this frontier which my Majesty hath made is indeed my son. . . . But he who shall have abandoned it, he who shall not have fought for it, behold! he is no son of mine, he is none born of me."[2] The southern frontier of Egypt had been extended substantially at Nubian expense.

It was during the period of the Thirteenth and Fourteenth Dynasties (c. 1785–1633) that the centralized state in Egypt began to fray once again and then virtually disintegrated under a series of internal and external blows. This period is characterized by a large number of weak and ineffectual rulers who not only permitted the royal authority to be arrogated by local princes once more, but who also were unable to respond effectively to the major threat that confronted Egypt from across its northern frontier with Asia.

The subsequent invasion and conquest of the country from the north constituted a major turning point in Egyptian history. Prior to this event, the histories of Egypt and the rest of the Middle East followed virtually completely independent courses. While there had been trade with Asia for millennia, and there is some evidence of Egyptian dominance over southern Palestine in this early period, there does not appear to have been any significant Egyptian political involvement in Asian affairs. The invasion from Asia was to change all this radically. Ignoring political developments in Asia would henceforth no longer be a realistic option for Egypt. For good or ill, Egypt was forced to move from the periphery to the core of the Middle East.

EARLY MESOPOTAMIA

The recorded history of ancient Mesopotamia begins with the appearance of the Sumerians, a non-Semitic people of uncertain origin who, sometime during the fourth millennium B.C.E., conquered and settled the region where the Euphrates and Tigris Rivers empty into the Persian Gulf. (It should be borne in mind that at that time the gulf most likely extended inland a considerable way from its present shoreline. In other words, the confluence of the Tigris and Euphrates in the Shatt al-Arab, at a point well below the sites of Sumerian settlement, probably did not exist at the time.) There they established a number of settlements that eventually became fiercely independent city-states. Ur, Erech, Lagash, Umma, and city-states at other locations in the southernmost part of Mesopotamia were ruled by dynasties that contended with each other for regional power and domination. At the same time, the northern part of southern Mesopotamia was subjected to the successful influx of Semitic peoples who established significant settlements such as Kish in the area that would become known as Akkad. These same peoples also established settlements such as Mari and Ashur farther north along the Tigris and Euphrates Rivers, in the area of northern Mesopotamia that would later become known as Assyria.

The early political history of Mesopotamia can only be inferred by extrapolation from bits and pieces of not very reliable information uncovered by scholars thus far. The first recorded event of interest in Mesopotamian political history concerns the defeat of the Elamites, a people whose homeland lay east of the Tigris in southwestern Iran, at the hands of Etana, a predynastic ruler of the northern city-state of Kish. This ruler is described in the Sumerian King List as "he who stabilized all the lands," suggesting that his reach may have extended beyond Sumer to the neighboring territories as well, possibly making him the world's first imperialist.[3] Similarly, there is some literary evidence that about 2600 B.C.E. a great military leader and conqueror named Lugalannemundu, who was a king of the city-state of Adab, defeated a coalition of thirteen city-states arrayed against him. He also claimed to have established an empire that spanned most of the Fertile Crescent, from the Zagros Mountains to the Mediterranean.

Although this ancient empire does not appear to have outlasted its founder, it is not inconceivable that such an empire existed. It seems quite clear that rather extensive communications and commerce existed throughout the Fertile Crescent for millennia prior to this period. We now know of a rather sophisticated commercial treaty negotiated about 2500 B.C.E. between the imperial city-state of Ebla, in western Syria, and the city-state of Ashur, in Assyria.[4] There is also evidence that Ebla's political reach had extended to the kingdom of Mari on the Middle Euphrates, which was reduced to being a vassal state of the Eblaite king Ar-Ennum. However, with the consolidation of political power in Mesopotamia and its subsequent imperial expansion, Ebla, a land-bridge power, was soon wiped off the map.

At about the same time that Ebla reached the peak of its power, a powerful ruler named Mesilim arose in Kish and appears to have dominated most if not all of southern Mesopotamia, including Adab, and may have extended his conquests as far as Hamazi in northern Iran. It is known that he served as arbitrator of a bitter boundary dispute between Umma and Lagash, an issue that plagued relations between the two city-states for generations, suggesting that both city-states acknowledged Mesilim as their overlord.

During this same period, another powerful political-military figure named Ur-Nanshe took control of Lagash, founding a dynasty that held sway there for five generations, making it an important political power in southern Mesopotamia for more than a century. Lagash was located in a highly fertile area watered by irrigation canals feeding off the Shatt al-Gharraf, a channel linking the Tigris and the Euphrates. This not only ensured Lagash bountiful crops but also placed it in a position to dominate river-borne commerce in the region, further ensuring its material prosperity. The security of Lagash, however, depended upon its relations with the nearby city of Umma, which was located a little north of Lagash on the western bank of the Shatt al-Gharraf and was therefore in a position to interfere with Lagash's water supply. To protect the source of its wealth, Lagash went to war with its neighbor on a number of occasions. For reasons that are not known, but presumably are related to its experience with Umma, about 2500 B.C.E., Eannatum, the ruler of Lagash, initiated a campaign of conquest of the city-states of the region that brought Ur, Erech, and Umma into a centralized Sumerian state. Before long, Lagash expanded its imperial reach north to Kish, a principal city of Akkad with which it had a long-standing rivalry, as well as to the lands of the Elamites east of the Tigris. These lands were rich in timber, stone, iron, and horses, commodities not readily available in large quantities in Mesopotamia.

Lagash's success, however, also set the stage for its downfall. The substantial revenues derived from the taxes and tribute imposed on the conquered cities enriched Lagash, but also demoralized its officials and priests who evidently became corrupted by their growing wealth. As Eannatum's successors began to be challenged repeatedly by Umma and other conquered city-states, which refused to continue to pay the required tribute and took up arms to reassert their independence, the need for revenue to finance Lagash's wars with them drove the officials and priests to become oppressors of their own people, imposing heavy taxes on every aspect of their lives.

After several decades of such exactions, the domestic situation in Lagash became intolerable and ripe for insurrection. A usurper, Urukagina (c. 2400), seized control of the state, overthrew the ruling dynasty, and promulgated a series of reforms that alleviated many of the burdens placed on the common folk. For example, he decreed that "an appointed priest may no longer go into the garden of a villein [sic] and fell a tree or take away the fruits."[5] While the elimination of such abuses made Urukagina popular among the powerless, he further alienated the societal elite upon whom the security of the state was dependent, creating internal instabilities that made Lagash increasingly vulnerable to external enemies. Ultimately, Lugalzagesi (c. 2400), the ruler of neighboring Umma, mounted a successful surprise attack on the city, bringing the reign of Urukagina and the regional predominance of Lagash to a definitive end in a single stroke.

With the fall of Urukagina, Lugalzagesi became the preeminent political leader in southern Mesopotamia. Moving his capital from Umma to Erech, he proclaimed himself king of Sumer, and initiated a campaign of conquest along the Fertile Crescent that brought him as far as the Mediterranean coast in Syria or Amurru, the Land of the West. He memorialized his achievement with the exaggeration typical of ancient times. "When the god Enlil, king of the lands, had bestowed upon Lugalzaggisi [sic] the kingdom of the land, and had granted him success in the eyes of the land, and when his might had cast the lands down, and he had conquered them from the rising of the sun unto the setting of the same, at that time he made straight his path from the Lower Sea, from Euphrates and Tigris, unto the Upper Sea. From the rising of the sun unto the setting of the same has Enlil granted him dominion."[6]

Notwithstanding his impressive achievement abroad, neither Lugalzagesi nor his successors were able to consolidate their power within Mesopotamia sufficiently to actually integrate Sumer and Akkad into a single imperial state. As a result, before long a new and formidable challenge to Sumerian domination came from Sharrukin, also known as Sargon of Agade (c. 2334–2279), a former official of Ur-Zababa, the king of Kish whom he apparently overthrew in a palace coup. Conducting a successful military campaign against the Sumerian heartland, Sharrukin conquered both Ur and Erech. Suzerainty over southern Mesopotamia was now transferred from Erech and Sumer to Agade (the city built by Sharrukin) or Akkad, by which name the northern part of southern Mesopotamia became known.

Building upon the imperial base established by Lugalzagesi, Sharrukin subdued neighboring Elam, which occupied the Susiana plain in the lowland region of southwestern Iran, and extended Akkadian control over most of Syria, as far north as the Taurus Mountains in Anatolia. Faced by the same difficulty as his predecessors in stabilizing the region of his power base in Mesopotamia, Sharrukin and his dynasty adopted a policy designed to achieve a more effective and permanent centralization of the Akkadian state and the dissolution of local autonomies. This policy called for the destruction of the walls of the cities in Mesopotamia. The aim of the policy was to deny potential rebels any strongholds from which to assert independence from the central government. Sharrukin also initiated the policy of appointing only citizens of his own town of Agade to high position, a policy still pursued by some contemporary Middle Eastern leaders in the hope of assuring greater reliability and trust among key officials. For similar reasons, he instituted the practice of bringing members of the families of local rulers to the capital where they remained as hostages to ensure the loyalty of their cities, another policy still followed in some parts of the region.

Despite his having taken these prophylactic measures, Sharrukin spent the latter years of his reign contending with a general revolt, one consequence of which was the destruction of the city of Babylon. Moreover, both of his immediate successors found it necessary to re-conquer Elam, which was evidently resilient enough not to permit itself to be absorbed by Akkad. They also had to contend with the problem of reasserting Akkadian authority in a number of the principal city-states of Mesopotamia, which defected during the periods of uncertainty that accompanied the dynastic transitions.

The Akkadian Empire reached its zenith under Naram-Sin (c. 2254–2218) and his grandson Shargali-Sharri (c. 2217–2193). They extended the reach of Akkad as far north as Diyarbekir in eastern Anatolia and the land of Guti or Gutium in the Zagros Mountains in western Iran, and as far south as Magan in eastern Arabia or Oman. Under their rule, Akkadian commerce and trade reached from Cyprus in the west to India in the east. Naram-Sin and his successor styled themselves, with justification, as kings of the Four Quarters of the World. In a sense, the stability of the Akkadian state became a function of its capacity for imperial growth. As Henri Frankfort observed:

If pressure from the outside world could be relied upon to bring about national unity, Mesopotamia would no doubt have become a single state on the lines laid down by the kings of Akkad. For the country was at all times exposed to great dangers. Civilized and prosperous, but lacking national boundaries, it tempted mountaineers and steppe dwellers with the possibilities of easy loot. Raids could be dealt with by the cities, but the large-scale invasions, which recurred every few centuries, required a strong central government to be repelled. The safeguarding of the trade routes, too, went beyond the competence of individual cities. . . . The Akkadian kings thus undertook a task which occupied all succeeding rulers of the land. . . . From Sargon of Akkad on, kings knew that it was necessary to maintain a unified and centralized state; it was necessary to dominate the borderlands sufficiently to meet aggression there; in short, imperialism was the only guarantee of peace.[7]

It appears that, to a large extent, the Akkadian Empire was able to thrive during the period from Sharrukin to Shargali-Sharri because as a centralized state it was able to overpower its smaller independent neighbors one at a time. However, even during the reign of Naram-Sin those opposed to Akkad began to recognize the need to unify, even if only temporarily, in their mutual self-interest. There is some evidence to suggest that, at one point, Naram-Sin was confronted by a substantial coalition of opposing forces, which was able to defeat the Akkadians, encouraging defections by others still under nominal Akkadian suzerainty.

In the east, a general revolt broke out along the frontier from Elam north to the Little Zab River, in the lands of the Elamites, Kassites, Lullubi, and the Guti. Although the insurrection was suppressed by Naram-Sin, it proved to be but a harbinger of things to come. Kutik-Inshushinak, an Elamite governor appointed by the Akkadian ruler to maintain order in Susiana, became the focal point for a resurgence of Elamite power, and the death of Naram-Sin served as the signal for a new revolt. Kutik-Inshushinak proclaimed the independence of Elam and invaded Mesopotamia, reaching as far as the upper Diyala River before being stopped. Although he was driven back into Iran by Shargali-Sharri, this was accomplished only with great difficulty. As a result, Elam was able to maintain its independence of Akkad as the empire began to wither under a seemingly endless series of assaults.

Following the death of Shargali-Sharri, the empire quickly disintegrated as conquered peoples not only threw off the Akkadian yoke but some also, as occurred in the case of the Lullubi and the Guti, went on the offensive against their former rulers by attacking Akkad itself. Even within Mesopotamia proper the power and authority of the rulers of Akkad diminished progressively until they lost effective control of the country. For a while, the center of power shifted from Agade back to Erech, a clear indication of growing instability in the state. Before long, Akkad had declined to the point where the Gutians were able to descend from their mountainous lands east of the Little Zab and invade and take possession of the core remnants of the disintegrated Akkadian Empire, including Elam, which they dominated for much of the following century.

Although the Gutians were able to impose their will on Akkad, they were not sufficiently powerful to maintain effective control over Sumer as well. As a result, much of the southern region of Mesopotamia reverted to local autonomy. Lagash, which had been rebuilt during the period of relative prosperity under the dynasty of Agade, now went through a political revival and for a brief period extended its dominion to other cities of Sumer. During the tenure of Gudea (c. 2143–2124), Lagash also conducted an indecisive campaign against the continually problematic Elamites.

The dynasty established by the Gutians was eventually overthrown by a prince of Erech, Utukhegal (c. 2120–2114), who sought to re-impose the centralized system of government developed earlier under Naram-Sin. His policy in this regard was predicated on the presumed fealty of the local governors to the central authority in Erech. However, it took no more than a half dozen years for the fallacy of this approach to be fully demonstrated. The centralized regime, which was instituted by Utukhegal, was in effect consigned to oblivion by a powerful local governor, Ur-Nammu (c. 2113–2096) of Ur. The center of power in Mesopotamia now shifted away from Akkad and back to Sumer once more. The Third Dynasty of Ur would hold sway in Mesopotamia for the next century.

Shulgi (c. 2095–2048), who succeeded Ur-Nammu, sought to consolidate control of both southern and northern Mesopotamia, and referred to himself as the king of Sumer and Akkad. He spent much of his long reign campaigning in Elam and the Zagros region in an effort to reconstitute the empire of Naram-Sin. By the middle of Shulgi's tenure the region of Khuzistan in western Iran came under the control of Ur, as did Susa, the principal center of Elam. Over a period of years, Shulgi extended his sway over the highlands near Susa and other centers along the coast of southwestern Iran through the politically arranged marriages of his daughters to the local rulers. By the time of Shulgi's successor, Amar-Sin (c. 2047–2039), Khuzistan was incorporated as a province of Ur and efforts were being made to push the frontier even farther eastward. However, the tide began to turn against Ur during the reign of Shu-Sin (c. 2038–2030), as its position in Elam deteriorated.

The kingdom of Sumer and Akkad remained intact for another twenty-five years before it started coming apart at its seams because of external pressures. During the reign of Ibbi-Sin (c. 2029–2005), whole tribes of semi-nomadic Amorites from Amurru, or eastern Syria, began making significant armed incursions into the country, capturing and retaining one fortified town after another. The authority of Ibbi-Sin's regime came under challenge repeatedly as an increasing number of cities, starting with Eshnunna and Susa, ceased to acknowledge Ur's suzerainty. The region quickly reverted to the ancient Mesopotamian pattern of competing autonomous ministates. As a result, the kingdom of Sumer and Akkad was progressively reduced in size until it encompassed only the city and adjacent lands of Ur itself. To make matters worse, the conquest of the corn lands and the disruption of commerce by the Amorites created famine and hardship in some parts of Sumer, precipitating uprisings against Ibbi-Sin. The situation soon became critical as the Elamites took advantage of Ur's growing weakness and began to conduct devastating raids against it. Ur was unable to cope effectively with the combination of unrelenting pressures it was exposed to on both its eastern and western flanks, and soon succumbed to a new power that emerged in the region.

The kingdom of Shimashki, the exact location of which remains unknown but which may have been established in the vicinity of Khorammabad in western Iran, had recently imposed its rule on Susa and Elam, and had seized Khuzistan. It then mounted a crippling attack on Ur, which was defeated decisively. The city was sacked, and Ibbi-Sin was taken captive and brought to Anshan, east of Susa, a region he had himself once ravaged. With his death in exile the once glorious Third Dynasty of Ur came to an abrupt end.

The collapse of Ur created a power vacuum in the area that soon produced a variety of contenders for regional supremacy. For a time, the dominant position in southern Mesopotamia was assumed by the rulers of the city of Isin, located in the center of the country. During Ur's waning years of dominance, Ishbi-Erra (c. 2017–1985) of Isin had continued to recognize the nominal suzerainty of Ibbi-Sin. But as Ur's decline became increasingly evident, Ishbi-Erra asserted Isin's independence and soon extended the area under his control to the important religious center at Nippur, without which it would have been extremely difficult to claim preeminence in Mesopotamia. Partly because of his control of Nippur, Ishbi-Erra was able to gain acceptance of Isin's supremacy in the region stretching from Arrapha (modern Kirkuk) in the distant north to Dilmun (modern Bahrain) in the south. About eight years after the sack of Ur, he was able to expel the foreign garrison that remained in the city and establish his authority there as the legitimate successor to the Third Dynasty.

The hegemony of Isin over southern Mesopotamia lasted for several generations, during which some of its international prominence and trade were restored, and some outlying city-states east of the Tigris such as Der (modern Badrah) were subjugated. However, by the time of Ishme-Dagan (c. 1953–1935) the supremacy of Isin began to come under challenge internally within Mesopotamia, and from new waves of Amorite tribes emerging from the fringes of the desert to the west that poured across the Euphrates into the region of Akkad. The seminomadic Amorite chiefs who took control of the major towns settled there and declared themselves kings of the city-states such as Kish and Nippur that they conquered, thereby becoming a new and permanent political force in the region.

Far to the south, the city-state of Larsa, located on the Euphrates between Ur and Erech, was beginning to achieve prominence as a new political power within southern Mesopotamia. The political fragmentation of Isin's power that began during the reign of Ishme-Dagan intensified under his successor, Lipit-Ishtar, whose authority came under sustained assault by Gungunum (c. 1932–1906), the king of Larsa. Gungunum succeeded in establishing his rule over Ur, thereby giving Larsa effective control over commerce between Bahrain and Mesopotamia. His successors added Erech and Nippur to their sphere of control, making Larsa the dominant power in the south.

During this same period a new power was beginning to emerge in the area east of the Tigris, north of Akkad. About 1900, Ilushima of Assyria made an incursion into southern Mesopotamia in the course of which he took Der and appears to have driven the Amorite clans out of Ur and Nippur. The cities of Der and Ur were both very important to the economy of Assyria. Der served as a major transit point for caravans traveling along the trade route to Elam, and Ur was the principal seaport serving all of Mesopotamia. From their capital at Ashur, on the Tigris between the Little and Great Zab Rivers, the Assyrians also carried on an extensive trade with the states of Asia Minor.

Despite the prominence achieved by rulers such as Sargon I (c. 1860), Assyria's growing power soon went into temporary eclipse as a consequence of the influx of Hittites and other peoples into the area, population movements and armed incursions that disrupted existing trading patterns. Several decades later, however, Assyria came under the control of an Amorite chieftain, Shamshi-Adad (c. 1814–1782), who restored some of its earlier luster. He added the once powerful kingdom of Mari on the Middle Euphrates to the growing Assyrian Empire, thereby extending its sphere of dominance to almost all of northern Mesopotamia.

At about the same time, an Amorite chieftain named Sumu-Abum (c. 1894–1881) established a new kingdom centered in the ancient town of Babylon, a few miles from Kish, which he fortified and transformed into a major political force that eventually gave its name to the regions of Sumer and Akkad. From Babylon, Sumu-Abum set out to extend his control throughout Mesopotamia, initially subjugating a number of other northern cities such as Kish and Sippar. Babylon's expansionism, however, ran head-on into similar ambitions on the part of Larsa, and a long struggle broke out between them for regional supremacy. It took about a century of intermittent conflict before the issue was resolved in favor of Babylon.

During that long period, both Babylon and Larsa were frequently preoccupied with other concerns that related to their immediate neighbors. To the north and east of Babylon, a number of independent city-states, from Mari on the Middle Euphrates to the frontier of Elam on the Diyala, were striving to expand their own areas of control, and thereby posed a challenge to Babylon's imperialist aspirations. Larsa too was faced with some serious challenges to its regional hegemony. The dynasty established by Gungunum was brought to an abrupt end when Larsa was overrun temporarily by the armies of Kazallu and Mutiabal, which were subsequently defeated by a tribal leader named Kudur-Mabuk, who may have been an Elamite. He restored Larsa's power and established a new dynasty to rule it. Under Rim-Sin (c. 1822–1763), Larsa finally conquered Isin and became the preeminent power in all of Mesopotamia south of Babylon. This development was of particular importance. With the elimination of Isin as a buffer between Babylon and Larsa, the resolution of the conflict between the latter two states would make the victor the virtually undisputed master, for the first time, of a single kingdom that encompassed all of southern Mesopotamia, from Sippar to the Persian Gulf. This was to be achieved through both military and political means by Hammurabi (c. 1792–1750) of Babylon.

When Hammurabi ascended the throne of Babylon, Mesopotamia was still divided among a number of powerful city-states, including a number of Amorite states such as Qatanum and Yamhad (Aleppo) that had emerged in northern Syria. As recorded in a document recovered from the ancient archives at Mari, "There is no king who of himself is strongest. Ten or fifteen kings follow Hammurabi of Babylon, the same number follow Rim-Sin of Larsa, the same number follow Ibal-pi-El of Eshnunna, the same number follow Amut-pi-El of Qatanum, and twenty kings follow Yarim-Lin of Yamhad."[8] However, within a few years there would be a significant change in the situation. About 1763, Hammurabi overthrew Rim-Sin, unified Sumer and Akkad, and proceeded to defeat the remaining independent city-states of the region, including the "army which Elam had raised en masse—from the frontier of Maharshi, including Subartu, Gutium, Eshnunna, and Malgium."[9] These were absorbed into the new Amorite kingdom of Babylonia that dominated most of Mesopotamia. Hammurabi's singular accomplishment was the effective elimination of the independent city-state as a significant political entity in Mesopotamia.

Although some of Hammurabi's political achievements, such as his code of laws, had lasting impact on the cultural development of the Middle East, the results of his military campaigns barely outlasted his reign. The basic building blocks of the Babylonian Empire were the major city-states that he had managed to subjugate and force into a centralized state. However, he was unable to completely suppress their attempts to restore the earlier era of autonomous city-states. Upon the death of Hammurabi, a series of revolts took place that set a process of political disintegration in motion.

Compounding the problem of stability in Babylonia at the time, this was also a period that witnessed the significant migration of Indo-European tribes across the Caucasus into southwestern Asia, a movement of peoples that created a variety of pressures on existing local and interstate political arrangements. Early in the reign of Hammurabi's son and successor, Samsu-iluna (c. 1749–1712), his empire came under assault by the Kassites, who descended from the foothills of the Zagros and swept across the Elamite frontier into Babylonia. Although the intruders were eventually repulsed, they did succeed in conquering Ur and Erech, and continued to infiltrate into Babylonia throughout the following century. Toward the end of Samsu-iluna's tenure a revolt against his authority took place in the southernmost part of the country, in the marshes of the northern littoral of the Persian Gulf, that he was unable to suppress. As a result, around 1740 the rebels were able to establish an autonomous Dynasty of the Sealands that dominated the southern end of Babylonia for the next two centuries. By the end of Samsu-iluna's tumultuous reign, the imperial sway of Hammurabi's kingdom had been substantially reduced to its original territories of Sumer and Akkad.

Samsu-iluna's successors devoted much of their efforts to sustaining the kingdom through strengthening Babylonia's defenses in anticipation of further assaults from beyond its borders. Abi-eshuh (c. 1711–1684) fought off a Kassite attempt to seize the country, but was unable to prevent them from establishing a foothold at Hana on the Euphrates, 200 miles from Babylon. His three successors seem to have been engaged in almost continual war with the Sealands to the south in a desperate effort to maintain the territorial integrity of the country. Although the Babylonian rulers were able to persevere in this struggle, the cause of their ultimate defeat was to come unexpectedly from the far north.

NOTES

1. Some recent scholarship suggests that it was under the aegis of the north that the unification first took place. See Nicolas Grimal, *A History of Ancient Egypt*, pp. 34–35. Note—all dates given for Egypt are based on the chronology given in the appendix to Grimal's work. It should also be noted that these dates are sometimes difficult to reconcile with those given for Mesopotamian and Hittite reigns by other scholars.

2. H. R. Hall, *The Ancient History of the Near East*, p. 162.

3. Samuel N. Kramer, *The Sumerians: Their History, Culture, and Character*, pp. 43, 328.

4. For text of treaty, see Giovanni Pettinato, *Ebla: A New Look at History*, pp. 229–237.

5. H.W.F. Saggs, *The Greatness That Was Babylon*, p. 47.

6. Hall, *The Ancient History of the Near East*, p. 183.

7. Henri Frankfort, *The Birth of Civilization in the Near East*, p. 87.

8. Saggs, *The Greatness That Was Babylon*, p. 67.

9. Elizabeth Carter and Matthew W. Stolper, *Elam: Surveys of Political History and Archeology*, p. 30.

2

Egypt and Asia

Sometime in the eighteenth century B.C.E., the period is a matter of contention among scholars, Egypt suddenly found itself drawn into the tangle of events transpiring to the north, in Asia. According to the ancient Egyptian historian Manetho, as recorded by Josephus:

It came to pass, I know not how, that God was averse to us, and there came, after a surprising manner, men of ignoble birth out of the eastern parts, and had boldness enough to make an expedition into our country, and with ease subdued it by force, yet without our hazarding a battle with them. So when they had gotten those that governed us under their power, they afterwards burnt down our cities, and demolished the temples of the gods, and used all the inhabitants after a most barbarous manner. . . . At length they made one of themselves king, whose name was Salatis; he also lived at Memphis, and made both the upper and lower regions pay tribute, and left garrisons in places that were most proper for them. He chiefly aimed to secure the eastern parts, as foreseeing that the Assyrians, who had then the greatest power, would be desirous of that kingdom and invade them.[1]

It seems clear that Manetho was referring to the largely Amorite invasion that quickly overran the country. The Amorites, as noted in the preceding chapter, had invaded Mesopotamia and founded a thriving kingdom in Babylonia. Hammurabi, preeminent among its rulers, had managed to bring virtually the whole of Mesopotamia under his sway, making the Amorite period the most dynamic in the country's long history. At the same time, however, the migration of Indo-European tribes from Anatolia along with Indo-Aryans from Iran into the Fertile Crescent placed heavy pressures on the Amorites who had settled in northern Mesopotamia, pushing them westward into the mountains and coastal regions of Syria, Lebanon, and Palestine. These lands, for the most part, came under the dominion of three powerful Amorite city-states. The most prominent of these was Yamhad, centered on Aleppo, which dominated northern Syria and was paid a certain deference by Hammurabi as well as by Zimri-lim of Mari. Sitting astride some of the major regional trade routes, Yamhad served as a gateway for the commerce transiting from as far to the east as Iran and as far to the west as Cyprus and the Aegean. One of the kings of Yamhad, Yarim-lim, is reported to have had a fleet of 500 ships that plied the Euphrates, enabling him to intervene directly in Mesopotamian politics.

On Yamhad's southern frontier there was the city-state of Qatanum, located on the upper Orontes River in central Syria, which had direct access to the Mediterranean coast through the Eleutheros Valley (Nahr al-Kebir). Qatanum maintained generally good relations with nearby Mari on the Middle Euphrates River, and the two states occasionally undertook joint military ventures. Farther south, Hazor, which was strategically located in the upper Jordan valley, dominated southern Syria and northern Palestine and maintained trade relations with virtually all the major cities in the Fertile Crescent. In essence, Amorite power had become supreme in southwestern Asia from the Zagros Mountains to the frontiers of Egypt. It was therefore to be expected that Egypt would be viewed by the Amorites and the melange of peoples under their domination and influence as a tempting target for further expansion.

THE HYKSOS

The alien force that seized control of Egypt during the eighteenth century B.C.E. is presumed to have been composed primarily of Amorites, along with an admixture of members of a number of tribes of Asian origin. These became known disparagingly as the Hyksos, a corruption of the Egyptian term for "rulers of foreign lands." According to Manetho's version of events, the Hyksos invaded and conquered the country without confronting any serious opposition. It is possible to explain this surprising circumstance if one assumes that the Egyptians capitulated quickly because they felt overwhelmed by the new military technology employed by the invaders. The Hyksos made extensive use of the horse-drawn war chariot, a terrifying instrument of war common in Mesopotamia but still unknown in Egypt at the time. However, Manetho's account of the invasion is considered untrustworthy by some modern scholars who maintain that it is more likely that the Hyksos were really Amorites who had settled in Egypt earlier, and had then managed to take control of the country from within.[2] In any case, the ability of the Hyksos to establish their complete dominance over Lower Egypt in a relatively short period may have been due in part to the assistance rendered to them by kinsmen who had settled in the area of the eastern Nile Delta in earlier times.

There had been a significant influx of immigrant workers into Egypt from Asia during the reign of Ammenemes III, and such immigration from the north continued as a consequence of the large population movements that were taking place at the time in Mesopotamia and Anatolia. These immigrant peoples tended to settle in the region of the eastern delta, close to Egypt's Asian frontier. Before long, the communities of these immigrants began to coalesce and dominate the territories of their settlement. As a result, by the end of the Middle Kingdom period the center of indigenous Egyptian power was being forced southward once again.

Around 1720, the Hyksos took control of and then fortified the ancient eastern delta town of Avaris, situated on the Pelusiac arm of the Nile. This became their principal power base from which they gradually extended their control over northern Egypt, a process that took about half a century. The ability of the Hyksos to take over the country without serious opposition may also be attributed in part to their tendency not to try to impose an Amorite social and political order on the indigenous populations that they conquered. Instead, they appear to have adopted Egyptian mores and institutions.

The Hyksos ruled Lower Egypt directly from the ancient capital at Memphis, but were evidently concerned about the increasing vulnerability of their position there as they pushed farther up the Nile Valley toward the territory that was under the control of the hostile princes of Thebes. The latter had never acknowledged the legitimacy of the regime imposed on the country by the invaders and never abandoned their own claims to Lower Egypt. Because they were unable to extend and consolidate their control over Upper Egypt, the Hyksos sought to establish alliances with the rulers of Nubia, outflanking and effectively neutralizing the Theban state. They accomplished this by seizing control of the trade routes through the desert to Nubia that permitted them to bypass the territory under Theban domination. Such alliances between the Hyksos and the Nubian kingdoms of Kush and Kerma prevailed until the end of the Hyksos period.

Although the Hyksos and the rulers of Thebes were generally at peace throughout the period, tensions between them continued to mount and were to erupt into open conflict in the late seventeenth century. Sometime during the reign of Inyotef VII in Thebes (c. 1620) the relationship with the Hyksos underwent a significant change. At about this time, the Hyksos king Apophis I began to be identified as the "King of Upper and Lower Egypt," suggesting that the status of the rulers of Thebes had changed from that of independent princes to vassals. The Hyksos now effectively dominated all of Egypt from the Mediterranean as far south as Elephantine. However, it seems ironic that at a time when they finally achieved their long-standing goal of bringing all of Egypt under their dominion the Hyksos should enter a period of rapid decline.

It is uncertain whether the Hyksos maintained any contacts with the Amorite kingdoms to the north. However, with the collapse of the powerful Amorite state in Babylonia, under the pressure of the sudden outburst of the Hittites from Anatolia, Amorite power along the entire Fertile Crescent appears to have disintegrated within a relatively brief period. This also seems to have occurred to the Hyksos. Once wielding great power, they now appeared to have lost the martial spirit that enabled them to defeat the Egyptians and seize and control the country in the first place.

The reaction to these developments in Upper Egypt was to kindle an insurrection against Hyksos rule. Senakhtenre Ta'a I (c. 1630–1605) repudiated the status of vassal, assumed the dignity of an independent king of Thebes, and initiated what was to be a long campaign to drive the Hyksos out of Egypt that was intensified under his successor Seqenenre Ta'a II (c. 1605–1580). According to a description of the situation in a document of the period, "the land of Egypt was in distress. There was no Lord . . . or King of the time. However, it happened that, as for King Seqenenre . . . he was Ruler . . . of the Southern City. Distress was in the town of the Asiatics, for Prince Apophis . . . was in Avaris, and the entire land was subject to him with their dues."[3] Nonetheless, it was not until Kamose (c. 1579–1571) succeeded to the Theban throne that the southern insurgency began to seriously threaten continued Hyksos rule in the country.

During the early years of Kamose's reign, the area under the control of Thebes extended as far south as Elephantine, near the First Cataract, and reached north to Cusae on the fringe of the Nile delta region. However, Kamose seems to have been prevented from making any further advances against the Hyksos in Lower Egypt because of the increasingly tenuous security situation that he faced on his own southern frontier.

The Nubian kingdom of Kush, which had always been an unstable region on Egypt's southern frontier and consequently a thorn in the side of successive Egyptian rulers, was in the hands of a prince allied to the Hyksos. This appeared to leave Kamose with few practical options, and with a great deal of frustration. He wanted to move against the Hyksos and was disturbed by his inability to do so. He is reported to have complained to his counselors: "To what purpose is my power, when one prince is in Avaris and the other in Kush [the Sudan]? I sit [here] linked with an Asiatic [on one side] and a Negro [on the other], while every man holds his own slice of Egypt. . . . My desire is to deliver Egypt, and to strike at the Asiatics."[4] However, his advisers urged caution. They were deeply concerned about the risks of a two-front war, and had doubts about the Egyptian ability to prevail in battle under such circumstances. Kamose, perhaps with more audacity than good judgment, put together an army made up primarily of Nubian mercenaries and launched a war of liberation. He soon confronted a Hyksos force at Nefrusi, north of Hermopolis, and emerged victorious from the battle. Although the Hyksos were still far from being defeated decisively, Kamose was sufficiently buoyed by his success to intensify and widen the conflict. He built a fleet of ships to enable his forces to harass the enemy deep in the delta region and eventually to pose a direct threat to the Hyksos main base at Avaris.

The Hyksos king Apophis (c. 1615–1575) became concerned about his apparently increasing vulnerability to attack and sent a message to his Nubian ally calling for the two-front campaign that Kamose's counselors so feared. He wrote: "Greetings to my son, the ruler of Kush. Why do you act there as ruler without letting me know whether you see what Egypt has done to me, how its ruler, Kamose, has set upon me on my own soil (though I have not attacked him)? He has chosen to ruin these two lands, my land and yours, and he has already devastated them. Come north, therefore; be not timid. He is here in my vicinity. There is none who can stand against you in this part of Egypt. Behold, I will give him no repose until you have arrived. And then we two shall divide up the towns of Egypt."[5] Unfortunately for Apophis, his message was intercepted by the Thebans and never reached his ally.

Without further concern about a coordinated attack on his rear, Kamose was able to prosecute the war against the Hyksos more freely, taking Memphis in about 1579. This forced the Hyksos to retreat to their bastion at Avaris, with Kamose in hot pursuit. But he was unable to penetrate the elaborate defenses that the Hyksos had prepared for the city. This led to a stalemate for the next twenty-five years, until Ahmose (c. 1552–1526) mounted the Theban throne and assumed leadership of the war effort. Under Ahmose's leadership, Hyksos domination of the Nile Delta was finally shattered. He eventually succeeded in breaking through the defenses at Avaris, forcing the Hyksos to relinquish their grip on Lower Egypt and to withdraw into southern Palestine.

Ahmose was determined to eliminate any future threat from the retreating Hyksos, and he pursued them into Palestine. His strategic goal appears to have been to secure the land approaches to Egypt from Asia. After a three-year siege, the Amorite fortress at Sharuhen (Tel Far'ah according to some scholars) on the Mediterranean coast near Gaza fell to the Egyptians. As a result, Ahmose was now in control of southern Palestine and the important trade routes that traversed the country.

Emboldened by his initial military successes, Ahmose became determined to keep up the expansionist momentum while consolidating his control over his fractious domestic opposition. His highest priority and greatest opportunity lay to the south where he sought to stabilize the frontier by subduing the perpetually troublesome Nubians. As recorded by a contemporary, Ahmose of Elkab, "after his majesty had killed the Asiatics, then he sailed southward to Khenti-hen-nefer, to destroy the Nubian nomads."[6] A move to the north seemed premature since it would have brought him into collision with the expanding Hurrian kingdom of Mitanni that was extending its reach from its base in the Zagros Mountains in the east to the Mediterranean in the west. At the time, Mitanni, which emerged as a major regional power in the wake of Amorite decline, was still the dominant state of northern Mesopotamia, the Jazirah. Mitanni's suzerainty was acknowledged by Assyria, and Egypt was in no position to challenge its hegemony in Syria. Ahmose's successor, Amenophis I (c. 1526–1506), similarly confined his expansionist ambitions to Africa, and undertook a series of campaigns along the Libyan frontier, repulsing the Berber tribesmen who had captured parts of the western delta region. According to Ahmose of Elkab, Amenophis was also challenged by a Nubian insurrection, and marched "southward to Kush in order to extend the boundaries of Egypt."[7] In fact, he pushed the Egyptian frontier up the Nile as far as the Third Cataract.

Nonetheless, the rulers of the Eighteenth Dynasty (c. 1552–1295) that was established by Ahmose were keenly aware that the greatest threat to the security of Egypt was from the volatile north. It was clear to them that it was essential that Egypt extend its military control to the African-Asian land bridge, that is, Palestine, Phoenicia, and Syria. Moreover, it was essential for Egypt to develop a navy that would be able to secure its coasts from a maritime invasion that might originate from Asia Minor, Phoenicia, Cyprus, or Crete. The pursuit of such far-reaching aims required a fundamental reorientation of Egyptian policy from its traditional focus on trade to geopolitics.

THE EGYPTIAN THRUST INTO ASIA

Under these expansion-oriented rulers, Egypt became transformed into an essentially militarist and imperialist state. After a lull of some thirty years during which primary attention was given to assuring internal peace in the country, Thutmosis I (c. 1506–1493) evidently concluded that Egypt was now strong enough to break out of its essentially self-imposed constraints and to begin expanding its frontiers in all directions. He subjugated Nubia and the lower Sudan, and moved the Egyptian frontier southward to a point just below the Fourth Cataract. He then took advantage of Mitanni's preoccupation at the time with the deadly challenge posed to it by the Hittites, and seized the opportunity to thrust northward into Syria, which he subjugated from the Mediterranean coast as far to the east as the Euphrates. He was able to return to his capital at Thebes loaded with tribute and the spoils of war.

However, Thutmosis did not succeed in decisively defeating Mitanni, a failure that was to contribute to continuing insecurity on the Egyptian Empire's northern flank, nor did he consolidate his control over the territories he conquered. As a result, no sooner did he withdraw his army from them than the territories reverted to their previous status, effectively wiping out whatever gains Thutmosis had achieved by force of arms.

During the reign of his successor, Thutmosis II (c. 1493–1479), another revolt against Egyptian domination erupted in Nubia and the region had to be pacified once again. In general, he continued the expansionist policies of his predecessors. He was succeeded by his consort Hatshepsut (c. 1478–1458), who initially ruled Egypt as regent for her infant stepson but ultimately usurped the throne for herself.

Hatshepsut is considered by many historians of the period to have deviated sharply from past precedent and to have pursued a peace policy in Egypt's foreign affairs for two decades. It is presumed that she required such a lull in order to devote herself to a major domestic construction program. This view is disputed by some modern scholars who suggest that she too followed the same basic foreign policy as her predecessors, but that the records of Hatshepsut's reign were tampered with so as not to detract from the importance of her more illustrious successor.[8] There appears to be some evidence that she personally led one campaign against the Nubians, and that at least three others in Africa and Asia were carried out during her reign. In any case, the period of her tenure appears to have witnessed erosion of Egyptian prestige among the states and peoples that had been subjugated and to have provided an opportunity for those who chafed under Egyptian domination to prepare for a struggle for liberation.

With the death of Hatshepsut and the succession of the now twenty-two-year-old Thutmosis III (c. 1458–1425),[9] the rulers of the numerous small principalities of Syria, aided and abetted by the remnants of the Hyksos, joined forces under the leadership of the king of Kadesh and revolted against Egyptian hegemony. Underlying the revolt was the presumption that Thutmosis, who had for so long been dominated by Hatshepsut, would be unable to maintain control of the empire established by his grandfather. This proved to be a serious error in judgment.

The very year he ascended to the throne, Thutmosis undertook not only to reassert Egyptian authority in Syria and Palestine but also to integrate these lands into an expanded Egyptian empire. With their strategically important harbors along the Mediterranean coast, and their controlling positions astride the major caravan routes traversing the area to both Asia Minor and Mesopotamia, Syria and Palestine represented the keys to dominance in southwestern Asia. Thutmosis was determined that those keys should be in Egyptian hands.

He took the ancient military road from Qantara along the coast of Palestine and engaged and defeated the rebel forces on the Plain of Esdraelon (Jezreel Valley) near the fortified town of Megiddo. The latter, a strategic crossroads in northern Palestine that dominated the route from Egypt to the Euphrates, fell after a seven-month siege. His victory, however, was not decisive because he failed to permanently occupy the conquered territory, which rebelled against Egyptian overlordship at every opportunity. As a result, this was to be only the first of seventeen military campaigns that Thutmosis had to undertake in support of his program of territorial aggrandizement.

Thutmosis eventually succeeded in wresting virtually undisputed control over the entire Syrian-Palestinian coastal strip from Mitanni, and battled and defeated its armies all the way across Syria. Equipped with prefabricated assault boats drawn on carts in the supply train of his army, Thutmosis crossed the mountains, moved down the Orontes, and headed for the Mitanni fortress at Carchemish on the Euphrates. When the Mitanni forces withdrew to safety across the river, the Egyptians brought up their assault boats, crossed the Euphrates, and completed the defeat of the Mitanni army.

Under Thutmosis III, Egypt became the preeminent power in the entire region, although it was plagued continually by rebellions of the conquered peoples and was unable to prevent the resurgence of Mitanni power. Indeed, by the end of the reign of Amenophis II (c. 1425–1401), Egypt was compelled to come to terms with Mitanni, ceding to the latter control of Syria north of a line drawn east from the Mediterranean coast at Tripoli. The peace treaty with Mitanni evolved into an alliance that effectively secured Egypt's northern frontier in Asia for the next hundred years.

Then, after having maintained a position of hegemony in the western Middle East for more than a century, Egypt suddenly became enmeshed in a debilitating internal crisis precipitated by the attempted religious reforms of Amenophis IV or Akhenaton (c. 1352–1338). He was opposed to the established Theban priesthood and the worship of Amon, and sought to institute his own version of the ancient cult of the sun. This caused serious internal dissension that pitted the palace against the temples, divided the national leadership, and confused the populace at large. Appearing to maintain an essentially nonactivist foreign policy, he unintentionally precipitated a break in relations with Tushratta, the king of Mitanni. This had the effect of immobilizing Egypt in face of the challenges to its imperial rule by the Hittites, who were busily engaged in attacking and conquering Egypt's vassals and dependencies in the north and east from their base in Anatolia. At the same time, sensing Egypt's waning determination to maintain control of its empire, the several subject states and peoples, with Hittite encouragement, began overthrowing their Egyptian governors and refused to pay further tribute. It was not long before the economic consequences were felt, as it soon caused the effective depletion of the Egyptian treasury. By the time of his death Akhenaton had steered Egypt into a steep imperial decline. Its empire in Asia quickly disintegrated as Egypt was forced to withdraw back toward its African frontier.

THE HITTITES

Throughout this volatile period, the number of independent states to the north and east constantly diminished under the unrelenting pressure of a handful of powerful expansionist states. It was truly a matter of the survival of the fittest, and by the middle of the fourteenth century most of the surviving states in the Middle East had been brought under the dominance of one of three major empires: Egypt, Assyria, or that of the Hittites.

The Hittites had established their foothold in the Halys River valley of Anatolia sometime in the early eighteenth century. They soon found themselves boxed in by the powerful Gasgas tribes of the Pontic Mountains to the north, the Luwians to the west, and the Hurrians to the east. The only way open for expansion lay to the southwest and southeast, and they began their expansion in these directions in the latter part of the following century under the leadership of Hattusilis I (c. 1650–1620). Sometime during the latter period of his reign, the Hittites struck across the Taurus Mountains and attacked Alalakh, a dependency of the rich and powerful city-state of Yamhad in northern Syria, and raided in the area just north of Carchemish on the Euphrates. Four years later, Hattusilis attacked the Yamhad capital, Aleppo, and crossed the Euphrates to raid in Mesopotamia.

Hittite expansionism took on a more substantial character at the outset of the sixteenth century under Mursilis I (c. 1620–1590). Penetrating into Syria about 1595, he took Aleppo and eliminated Yamhad as a political factor in the region. As noted in a later treaty between the Hittites and Aleppo: "Formerly the kings of Aleppo had acquired a great kingship; but Hattusilis, the great king, the king of the land of Khatte, terminated their kingship. After Hattusilis the king of the land of Khatte, Mursilis the great king, the grandson of Hattusilis, the great king, destroyed the kingship of Aleppo and Aleppo (itself)."[10] Mursilis also mounted a military expedition down the Euphrates that left a wide trail of destruction in its wake. He reached as far south as Babylon, where he overthrew the Amorite king, Samsu-ditana (c. 1625–1595), occupied and plundered the city, and then withdrew from it almost as suddenly as he had first appeared at its gates. This was done, presumably, to deal with a challenge to his authority that had arisen during his absence from Hatti. However, no sooner did Mursilis return to the Hittite capital at Hattusas with the wealth of Babylon in his train than his brother-in-law Hantilis (c. 1590–1560) murdered him. It seems that it was clearly dangerous for a Hittite ruler to be away from his capital for more than a very short period without having to face internal challenges to his rule.

Mursilis remained in Babylon long enough, however, to disrupt its governmental apparatus and completely undermine the previously existing regional political arrangements. Babylon was thus left virtually defenseless in the face of the invasion of a Kassite horde that swept down out of the Luristan region of the central Zagros to the east to fill the vacuum created by the Hittite withdrawal. A Kassite dynasty was established in Babylonia under Agum II (c. 1602–1585) in place of the Amorites who had ruled the country for centuries. The Kassites managed to consolidate and unify the kingdom once again, and to maintain its security in the face of continuing threats from Assyria and Elam for another four centuries. The troublesome Sealands at the head of the Persian Gulf were finally re-conquered and reintegrated into Kassite Babylonia by Ulamburiash (c. 1500).

The assassination of Mursilis had the unintended consequence of destabilizing the Hittite state for several generations until the resulting succession crises were resolved. It was during this extended period of internal Hittite turmoil that the neighboring Hurrians formed the nucleus of the new state of Mitanni, a Hurri confederation that took control of northern Syria and much of Assyria after the collapse of Amorite power in Mesopotamia. In northern Syria, the Mitannians sought to consolidate their grip by creating instability in Aleppo as a means of insuring that it would not reemerge as a pivotal power in the region aligned with Hatti.

For the next two centuries the Hittites were heavily preoccupied with a series of wars against Mitanni. The struggle was over domination of the northern part of the Fertile Crescent. By the time of the accession of Telepinus (c. 1525–1500) to the Hittite throne, the empire had effectively contracted to its original heartland in central Anatolia. Arzawa on the western coast of Anatolia had broken away, and there was little that the Hittites could do about it at the time. More significantly, the Hittites had been unable to prevent the Hurrians from founding the state of Kizzuwadna in Cilicia, blocking the Hittite route to the southeast through the Taurus Mountains. However, this development also had a positive aspect for the Hittites. Kizzuwadna served as a buffer state protecting a weakened Hatti from invasion by Mitanni, an arrangement that was solemnized by a treaty between Telepinus and Ishputakhshu, the Hurrian ruler of Kizzuwadna, a pact that was subsequently renewed by their successors.

Around the beginning of the fourteenth century B.C.E., a new ruling house seized power in Hattusas, presaging the reemergence of Hatti as a power in the region. With a more aggressive Egypt clearly evidencing expansionist aims in Asia, as became manifest in the campaigns of Thutmose III and Amenophis II, the rulers of Mitanni found themselves facing the likelihood of being drawn into simultaneous but unconnected wars with Egypt and Hatti. The unpleasant prospect of fighting wars on two fronts at the same time was sufficient to make the Hurrians anxious to eliminate at least one of these threats, diplomatically if possible. Of the two potential enemies, the threat from Egypt seemed less imminent and the Hurrians decided to seek a treaty of peace and alliance with it. The Hurrians and Egyptians thus entered into a period of close, even if occasionally erratic, relations. The Hurrian ruler Artatama gave his daughter in marriage to Amenophis' son Thutmosis IV (c. 1401–1390) to seal an alliance between the two states, a pact that was later renewed by their successors, Suttarna II and Amenophis III (c. 1390–1352), with the marriage of the latter to the Hurrian king's daughter. The combined presence of Hurrian and Egyptian power in Syria effectively slowed the pace of the Hittite advance southward. Nonetheless, during the latter part of Amenophis' reign he had to deal with a revolt by the Amorite state of Amurru, whose ruler Abdi-Ashirta had joined a coalition with the Hittites in an effort to throw off the Egyptian yoke.

The stability of the Egyptian-Hurrian alliance had always been tenuous, subject to the highly erratic character of Mitanni politics. A pro-Hittite group assassinated Artashumara, the heir to the Hurrian throne. The leader of the group, Tuhe, proclaimed himself as regent of the kingdom. However, he did not remain in office for very long and was deposed by Artashumara's son Tushratta. The latter sought to reestablish good relations with Amenophis. He too gave a daughter in marriage to the Egyptian pharaoh to seal the alliance again. At the same time, concerned about the lingering threat posed to it by Mitanni, Babylonia attempted to strike its own alliance with Egypt as a means of placing constraints on Hurrian freedom of action. It arranged for Amenophis to marry both the sister and daughter of the Babylonian king, Kadashman-Enlil I. The latter arrangement put new pressure on Assyria, which was nominally a vassal state of Mitanni but was also the object of Babylonian ambitions. The Assyrian king Ashuruballit (c. 1360–1300) was forced to show conspicuous deference to Egypt as a means of assuring his continued independence. Through this complex of alliances, Egypt became the effective arbiter of power in much of northern Syria.

It was this position that was squandered by Akhenaton, who unintentionally destroyed the defensive alliance with Mitanni because of his failure to deliver on certain commitments promised to the Hurrian king by his father. This took place just at a time when the prospects for Hittite expansion had improved considerably as a consequence of a Hurrian dynastic succession crisis that exploded in civil war. The problem was exacerbated by sharp internal disagreements among the Mitanni elite over the wisdom and desirability of the alliance with Egypt. The outcome of the crisis involved the ultimate dissolution of Mitanni into several smaller states, the major one being Hanigalbat. This made it feasible for the Hittites to pursue a strategy of "divide and conquer." In addition, the power vacuum that developed as a consequence of the debilitating internal crisis in Egypt during the reign of Akhenaton made it a particularly opportune moment for the Hittites to break out of their northern confines once more.

Under Suppiluliumas I (c. 1375–1335), the Hittites undertook to exploit fully the opportunities presented and soon reached the zenith of their power. They consolidated their grip on Anatolia and northern Syria from the Halys to the Euphrates. To neutralize Egypt, Suppiluliumas contrived to reach an accord with Akhenaton that completely opened the breach between Egypt and Mitanni, leaving the latter without a major ally and vulnerable to a Hittite attack. He sought to ensure that Egypt would have no excuse for intervening in the north by initially avoiding any overt interference in Egypt's dependencies in southern Syria, or in the trading ports along the Mediterranean coast. This policy proved successful. Egypt refused to come to the aid of the numerous small Syrian states like Byblos that appealed to the pharaoh for help, leaving them exposed to the expected Hittite onslaught.

Some of these small Syrian states, such as Ugarit and Amurru, situated in the buffer zone between the Egyptian and Hittite frontiers, had little alternative but to switch alliances and become Hittite vassals. It is known that Aziras, king of Amurru, who had seized control of Phoenicia, entered into a defense pact with Suppiluliumas. Under the terms of the agreement, Suppiluliumas committed himself to a guarantee of Amurru's security. "If somebody presses Aziras hard ... or if somebody starts a revolt, if you then write to the king of the Hatti land: 'send troops and charioteers to my aid!' I shall hit that enemy for you."[11] Niqmaddu of Ugarit had previously signed a mutual security pact with Aziras, and when the latter turned to the Hittites, the former had little choice but to do so as well. Niqmaddu, who apparently was married to an Egyptian princess, had sought to remain neutral in the Egyptian-Hittite struggle for supremacy but found himself unable to do so.

It was only when the Hittites had already put Carchemish, the last Mitanni stronghold west of the Euphrates, under siege that Suppiluliumas sent forces across the line marking the Egyptian sphere of interest in Syria at Kadesh. Hittite control extended as far south as Lebanon, thereby setting the stage for a struggle with Egypt for regional supremacy. At issue was the undisputed control of the intercontinental land bridge and therefore mastery of the major trade routes between Africa and Asia. To offset the emergence of Assyria as a power to be reckoned with while he was preoccupied with Egypt, Suppiluliumas seems to have gotten involved in Hurrian dynastic politics. He threw his support behind a claimant to the Mitanni (Hanigalbat) throne as a means of using the much reduced state as a buffer between Assyria and the Hittite Empire.

For the most part, Hittite expansion was kept within relatively modest bounds. Their kings recognized that their position in central Anatolia had both advantages and disadvantages. On the one hand, they were virtually surrounded by enemies, all of whom were vying for control of the same valuable trade routes. On the other hand, by keeping the empire relatively compact, and assuming that significant multilateral alliances against them were unlikely, they were in a position to shift their powerful military forces in whatever direction circumstances demanded, giving them great flexibility. Accordingly, it served their interests well to develop and maintain a network of small buffer states along the Hittite frontiers. One of the more troublesome of these was Arzawa in western Anatolia.

It was not until Suppiluliumas' successor, Mursilis II (c. 1334–1306), who proved to be one of the most able military leaders of the ancient world, came to power that the Hittites were able to dispose of the Arzawa problem decisively. The Hittites were heavily dependent on tin for the manufacture of weapons and other goods essential to their economy, and the primary source of their supply of the metal appears to have been Bohemia in central Europe. The metal was transported from the Bohemian mines across the Balkans into Thrace, and then across the Bosphorus into Anatolia. As long as an aggressive Arzawa was able to control the tin route at its point of entry into Anatolia, Hittite power was contingent to a significant degree on its ability to keep the route open. Mursilis finally succeeded in restoring Hittite control over Arzawa after more than a century of struggle.

Mursilis also vigorously pursued a campaign to seize control of the Syrian-Palestinian coastal strip. The struggle for dominance over this strategically important region was long and bitter, dragging on inconclusively for a generation. By the beginning of the thirteenth century, Egypt once again emerged as a major factor in the regional power equation and the struggle for supremacy was renewed under Sethos I (c. 1294–1279). Although Palestine and Phoenicia were recovered for Egypt, the Egyptian-Hittite conflict went on inconclusively for several years culminating in a major but ultimately indecisive battle fought at Kadesh on the Orontes between the armies of Rameses II (c. 1279–1212) and the Hittite king Muwatallis (c. 1306–1282).

The Egyptian king viewed this battle as the high point of his career, celebrating it as a great victory. In fact, it was nothing of the sort. Rameses was simply outclassed as a general by Muwatallis, who contrived to be in position to attack the flank of the long Egyptian army column with a mass of chariotry. At best, Rameses managed to retreat with the remnants of his army. No sooner had he returned to Egypt than Muwatalis deposed the prince of Amurru enthroned by Rameses, placed his own man in the position, and transformed the area into an anti-Egyptian buffer zone. At the same time, many of the small states of Palestine exploited the opportunity to revolt against Egyptian hegemony. But before Rameses could react to these events, he was forced to divert his attention to his western frontier in Africa where he had to take steps to stop the damaging raids that were being carried out against the delta region by marauding tribes from Libya.

Rameses was also confronted by the need to rebuild the economic and military foundations of Egyptian power, which were in a serious state of disrepair as a direct consequence of the loss of revenues from tribute paid by the former imperial dependencies. He resolved Egypt's immediate problems by sending an expedition to Nubia to exploit the gold mines that were to be found there, and by using the gold retrieved to finance the reconditioning of Egypt's military capabilities. With his army rebuilt and re-equipped, Rameses sought to undertake the re-conquest of the Syrian provinces but was sidetracked by the need to deal with a number of small but nettlesome kingdoms that had come into being in southern Palestine under Hittite suzerainty. This led to the Egyptian conquest of Edom and Moab and ultimately to the recapture and re-incorporation of Kadesh and Amurru into the Egyptian Empire.

It soon became apparent to both Egypt and Hatti that the long-standing conflict over control of Syria and the coastal trade routes had, for all practical purposes, resulted in a stalemate. Neither party seemed capable of decisively defeating the other, and a negotiated settlement became desirable. The belligerents may have been aided in reaching this conclusion by a common concern that while Egypt and Hatti were bleeding each other dry, a formidable threat to both was emerging in Assyria to the east. It seems reasonable to assume that they were well aware that they would be in a weak position to deal with such a threat if they continued the seemingly hopeless conflict in which they had for so long been engaged. Hattusilis took the initiative and sent a messenger to the Egyptians proposing to resolve their outstanding issues through negotiation. The latter responded positively, and the Egyptian-Hittite conflict was quickly and formally settled by a pact concluded between Rameses II and Hattusilis III (c. 1275–1250).

It is noteworthy that the Egyptian-Hittite accord clearly reflects a concern about a common enemy. The pact was in essence both a non-belligerency treaty under which each state agreed to refrain from attacking the other, and a mutual security pact under which each agreed to come to the other's assistance in the event of external aggression, presumably by Assyria, or internal revolt. Its relevant extant clauses stated:

But thus shall it be henceforth, even from this day . . . concerning the land of Egypt, with the land of Kheta [Hatti] to cause no hostility to arise between them for ever. Behold, this it is—Khetasira [Hattusilis], the Grand-Duke of Kheta, covenants with Ra-user-ma [Rameses], approved by the Sun, the great ruler of Egypt, from this day forth, that good peace and good brotherhood shall be between us for ever. . . . The Grand-Duke of Kheta shall not invade the land of Egypt for ever, to carry away anything from it; nor shall Ramesu-Meriamen, the great ruler of Egypt, invade the land of Kheta for ever. . . . If any enemy shall come to the lands of Ramesu-Meriamen, the great ruler of Egypt, and he shall send to the Grand-Duke of Kheta, saying, Come and give me help against him, then shall the Grand-Duke of Kheta . . . smite the enemy; but if it be that the Grand-Duke of Kheta shall not come (himself) he shall send his infantry and his cavalry.[12]

Although no demarcation of their respective spheres of interest was contained in the treaty, it is assumed that as a practical matter the line separating Egypt from the Hittites was drawn at Byblos, on the Mediterranean north of Sidon. A decade later, Egyptian-Hittite ties were strengthened by the marriage of Rameses II to the daughter of the Hittite king. These moves established a short-lived balance of power in the eastern Mediterranean and a brief period of stability along its littoral.

The picture was somewhat different further inland where the Assyrians began to encroach on the approaches to Anatolia and succeeded in wresting control of the Ergam Maden copper mines of Isuwa. However, the Hittites were able to block the Assyrian advance farther south near Carchemish, and were therefore able to retain control of the Syrian coast. To compensate for the loss of their copper sources to the Assyrians, Tudhaliyas IV (c. 1250–1220) invaded and conquered Cyprus, which provided access to an alternate source of copper that was not subject to interdiction by Assyria.

Despite its apparent ability to maintain a favorable power position in the region, the Hittite Empire barely lasted until the end of the thirteenth century, although small neo-Hittite states persisted until the eighth century B.C.E. While it is unclear as to what constituted the specific causes of Hittite decline, it is generally assumed that it came about primarily as a consequence of the intrusion of a new power into the Middle East. The "Sea People" appeared on the scene at a time when the Hittites were exhausted by the centuries of virtually unrelenting conflict with Egypt and with their various enemies in Asia.

THE SEA PEOPLE

The intrusion of the Sea People into the core zone of the Middle East appears to have been the result of momentous events taking place elsewhere in the eastern Mediterranean and Aegean regions. At the beginning of the fifteenth century B.C.E., these regions, and the trade passing through them, were dominated for about a hundred years by an alliance of Aegean states under the leadership of Minoan Crete. The regional hegemony of Crete came to an end with the destruction of its center at Knossos, most probably by an alliance of city-states of the Aegean littoral, that sought to rid themselves of Cretan interference in their affairs. There is reason to believe that this turn of events may have been instigated and orchestrated by the Peloponnesian kingdom of Mycenae in conjunction with Egypt as a means of eliminating Crete's role as middleman in the lucrative trade between them. In any case, Mycenae now replaced Crete as the dominant power in the Aegean, supplanting its hegemony throughout the region.

One particularly significant consequence of the fall of Minoan Crete for the history of the region was the dissolution of its formidable navy, which had policed the waters of the Aegean and eastern Mediterranean for a thousand years. This had the effect of creating unemployment among the maritime tribes of Lycians and Shardana from the coasts of Asia Minor who had been engaged by Crete in the control of piracy. Deprived of their traditional employment, these maritime marauders turned to the trade of piracy themselves, destabilizing the trade routes throughout the region and posing a threat to the security of those settlements in close proximity to the sea from Mycenae to Egypt. By the thirteenth century, the Mycenaean Empire itself was in a state of disarray as a result of the mounting pressures on it. These came both from Lycian sea raiders and from the substantial migration at the time of Indo-European peoples southward into the Balkans and Greece. These pushed in the direction of the sea, displacing the peoples they found in their path.

The Sea People who burst onto the scene of Middle Eastern history at this juncture are generally thought to have formerly been inhabitants of Greece and the Aegean Islands. They are assumed to have been primarily Achaeans from Thessaly who were displaced by the increasing population pressures on their small littoral enclaves that resulted from the influx of Dorians from the north. It would appear to have been these Achaeans, in company with others from the region, who took to their ships to conquer new lands for settlement. However, given their numbers and typical mode of transportation—ox carts, a means most unlikely for seafaring peoples—these newcomers most likely represented a more complex migratory wave into the Middle East from Europe, and were called Sea People by the Egyptians simply because they came from across the sea.

The mix of peoples moving into the Middle East during this turbulent period included Thracians and Phrygians as well as Armenians who forced their way into Anatolia from the Balkan Peninsula and the Caucasus Mountains. One significant consequence of the influx of these aggressive migrants into Asia Minor was their interruption of the northwestern trade route to Europe from Hatti, which had serious economic impact on the latter's economy. The subsequent conquest of Cyprus and its copper mines by the Sea People proved disastrous for the continued economic and military viability of the Hittite Empire, which was exhausted by centuries of unrelenting struggle for dominance in the Fertile Crescent. The imperial heartland itself could be kept secure from invasion from the east only as long as the Hittites controlled the passes through the Taurus Mountains. However, Hatti was highly vulnerable to attack from across the plains of western Anatolia, and that vulnerability increased as large numbers of diverse peoples from abroad moved into the peninsula. The Hittites simply were unable to prevent them from crossing the Bosphorus into Anatolia, or from sailing to and landing at different points along the extensive Anatolian coastline, and establishing tenaciously held footholds there from which they expanded inland at Hittite expense.

The Sea People, probably including Phrygians and Lycians from Asia Minor, and perhaps an admixture of recruits from Italy and Sicily as well, also established a substantial presence on the North African coast west of Egypt. Before long, having joined forces with the Berber Libu (Libyans), they advanced on Egypt from Cyrenaica bent on the conquest of the rich lands of the delta region. Overrunning the Egyptian frontier forts, they managed to reach the Canopic branch of the Nile before being stopped by the forces of the pharaoh. Although the Egyptians made much of their victory over the Libyans, at best it provided only a temporary respite. About 1174, and again a mere half-dozen years later, Rameses III (c. 1186–1154) had to beat back attacks by the Libu and the Meshwesh, the latter for a time occupying much of the western delta region as far south as Memphis.

To make matters worse, during the same period Rameses had to confront the threat posed by the onslaught of another wave of Sea People that struck the shores of the eastern Mediterranean. The Hittite Empire had collapsed under the pressure of their unrelenting assault, and they now turned southward, approaching Egypt through Syria and Palestine. Fortunately for the Egyptians, the Sea People were unable to coordinate their attacks on Egypt from opposite directions. Had they done so, the subsequent history of the region would have been rather different, since it is unlikely that Rameses would have emerged victorious from a two-front war. As it was, he proved able to deal with each assault separately.

The impact of the advance of the Sea People on the region is reflected in the contemporary account recorded in the temple of Rameses III at Thebes: "The foreign countries made a conspiracy in their islands. All at once the lands were removed and scattered in the fray. No land could stand before their arms, from Hatti, Kode [Cilicia], Carchemish, Arzawa, and Alashiya [probably Cyprus] on, being cut off at [one time]. . . . They were coming forward toward Egypt, while the flame was prepared before them. Their confederation was the Philistines, Tjeker, Shekelesh, Denye(n), and Weshesh, lands united. They laid their hands upon the lands as far as the circuit of the earth, their hearts confident and trusting: 'Our plans will succeed!' "[13]

The Sea People sacked the coastal region of Syria, Phoenicia, and Palestine, destroying a number of city-states such as Alalakh and Ugarit in the process, and then attacked Egypt simultaneously by land and sea. The maritime assault, led by the Philistines, turned into a disaster for them in the delta as their ships were trapped and destroyed in the inlets of the Nile at Pelusium by the Egyptian fleet. At the same time, the armies of Rameses succeeded in repelling the land-based attack before the Sea People were able to cross the Egyptian frontier in the Sinai. Rameses was able to boast: "Those who reached my frontier, their seed is not. . . . Those who came forward together on the sea, the full flame was in front of them at the rivermouths, while a stockade of lances surrounded them on the shore. They were dragged in, enclosed, and prostrated on the beach, killed, and made into heaps from tail to head. Their ships and their goods were as if fallen into the water."[14]

Although Egypt still seemed capable of protecting its frontiers, its power was nonetheless in a state of steady decline and it could not force the Sea

People to withdraw from the vicinity of its northern frontier. As a result, it was not long before a practical accommodation was reached with the Philistines, who remained entrenched on Egypt's doorstep in southern Palestine. The Philistines thus took control of the coastal region at the southern end of the African-Asian land bridge and established a buffer state there that effectively dominated the land approaches to Egypt from Asia.

The Philistines sought to expand the area under their control to all of the coastal plain of Palestine. This brought them into direct conflict with the Israelites who were at the time in the process of establishing their own state in the area, triggering a centuries-long struggle between them for dominance of the southern land-bridge region. At the same time, other elements of the Sea People settled farther north along the Mediterranean coast. There they assimilated to the indigenous population and thereby gave birth to a new Phoenician nation that emerged as a thassalocracy that dominated maritime traffic and commerce in the eastern Mediterranean and the Aegean Seas for centuries.

NOTES

1. Flavius Josephus, *Against Apion*, Bk. I:14.

2. John Van Seters, *The Hyksos: A New Investigation*, pp. 191–195.

3. James B. Pritchard, ed., *Ancient Near Eastern Texts Relating to the Old Testament*, p. 231.

4. Arthur Weigall, *A History of the Pharaohs*, Vol. 2, p. 221.

5. George Steindorff and Keith C. Seele, *When Egypt Ruled the East*, 2nd ed., p. 31.

6. James B. Pritchard, ed., *The Ancient Near East*, p. 174.

7. Steindorff and Seele, *When Egypt Ruled the East*, p. 33.

8. Donald B. Redford, *History and Chronology of the Eighteenth Dynasty of Egypt*, pp. 57–87.

9. The reign of Thutmosis III is usually dated from the death of Thutmosis II, ignoring the twenty-two-year reign of Hatshepsut. However, this convention confuses the issue and is not followed here.

10. Donald B. Redford, *Egypt, Canaan, and Israel in Ancient Times*, p. 134.

11. Pritchard, ed., *The Ancient Near East*, Vol. II, p. 44.

12. William Wright, *The Empire of the Hittites*, pp. 28–30.

13. Pritchard, ed., *The Ancient Near East*, p. 185.

14. Ibid., p. 186.

3

The Rise and Decline
of Assyria

The decline of Mitanni, followed by the sudden collapse of the Hittite Empire, created a power vacuum in Syria that a number of petty and local Aramaean states attempted to fill. None, however, was strong enough to dominate the area, a circumstance that made it a tempting target for Assyria, which was reemerging as a major force in the geopolitics of the Fertile Crescent.

From its earliest history, Assyria's principal orientation was toward the west, even though it was often most preoccupied with problems in other directions. This orientation was dictated in great measure by its geostrategic position. East and north of the narrow Tigris Valley lay a mountainous region peopled by hardy raiding tribes such as the Guti and Lullubi, which always proved troublesome and difficult to restrain. To the south, of course, lay the rich Mesopotamian plain. But it was home to the more populous Akkadians, Sumerians, and Babylonians who had consistently sought to expand their kingdoms northward into Assyria, making it an imperative of Assyrian policy to fortify the frontier separating them. It was in the west, however, that both the greatest threat and greatest opportunity were to be found. The steppe of the Jazirah, which stretched westward for hundreds of miles, left Assyria exposed to attack by marauding armies or nomadic bands from the fringes of the vast Arabian Desert. Stability in this broad region was critical to Assyria's security and, absent any natural formations that could serve as the basis for a fortified frontier, could be assured only through direct control.

Control of the Jazirah, however, would also bring Assyria within striking distance of the rich sources of copper, iron, lumber, silver, and stone that were to be found just a bit farther to the northwest in Anatolia. Moreover, it would provide direct access to the eastern Mediterranean coast, which boasted some of the major ports of the Middle East and the international trade routes that passed through the region. It was surely a tempting prospect for a state with expansionist ambitions.

At the time of the decline of the Hittites, the Assyrians were still nominally vassals of Kassite Babylonia, an arrangement brought about as a result of an agreement concluded in the latter part of the fifteenth century B.C.E. between the Kassite king Karaindash (c. 1445–1427) and Ashur-rimni-sheshu, king of Assyria. It is significant that the treaty solemnized a mutual oath to respect the boundary demarcated between them. This suggests that Assyria was already sufficiently powerful to prevent the Kassites from any further northward expansion. Assyria may thus be seen as gaining the upper hand in the perennial struggle for dominance in Mesopotamia. Before long, it was in a position to influence the internal affairs of Kassite Babylonia, notwithstanding the fact that it continued to acknowledge itself to be a nominal vassal of the latter. Indeed, the Kassite king Burnaburiash II (c. 1375–1347), who kept up a correspondence with the pharaohs of Egypt, had earlier remonstrated with Amenhotep III for having accorded recognition to Ashur-uballit (c. 1360–1300) as an independent monarch at a time when Babylonia still claimed formal supremacy over Assyria. Ashur-uballit sought to strengthen his hand in Babylonia by giving his daughter in marriage to Burnaburiash. When Kara-hardash, their son and heir apparent to the Babylonian throne, was killed in a *coup d'etat* that overthrew Burnaburiash, Ashur-uballit invaded Babylonia, removed and executed the usurper Nazibugash, and placed another of Burnaburiash's sons, Kurigalzu II (c. 1345–1324), on the throne.

Nonetheless, the competition for regional hegemony was such that relations between Assyria and Babylonia broke down completely after the accession of Enlil-nirari (c. 1329–1320) to the Assyrian throne, and war erupted between him and Kurigalzu. Assyria emerged from the conflict with the upper hand and, under its next two rulers, Arik-den-ilu (c. 1319–1308) and Adad-nirari I (c. 1307–1275), it began to extend its control to the peoples on the fringes of its eastern and northwestern frontiers. Arik-den-ilu subdued the Guti in the Zagros and the Hittites on Assyria's western frontier. He also drove the Bedouin tribes that were beginning to encroach on his territory in the southwest back toward the desert.

The growing power of Assyria became a matter of increasing concern to its neighbors to the north and south, and served as a spur to the restoration of relations between the Kassites and the Hittites, presumably to serve as a constraint on Assyria's freedom of action. Shalmaneser I (c. 1274–1245), however, dispensed with all further pretense of even nominal deference to Babylonia and openly proclaimed Assyrian supremacy in western Asia. He mounted repeated campaigns against the still powerful Hittites, and also took to the field against Hanigalbat, now an Assyrian vassal state that had rebelled against its overlord. After the defeat of Shattuara II, the last of the Hurrian kings, Shalmaneser annexed Hanigalbat and transformed it into an Assyrian province. He boasted of this achievement: "I fought a battle and accomplished their defeat. I killed countless numbers of his defeated and widespreading hosts. . . . Nine of his strongholds and his capital city I captured. One hundred and eighty of his cities I turned into tells and ruins. . . . Their lands I brought under my sway, and the rest of their cities I burned with fire."[1] Shalmaneser had finally wiped the remnants of the once powerful empire of Mitanni off the face of the map.

Shalmaneser's son and successor Tukulti-Ninurta I (c. 1244–1208) continued to expand in the north, and extended Assyrian control as far as the region southwest of Lake Van. He then turned his attention to Babylonia, which was in a particularly vulnerable position at the time. The Babylonian king Kashtiliashu IV (c. 1242–1235) was already under assault by the newly invigorated Elamite state that had reemerged as a major political force in the region after a hiatus of some four centuries. Under Kiten-Hutran (1235–c. 1205), the Elamites sought to gain control of the frontier region between Elam and Babylonia. In 1226, Kiten-Hutran struck across the Tigris and conquered Nippur. Then, marching north, he re-crossed the Tigris and seized Der.

Attacked simultaneously from the east and the north, Kassite Babylonia collapsed, with the Assyrians winning the race to the capital. By occupying the heart of the country the Assyrians were able to prevent the Elamites from consolidating their gains. They brought Babylonia directly under Assyrian control for the first time, reversing the historic relationship between the two states. Tukulti-Ninurta declared: "I forced Kashtiliash, King of Kar-Duniash, to give battle; I brought about the defeat of his armies, his warriors I overthrew. In the midst of that battle my hand captured Kashtiliash, the Kassite king. . . . Sumer and Akkad to its farthest border I brought under my sway. On the lower sea of the rising sun [the Persian Gulf] I established the frontier of my land."[2]

At about this same time, for reasons that are as yet unclear, Tukulti-Ninurta appears to have made a policy decision that brought Assyrian military activity to a halt, a policy that soon encouraged Babylonia to revolt and generated serious internal repercussions in Assyria. Tukulti-Ninurta was eliminated by his son Ashur-nasirpal I (c. 1207–1204), who attempted to arrest the decline in Assyrian power, but he was unable to do so. The erosion of Assyria's position continued steadily, and by the time of Ninurta-apal-ekur (c. 1192–1180) the empire had contracted physically to the size of the original Assyrian homeland. Once again Kassite Babylonia was able to reassert its hegemony over the region as Assyria reverted to a subordinate position.

However, the days of renewed Kassite preeminence were numbered as Babylonia came under continuing attack by the Elamites, who had also undergone a political revival at the beginning of the thirteenth century with the establishment of a new dynasty of highly competent and effective rulers. Shutruk-nahunte I (1185–1155) invaded Babylonia in 1160 with a vast army and wreaked havoc to an extent not previously experienced there. Babylon was taken and given as a prize to the Elamite ruler's son, Kuturnahhunte. A Kassite puppet prince, Enlil-nadin-ahne, was subsequently placed on the throne but was soon overthrown by another Elamite ruler, Shilhak-Inshushinak (1150–c. 1120), bringing to an end the more than 500-year rule of the Kassites in Babylonia.

Under Shilhak-Inshushinak the Elamites extended their reach to most of the Tigris Valley, the eastern littoral of the Persian Gulf, and to the Zagros, thereby constituting a substantial Elamite empire for the first time. But for reasons we are unable to discern with any clarity, the Elamites failed to establish effective dominion over their empire for more than a very brief period. Perhaps it was because they exhausted themselves in the wars for control over western Iran, or because of the need to deal with the hordes of Medes and Persians that were beginning to pour into Iran from Transcaspia to the northeast.

During the latter part of the reign of Shilhak-Inshushinak the Elamite grip on southern Mesopotamia relaxed and a dynasty of indigenous princes of Isin managed to seize control of Babylonia. Nebuchadrezzar I (c. 1124–1103), assisted by an Elamite noble who defected to him, succeeded in invading Elam and defeating the Elamite king Hutelutush near Susa in 1115. He took the Elamite capital and plundered the countryside. Nebuchadrezzar effectively eliminated Elam as a political force of any consequence in regional politics for the next three centuries. Nonetheless, the Babylonians were unable to capitalize on their success and retain control of Elam because their attention was soon drawn to the greater threat posed by the resurgence of Assyrian power on their northern frontier.

The collapse of the Kassite kingdom, and the instability of the Elamite rule that succeeded it, gave Assyria the opportunity to begin to reassert itself once more. This resurgence of Assyrian power started to become evident during the reign of Ashur-dan I (c. 1179–1134), who began to take steps to protect the northern trade routes in the region of the Little Zab when Babylonia proved incapable of doing so effectively. His successor, Ashur-resh-ishi (c. 1133–1116), was finally able to free Assyria from its subordination to Babylonia. Assyria now began the development of an awesome military capability that soon far exceeded anything previously known in the ancient Middle East.

The architect of Assyrian power was Tiglath-pileser I (c. 1115–1077), who mounted the throne at a time when Assyria was faced with serious challenges to its continued viability from all directions. In the east, the tribes of the Zagros were gnawing away at the fringes of the kingdom. To the south, he was faced with a new and reinvigorated Babylonian state that had successfully challenged the Elamites, and had already penetrated into Assyrian territory as far north as the Little Zab, only about twenty miles from the Assyrian capital, which became the new frontier between them. In the north, a force of some 21,000 Anatolian tribesmen (probably Phrygians) crossed the Taurus and began marching down the Tigris Valley toward Nineveh. And in the west, there were the Aramaeans who were busy establishing their control along the Euphrates and threatening to pour into Mesopotamia.

Tiglath-pileser began to deal with these simultaneous challenges systematically. Most critical was the threat to Nineveh, which he gave highest priority. He marched against the invading force coming down the Tigris Valley and succeeded in destroying it along with the allies it had garnered along the way. Determined to assure the security of his northern frontiers, Tiglath-pileser penetrated into Armenia as far as Malazgird, well beyond Lake Van, at the same time that part of his forces pacified the tribes of the northern Zagros. He boasted of these victories: "There fell into my hands altogether, between the commencement of my reign and my fifth year, forty-two countries with their kings, from the banks of the River Zab to the banks of the River Euphrates, the country of the Khatti, and the upper ocean of the setting sun. I brought them under one government; I took hostages from them; and I imposed on them tribute and offerings."[3]

With his frontiers in the north secured, he turned his attention to Babylonia, which he disposed of in relatively short order according to the record he left of his achievement. "I marched against Kar-Duniash . . . I captured the palaces of Babylon belonging to Marduk-nadin-ahhe, King of Kar-Duniash. I burned them with fire. The possessions of his palace I carried off. The second time, I drew up a line of battle chariots against Marduk-nadin-ahhe, King of Kar-Duniash, and I smote him."[4]

Having established a dominant position in Mesopotamia and its adjacent regions, Tiglath-pileser then attempted to sweep westward to the Mediterranean. No doubt to his great surprise, he not only was effectively blocked from doing so but also found himself under attack by a vast confederation of Aramaean tribes of uncertain origin that emerged out of the Syrian Desert. The collapse of the Hittite state, coupled with the relative weakness of both Babylonia and Assyria, had created a power vacuum in Syria that the Aramaeans sought to fill. Tiglath-pileser is said to have fought some twenty-eight campaigns against the Aramaeans, and may have actually reached the Phoenician coast during one of them, as he claimed. However, he clearly was unable to consolidate Assyrian control of Syria or even to secure his western frontiers against Aramaean attack before he was assassinated.

Over the next century incremental Aramaean expansion eastward continued unabated. During the reign of Tiglath-pileser's successor Ashur-bel-kala (c. 1074–1057), the Aramaeans appear to have been held in check at the Middle Euphrates. It seems that the Assyrians may have attempted to deflect the Aramaean thrust southward to Babylonia, where they installed an Aramaean, Adad-apal-iddina (c. 1067–1046), as king. While this may have delayed the Aramaean movement eastward for a time, it did not stop it. By the time of Ashur-rabi II (c. 1010–970), the Assyrians were no longer able to offer any effective opposition to the Aramaean advance. They crossed the Middle Euphrates and proceeded to establish a network of autonomous but interrelated kingdoms that began to encroach directly on the Assyrian heartland, posing a serious threat to the continued viability of the Assyrian Empire. During the reign of Tiglath-pileser II (c. 966–935), the Aramaeans reached Nisibis, midway between the Khabur and the Tigris. Within a few decades they were settled throughout the Jazirah and achieved effective control of a zone stretching from the Mediterranean to the Zagros. This also gave the Aramaeans the ability to interfere with the international trade routes that passed through the area, thereby directly affecting the Assyrian economy.

THE RISE OF ISRAEL

It was during this same period that the Israelites under David (c. 1010–970) began to successfully challenge the Philistine position in southern Palestine. David intended to unify the tribal confederations of Israel (Samaria) and Judah (Judaea) into a single state that would completely dominate the southern end of the African-Asian land bridge. By controlling this strategic junction, the Israelites, if they could hold on to it, would become a major player in the international affairs of the entire region and presumably derive substantial economic benefits from its position astride the major trade routes passing through it. To this end David undertook a systematic conquest of the key points of strategic importance for maintaining control of the area. However, he was without any existing naval capability. And, absent any Israelite tradition of seafaring that might have permitted the development of an effective naval force, David elected to run the risk of permitting the Philistines and the Phoenicians to continue to dominate the coastline from the Egyptian frontier as far north as Sidon. In effect, he preferred to make allies of the Philistines and Phoenicians, giving them the burden of defending the coastal area while the Israelites controlled the heights to the east, which permitted them to swoop down on the coastal plain whenever such might be considered necessary. Moreover, by leaving these basically maritime states intact, he was able to benefit from the revenues derived from the east-west transit trade across his territory from the coastal ports, in addition to the income resulting from his control of the north-south caravan routes. As discussed by two contemporary military historians:

If we try to reconstruct the strategic concept behind David's conquests, we may conclude that David was the first ruler of the Palestinian land-bridge who firmly grasped the fact that complete and secure mastery of the area—and consequently reasonably secure existence in it—required command over all the three major routes that connected Egypt with Asia Minor and Mesopotamia: the Via Maris, the watershed road and the King's Highway [in Trans-Jordan]. Secondary routes, such as the Jordan Valley road, were, of course, included in the Davidic dominion; and most important, at least stretches of the desert-fringe road that skirts the portion of the Trans-Jordan plateau inhabited by a sedentary population were also under his sway.

David's empire thus extended between the Mediterranean on the west and the desert on the east, while he was free to move his forces on interior lines along the above-mentioned parallel routes to meet any external threat from either north or south.[5]

David's grand strategy proved to be a sound one, and he succeeded in building a relatively powerful state that established its mastery over the strategically important land bridge. However, he was unable to fuse Samaria and Judaea permanently into a unified Israelite state, and it came apart at the seam after only about eighty years. The united monarchy split apart in about 931, producing two Israelite states that, in the aggregate, were weaker and more susceptible to invasion and conquest than the unified state left behind by David's son and heir Solomon (c. 970–931). By the time of the death of Solomon, who had managed to maintain reasonably good relations with Egypt, the specter of a renewed Assyrian drive for regional dominance could already be seen on the geopolitical horizon. It would have been very difficult for the unified Israelite state of David and Solomon to withstand the coming Assyrian onslaught. Ultimately, it was to prove impossible for the divided state to do so.

THE RESURGENCE OF ASSYRIAN POWER

The century and a half following the death of Tiglath-pileser I witnessed the contraction of Assyria from a major empire to a strip of land about 100 miles long and 50 miles wide along the western bank of the Tigris. However, although Assyria had shrunk significantly in size and power, it remained a potent force awaiting leaders who would be able to bring it out of the doldrums. This began to happen with the ascension of Adad-nirari II (c. 911–891) to the Assyrian throne.

In a series of hard-fought campaigns, he succeeded in extending Assyria's dominion once again to the lands of the Little Zab. He drove the Aramaeans out of the Tigris Valley, eliminated the threat to Nineveh, and re-imposed Assyrian hegemony over Babylonia, annexing a large chunk of the territory of the latter north of the Diyala River. Adad-nirari partially restored Assyria's dominance of the Jazirah, recovering several cities in its eastern portion. He also pushed the Aramaeans out of the former Assyrian towns along the Middle Euphrates, which allowed Assyria to restore its domination of the important trade routes through the region. He also struck beyond the Euphrates, where he subjugated and extracted tribute from the coalition of Aramaean tribes and others who had taken control of northern Syria.

The restoration of Assyria's regional position continued to progress during the brief reign of Tukulti-Ninurta II (c. 890–884), who consolidated its control over all of northern Mesopotamia. This expansionist policy was pursued vigorously by his successor, Ashur-nasirpal II (c. 884–859), who systematically destroyed the Aramaean states in the west and imposed Assyrian rule over all of northern Syria. He also struck farther north into Asia Minor, marching through Commagene as far as Malatia. In addition, he enabled Assyria to assert its suzerainty over the Phoenician city-states along the Mediterranean coast. It seemed that Assyria had now achieved complete control of virtually all the major trade routes in the Middle East. However, at this time the Assyrians still skirted around the kingdoms of Damascus and Israel, where they expected to encounter strong opposition to their imperial aims. Their preferred strategy was to establish a cordon around the two kingdoms that could be tightened whenever circumstances favored it.

The new ruler of the northern Israelite kingdom, Omri (c. 886–875), sought to reestablish Israel as the major regional power in southern Syria and Palestine. He built a new capital at Samaria, which later became the name of the territory of the kingdom of Israel, and entered into close collaboration with the kingdom of Judah. He then strengthened the traditional alliance with the Phoenicians, cementing it with the marriage of his son and heir, Ahab (c. 874–852), to the daughter of the king of Tyre. This gave him the economic resources he needed to achieve his ambitions, and the opportunity to wrest control of the trade routes from the Phoenician coast inland—away from the Assyrians.

The reemergence of Israelite power on its southern frontier was watched with growing concern in Damascus. It was perceived there as the beginning of an attempt by the rulers of Samaria to re-create the Davidic and Solomonic kingdom, which would be a direct threat to the interests of Damascus. Around 870, Ben-Hadad II (Hadadezer or Adadidri), the Aramaean king of Syria, formed a coalition with a number of minor principalities that similarly felt threatened and launched a preemptive war against Samaria. As recorded in the Bible: "And Ben-hadad the king of Syria gathered all his host together: and there were thirty and two kings with him, and horses, and chariots: and he went up and besieged Samaria, and warred against it."[6] Although the Samarian forces were greatly outnumbered by those of the Syrian alliance, Ahab emerged victorious from the conflict primarily because of his superiority as a tactical commander. However, anticipating a strong Assyrian reaction to any changes in the political configuration of the region that might challenge its hegemony, Ahab treated Ben-Hadad, who was taken captive, with magnanimity and entered into a defensive alliance with him. The expected attack by Assyria was not long in coming.

Shalmaneser III (c. 858–824), who campaigned relentlessly for almost his entire reign, marched into Syria and Palestine and confronted the coalition headed by Ben-Hadad and Ahab that had been forged out of the minor states of the region. Although Shalmaneser prevailed against the coalition in 853 at the battle of Qarqar in the Orontes Valley, it was not a definitive victory and the Assyrian king was unable to press his advantage to defeat the alliance decisively. Preoccupied elsewhere for a number of years, he attacked Damascus once more in 841, but again failed to take the city. It would be misleading, however, to assume that the fundamental reason for the Assyrian failure to conquer southern Syria and Israel at this time was because of the intrinsic power of the temporary Aramaean-Israelite coalition. A more geopolitically realistic explanation is that Shalmaneser was not in a position to devote the energy and resources needed to decisively defeat the coalition because he was simultaneously preoccupied with larger and more dangerous challenges on Assyria's southern, northern, and eastern frontiers.

During the reign of Shalmaneser's predecessor, the Babylonian king Nabu-appal-iddina (c. 885–852) was left free to repair some of the devastation caused by the Aramaean invasion, enabling Babylonia to rebuild its military capabilities to the point where it soon achieved a balance of power with its northern neighbor. However, with the succession of Marduk-zakir-shumi to the throne of Babylon in 851 a civil war broke out between him and his brother who was backed by the Aramaeans. The former turned to Shalmaneser for assistance in securing his succession to the throne. The Assyrian ruler readily agreed and mounted a police action in Babylonia that brought Assyrian forces as far south as the Persian Gulf. Good as his word, Shalmaneser allowed Marduk-zakir-shumi to sit on the throne of Babylonia, but only as a vassal of Assyria.

Shalmaneser's imperial ambitions also ran into unexpected problems on other fronts as well. In the east, he was confronted by the Iranians, that is, the Persians and Medes who were concentrating in the area south of Lake Urmia and were evolving into a formidable force in the region. In 844 and 836, the Medes had interfered effectively with Shalmaneser's attempts to extend the Assyrian frontier beyond the Zagros and were proceeding to bring the region into their own grip.

Another impediment to the achievement of Assyrian ambitions was the fledgling state of Urartu (Ararat or Armenia) to the north, which had been forged out of remnants of the defunct Hurri kingdoms in the vicinity of Lake Van. Under its first known king, Aram (c. 858–844), Urartu stretched from the Euphrates in the west to Lake Urmia in the east, reaching as far north as the Araxes River in the Caucasus. Shalmaneser campaigned against the Urartians in the very first year of his reign. "I drew near Sugunia, the stronghold of Aramu, the Urartian; I invested the town and captured it; I killed many of his warriors and carried off plunder . . . fourteen settlements in its territory I gave to the flames."[7] Nonetheless, Shalmaneser was unable to establish his control over the nettlesome Urartians or his dominion over any of the lands north of Carchemish in the west and the Zagros in the east.

Toward the end of Shalmaneser's reign, Assyria became wracked by serious internal disorders. One of his sons, Ashur-danin-aplu, rebelled with the support of twenty-seven cities including Ashsur, Nineveh, Erbil, and Arrapha. The result was a civil war that went on for about five years. It was finally suppressed by Shamshi-Adad V (c. 823–810), but not before the kingdom was seriously weakened. It seems that Shamshi-Adad had to turn to the king of Babylonia for assistance in defeating his brother, for which Assyria had to pay a steep price in tribute. Taking advantage of the window of opportunity created by Assyria's internal problems, Urartu, under Ishpuinis (c. 828–810), consolidated its power and then began to project it throughout the wider region. Shamshi-Adad spent most of his reign restoring Assyria's hegemony over Babylonia and the other vassal states on its immediate frontiers.

By the end of the ninth century, Adad-nirari III (c. 810–783) came to believe that Assyria's flanks were sufficiently secure to permit it to enter the contest for control of the east-west trade routes once again. He marched into Syria, capturing Damascus in 804, and then proceeded toward northern Palestine where he demanded and received tribute from Samaria. Within a short period, he extended his suzerainty to the Phoenicians, Philistines, and Edomites as well. However, the Assyrians failed to use their power to actually conquer these territories. Their incursions were more in the nature of raids, the effects of which dissipated soon after their forces were withdrawn. In effect, over time, there was little to show for the effort. Moreover, the redirection of Assyria's attention from its northern and eastern frontiers toward the Mediterranean had serious unanticipated long-term geopolitical consequences. Neglect of those regions soon precipitated the steady erosion of Assyrian power there and permitted the emergence of political forces that ultimately would hasten the end of the Assyrian Empire.

As Assyrian power receded from its northern periphery, Ishpuinis of Urartu initiated an imperial expansion of his own. This soon cost Assyria all of the districts along the upper Tigris and the Great Zab, as well as the region immediately south of Lake Urmia. Anticipating a strong reaction, Ishpuinis built a series of fortifications in the Urmia region that were intended to contain the Assyrians. These defensive measures proved to be of questionable value since Assyria no longer seemed capable of simultaneously conducting an effective offensive war in the west and a defensive war in the north. Unwilling to cease its campaigns in Syria, Assyria was simply unable to concentrate the forces necessary to eliminate the threat from Urartu.

Under Menuas (810–785), Urartu took effective control of the lucrative caravan routes between central and southeastern Asia as well as Elam to the Mediterranean and the Black Sea, causing them to pass through its territories rather than through Assyria as before. Although Menuas was able to consolidate his control of parts of Media and Parsua, he was unable to gain the upper hand over Assyria's northern dependencies. The contest between Assyria and Urartu for power in the region thus continued inconclusively for decades. However, during the reign of Shalmaneser IV (c. 782–772), Urartu, under Argishtis I (c. 785–753), finally tipped the balance of power in its favor. Argishtis was able to extend Urartian supremacy over most of the small neo-Hittite states of the Taurus region that had previously been vassals of Assyria, as well as over the Cimmerians in the Caucasus and the Mannai in Kurdistan. His successor, Sarduris II (c. 753–735), further extended Urartu's sphere of influence to the Aramaean kingdoms of northern Syria. He also conquered Colchis on the southeast coast of the Black Sea. Control of the copper and iron mines of Armenia, Georgia, Commagene, and Azerbaijan gave Urartu the wealth it needed to constitute a major threat to Assyria's preeminent position in the Fertile Crescent.

Assyria's rapid decline as an empire under a series of relatively ineffectual rulers was reversed dramatically with the accession of Tiglath-pileser III (c. 745–727) to the throne. Previously, the underlying policy governing Assyrian aggression was primarily economic in character. The objective had been to obtain booty and regular tribute from the conquered states, which were forced to acknowledge Assyrian suzerainty in tangible terms. Tiglath-pileser instituted a fundamentally different approach to the matter. His policy, which was followed by his successors as well, was one of unadulterated military and political imperialism. He recognized that the only way he could successfully confront the growing challenge from Urartu was to first consolidate his grip on the latter's flanks in Syria and western Iran. His principal objective became the establishment of clear and unchallenged Assyrian hegemony over western Asia and its trade routes. This was to be achieved by the significant improvement of the security of Assyria's exposed northern and eastern frontiers. It involved the completion of the destruction of the Hittites as a political force in Syria, the subjugation of perennially troublesome Babylonia, and the pacification and control of Syria, Palestine, and the Phoenician cities along the Mediterranean coast.

In a series of swift and devastating campaigns, Tiglath-pileser defeated Sarduris of Urartu, who had gone to the aid of his Aramaean allies in Syria, in a battle near Samsat on the Euphrates, forcing him to retreat back to Urartu. Tiglath-pileser re-conquered the territories that were previously lost and brought the war into the heart of the enemy country in 736, besieging but failing to take the Urartu capital at Tushpa on Lake Van. Although he had defeated Urartu in battle, Tiglath-pileser failed to translate the defeat into practical political outcomes and left most of the Urartian Empire intact.

When trouble broke out in Babylonia once again in 734 with the death of the pro-Assyrian ruler Nabu-nasir (c. 747–734), Tiglath-pileser intervened. It took about three years to pacify the country, which he placed under direct Assyrian administration after having himself declared king of Babylon. He then undertook another series of campaigns across the Zagros, defeated the Medes in the region northwest of Ecbatana (Hamadan), and pushed eastward as far as the fringes of the Salt Desert southwest of Tehran. No previous Assyrian force had ever penetrated that far to the east.

Once having reestablished Assyrian domination, Tiglath-pileser also made it his policy to assure continuing control of the conquered and annexed territories. He did this by establishing Assyrian colonies there, effectively integrating the territories as provinces within the empire with their governors reporting directly to the king. He also changed the fundamentally feudal structure of the Assyrian army, which was based on conscription of levies supplied by the lords of the land for the duration of the annual campaign season, to that of a professional standing army formed of contingents from the various dependencies of the empire. This change dramatically increased the capabilities of the Assyrian army, but was to prove a long-term liability as the loyalty of such troops became questionable when they were needed the most.

To forestall the emergence of indigenous liberation movements and to reduce the prospects for future rebellions, Tiglath-pileser made it his policy to transplant the elite elements of the conquered populations from their home territories to other locations within the Assyrian Empire. Accordingly, he ordered the transfer of some 65,000 Medes to settlements along the Diyala, while similarly transplanting large numbers of Aramaeans from Syria to occupy the lands vacated by the Medes. At the same time, Tiglath-pileser's drive toward the west prompted the threatened states of the region to join forces in an effort to block the Assyrian advance. However, the most they were able to accomplish was to slow it down a bit. In 732, Damascus, the most important city of the west, fell once again to the Assyrian armies. By the time of his death in 727, Tiglath-pileser had left to his successors an empire stretching from the Egyptian frontier to the Persian Gulf and as far north as Cilicia in Asia Minor.

Tiglath-pileser's successes created serious problems for the two powers that had so far managed to remain out of Assyria's grasp, Egypt and Elam. In both cases, Assyrian expansionism had significant effects on their economies. The Assyrian occupation of Phoenicia affected Egypt's commercial relations with one of its major trading partners, while Tiglath-pileser's drive into Iran interrupted the major trade routes between Elam and the north. Neither country was in a position to go to war with Assyria, which was then at the height of its power. Instead, they chose the next best alternative of lending support surreptitiously, in both arms and men, to the numerous vassal states and sheikdoms that seemed to be in continual revolt against Assyrian rule.

Under great pressure, Egypt managed to forestall an invasion by reaching an accommodation with Assyria. In effect, Egypt was compelled to renounce all claims that it had on territories in Asia, and to desist from any provocative behavior beyond its northern frontier. This had an immediate and tangible effect on Samaria, under the rule of Hoshea (732–724) at the time. Unable to resist Assyria without Egyptian support, Samaria was forced to acknowledge Assyria's suzerainty and to become one of the latter's vassal states.

The situation changed dramatically, however, with the accession of Shalmaneser V (727–722) to the Assyrian throne. Coincidentally, a serious upheaval took place on the western imperial frontier. Egypt was overrun at the time by a Kushite invasion from the south, which placed a more aggressive regime under Shabak I in power in Memphis. In Samaria, Hoshea, restless under the Assyrian yoke, saw this as an opportune moment to forge an anti-Assyrian alliance with Egypt and Tyre, and to declare his repudiation of Assyrian suzerainty by refusing any further payment of the required tribute. This, of course, was quite unacceptable to Shalmaneser. "And the king of Assyria found conspiracy in Hoshea: for he had sent messengers to So king of Egypt, and brought no present to the king of Assyria, as he had done year by year."[8] The Assyrian reaction was swift and violent. Samaria was invaded, and the capital was placed under a siege that lasted some three years and was still in operation when Shalmaneser died.

When his successor Sargon II (722–705) mounted the throne, the consolidation of the Assyrian position in the west was undertaken in earnest. The kingdom of Israel in Samaria was finally and completely destroyed in 722–721 and some 30,000 Israelites were uprooted and dispersed throughout the empire. Sargon then turned to deal with the Phoenicians, who were quickly subdued, with the exception of Tyre which because of its offshore location was able to hold out for another twenty-one years. The Assyrians then took on the alliance of the Philistines and Egyptians, under Hanuna of Gaza and Shabak respectively, and defeated it decisively at Rafah on the Egyptian-Palestinian frontier in 720. For all practical purposes, Sargon succeeded in imposing undisputed Assyrian control of the entire Mediterranean coastal region of Syria and Palestine, extending his reach into the sea as far as Cyprus.

However, and despite its great power, Assyria was still incapable of dealing with the security challenges it faced on its eastern and western flanks simultaneously. Thus, while Sargon was distracted by his wars in the west, Merodach-baladan (Marduk-apla-iddina II), the paramount leader of the Chaldeans, the people of the lands of the northwestern littoral of the Persian Gulf, placed himself on the throne of Babylonia. The latter then formed an alliance with Humban-nikash (742–717), king of the Elamites who had their own score to settle with Assyria. Merodach-baladan seized the opportunity afforded by Sargon's preoccupation in the west to revolt against Assyrian domination. The Babylonian-Elamite forces fought a major battle with the Assyrians in 720, the net result of which, notwithstanding Sargon's claim of an Assyrian victory, was that Babylonia recovered its independence, at least temporarily. Once again Sargon was distracted by events in the west. He was forced to redirect his attention to Syria where a rebellion had broken out, as well as to the north where Urartu was developing an anti-Assyrian coalition with the Medes. Merodach-baladan was therefore able to rule Babylonia for a dozen years, relatively undisturbed, before Sargon finally deposed him.

At about this same time, a new threat appeared in the north. Hordes of Cimmerians invaded the region from southern Russia. One contingent, perhaps constituting the majority of the migrating tribesmen, crossed the Bosphorus into Anatolia and attacked and sacked Ephesus, the kingdom of Lydia, and a number of Ionian cities. Another smaller group descended on Armenia from the Caucasus. The Urartians succeeded in diverting the latter to Anatolia where they were confronted by the Phrygians, with whom they struggled for years and finally defeated, and to Assyrian territory to the south. Rising to the challenge, the Assyrians engaged and defeated the Cimmerians in a major battle at Tabal in 705, during which Sargon was killed.

The Cimmerian invasions had brought about the destruction of Phrygia and the weakening of both Lydia and the Ionian cities of Asia Minor. They also contributed significantly to the weakening and ultimate collapse of the kingdom of Urartu. The Cimmerians appear to have left no lasting impression on the region. They sowed a good deal of destruction and chaos and then vanished almost as suddenly as they first appeared.

Sargon's successor, Sennacherib (705–681), inherited the problem of trying to keep the relatively vast empire intact. Babylonia, with the connivance of the deposed Merodach-baladan who had renewed the alliance with the Elamites under their king Shutruk-nahunte II (717–699), once again attempted to challenge Assyrian suzerainty by taking advantage of the simultaneous outbreak of another rebellion in Palestine. Hezekiah (c. 720–692), king of Judah, aware of the mutinous stirrings in Babylonia, entered into an anti-Assyrian alliance with Shabak of Egypt, against the advice of the prophet Isaiah. The latter argued that Egypt was not a reliable ally, and that it would be a serious mistake for the king to base his foreign policy on the presumption of tangible Egyptian support. Indeed, according to Isaiah, Sennacherib sent an emissary to Jerusalem warning about the folly of relying on Egypt. "Behold, thou trustest upon the staff of this bruised reed, even upon Egypt; whereon if a man lean, it will go into his hand, and pierce it; so is Pharaoh king of Egypt to all that trust on him."[9] Isaiah's assessment of Egypt was to prove quite accurate. Judah's alliance with Egypt once again threatened Assyrian dominance of the vital trade routes of the region. If Hezekiah believed that Sennacherib would be unlikely to react very strongly in the west while a simultaneous threat was emerging on his very doorstep in the east, he apparently misjudged the importance placed on control of the trade routes by the Assyrians. Sennacherib marched against the alliance in 701 and soon placed Jerusalem, which received no significant support from Egypt, under siege. Notwithstanding Egypt's failure to meet its treaty obligations, it seemed that Hezekiah's policy was going to succeed anyway. The pressure of events in Babylonia forced Sennacherib to abruptly break off his campaign in Palestine in order to suppress the rebellion that had erupted on his doorstep in Babylonia once again.

This time Sennacherib placed his eldest son Ashur-nadin-shumi (699–694) on the Babylonian throne, hoping thereby to forestall further challenges to Assyrian suzerainty. Nonetheless, repeated uprisings took place over the next dozen years, particularly by the Elamites under Hallushu-Inshushinak (699–693) and Humban-nimena (692–687). Elam had now become a major factor in the politics of Babylonia and a serious thorn in Assyria's side.

To punish Elam, Sennacherib launched an audacious amphibious invasion of the country in 695. Syrian craftsmen were brought to Nineveh where they constructed a large fleet of ships that were ferried down the Tigris as far as Opis. From there they were then dragged on rollers for some 28 miles to the Euphrates from which they proceeded to the mouth of the river while the Assyrian army proceeded south by land. The Assyrians were thus able to bring their forces across the Persian Gulf and mount a successful surprise assault on Elam, conquering a few cities and accumulating a good deal of booty before returning to Assyria. However, in 694, while the Assyrians were still preoccupied in the south, the Elamites retaliated by launching a daring raid of their own across the Tigris during which they took Sippar and captured Sennacherib's son. They also managed to place an Elamite puppet on the Babylonian throne for a few months. However, they were unable to successfully contain the far more powerful Assyrians for more than a short while. Then, in 689, with the support of the king of Elam, the Babylonians revolted once again. This time, having nearly suffered a defeat in suppressing the rebellion, Sennacherib retaliated by virtually destroying the ancient Mesopotamian capital of Babylon after a siege that lasted almost a year. The net effect of this was to pacify the country for another eight years.

No sooner had Sennacherib restored order in the south than he was forced to direct his attention to a new threat that was emerging in the distant northwest. It was at about this time that the coasts of Anatolia became subject to intense colonization and settlement by Ionian Greeks, who began to expand eastward along the Mediterranean. About 698, Kirua, the governor of Cilicia, revolted against Assyria and aligned himself with the Ionians who had landed on the Cilician coast and established bases at Tarsus and Ingira. They seized the Cilician Gates, thereby interrupting the great trade route through the Taurus Mountains from Syria to Anatolia and the Black Sea coast.

Sennacherib's armies engaged and defeated the Greeks in a major battle, blocking their attempts to gain control of the important Syrian-Palestinian coastal trade routes as well as any further eastward expansion of their colonies. Nonetheless, by the end of the seventh century Ionian expansion into the Middle East had become a significant factor that would greatly affect its future history. Not only had the Ionians driven the Phoenician traders out of Greek waters, but also they had severed the Phoenician trade routes that linked the motherland with its major trade centers and colonies in Carthage, Sicily, and Spain, thereby permanently reducing the previously preeminent role of the Phoenicians in international maritime commerce.

The Assyrian Empire reached its zenith under Sennacherib's successor Esarhaddon (681–668), whose first major act was to rebuild Babylon. This proved very popular and helped keep Babylonia generally quiet during his reign. Elsewhere, however, he took a rather harsher approach to dealing with the problems he inherited. When Abdmilkut, king of Sidon, revolted in 678, Esarhaddon completely destroyed the city and annihilated the population and replaced it with settlers imported from the Persian Gulf region. In retaliation for its repeated interference in Palestine and Phoenicia, where it was constantly promoting rebellion, Esarhaddon invaded Egypt in 671, defeated Taharqa, the Nubian king of the country, and conquered and occupied the Nile Delta as far south as Memphis. Although Egypt was to remain under Assyrian rule for fifteen years, it was not a trouble-free occupation. In 669 Taharqa returned from the south where he had sought refuge. He triggered a revolt against the Assyrians and retook Memphis. Esarhaddon was on his way back to Egypt to quell this rebellion when he died en route in Syria, leaving the task to his successor.

Early in his reign Esarhaddon was faced with a new threat in the north that would ultimately have major impact on the history of the Middle East. A nomadic people from southern Russia, the Scythians, came across the Caucasus following the Cimmerians, with whom they were closely related and who had already established themselves in Anatolia, Armenia, and Iran. The Cimmerians pushed through the Taurus passes in 679 and descended on the Assyrian vassal states in Cilicia. Esarhaddon counterattacked swiftly, driving the Cimmerian hordes back across the Halys River where, three years later, they conquered the kingdom of Phrygia.

Concerned about the succession crises that seemed to be endemic in the kingdoms of the Middle East, Esarhaddon took steps in 672 to ensure a peaceful succession by effectively dividing the empire between his two principal heirs. He made Ashurbanipal his successor in Assyria and Shamash-shum-ukin the viceroy of Babylonia. So that the empire might remain intact, it was agreed that each of these rulers was to remain sovereign in his kingdom, although Babylonia was expected to show formal deference to Assyria. Under this arrangement, Assyria was to be responsible for the non-Mesopotamian components of the empire, its foreign policy, and the leadership of the imperial army. Surprisingly, this arrangement worked for seventeen years.

Ashurbanipal (668–626) also inherited the responsibility for restoring order in rebellious Egypt. Taharqa attempted to block the Assyrian advance but was defeated and forced to flee to Thebes in Upper Egypt, with the Assyrians in hot pursuit. Ashurbanipal's army reached Thebes but was unable to capture the elusive Egyptian king. Ashurbanipal, however, found himself in an awkward situation. The Assyrian forces were now about 1,300 miles from home and as a practical matter were in no position to maintain direct control of the vast territory they had traversed. Moreover, Ashurbanipal was soon beset with problems closer to home in Elam and Arabia that demanded his undivided attention. Accordingly, he had little choice but to reappoint some twenty local kings and governors who had not joined the rebellion to rule Egypt on his behalf, bolstered by some Assyrian garrisons and a number of harsh regulations that were to be imposed on the defeated Egyptians.

Once again, the slightest relaxation of the Assyrian grip precipitated rebellion. No sooner had the bulk of the Assyrian forces withdrawn than a plot was hatched for a new revolt. "All the kings . . . talked about rebellion and came, among themselves, to the unholy decision: 'Taharqa has been driven out of Egypt, how can we, ourselves, stay?' And they sent their mounted messengers to Taharqa, King of Nubia, to establish a sworn agreement: 'Let there be peace between us and let us come to mutual understanding; we will divide the country between us, no foreigner shall be ruler among us.' "[10] Unfortunately for the Egyptians, the plot was discovered and the plotters were arrested and sent to Nineveh where they were executed.

This did not put an end to the problem, however, because immediately upon Taharqa's death in 665, his successor Tanuatumun triggered yet another revolt and managed to seize Memphis. This forced Ashurbanipal to return to Egypt with a powerful army and to pursue the rebel leader to Thebes once again. This time, however, the Assyrians inflicted such damage on the city that it never recovered. Nonetheless, the most Ashurbanipal achieved by this campaign was a temporary respite during which he was able to turn his attention to Assyria's volatile eastern and northern frontiers.

About 655, taking advantage of the opportunity presented by Ashurbanipal's preoccupation with conflicts at the other end of his empire, Egypt and Lydia, both of them Mediterranean naval powers with common commercial interests, formed an alliance directed against Assyria. Psammetichus I (663–609), with the aid of his ally Gyges (c. 687–652) of Lydia, supported by a substantial number of Ionian and Carian Greek mercenaries, finally drove the Assyrians out of Egypt and pursued them into Palestine as far as Ashdod. Faced with an invasion of Akkad by the Elamites, and unable to deal effectively with both crises simultaneously, Ashurbanipal chose to save Mesopotamia rather than reinforce his garrisons in Egypt.

No sooner had the crises of 655 subsided than Ashurbanipal was confronted by a revolt in Babylonia. His brother Shamash-shum-ukin had remained faithful to the succession arrangement made by his father for some seventeen years, but ultimately came or was led to believe that Assyria was eclipsing Babylonia's rightful place as head of the empire. In 651 he closed the frontier with Assyria and entered into a series of alliances with a number of Ashurbanipal's enemies from Elam to Egypt. Unfortunately for him, however, Ashurbanipal learned of the plot before it could be put in effect and attacked Babylonia. The war went on for three years until 648, when Shamash-shum-ukin realized that it was a lost cause and set fire to his own palace in Babylon, perishing in the flames. Having disposed of Babylonia, Ashurbanipal then proceeded to retaliate against the various other parties to the cabal. He fought a difficult war against Arab tribes in the desert and a long war against Elam that went on until 646, ending with the destruction of Susa and the virtual obliteration of the country.

Although Ashurbanipal had managed to sustain the powerful empire he inherited, his successors found themselves increasingly incapable of maintaining it. Upon his death in 627, a revolt broke out in Assyria that had to be suppressed before his son Ashur-etil-ilani could take the throne. A similar crisis occurred a few years later when his brother Sin-shar-ishkun succeeded him about 623. Although the empire appeared to be intact, it was clearly decaying from within and would soon collapse under the blows it was to receive from the east.

In retrospect, the Assyrians had committed the same fundamental errors that were to plague many future empires as well. The incessant wars of conquest had the unanticipated and unacknowledged consequence of effectively undermining the state's primarily agricultural economic base. In the period preceding the adoption of Tiglath-pileser's policy of imperial expansion, the standing army was limited in size and could be supported by the booty and tribute garnered through its campaigns. When the security of the state was threatened along its frontiers, the farming population might be mobilized for short periods of time to help defend the country without seriously affecting the economy. However, with the new policy of territorial expansion and control it soon became necessary to expand the size of the army significantly. This meant drawing people away from their agricultural pursuits for longer periods of time, in many cases permanently, to meet the continually expanding military manpower requirements. The economic as well as social consequences for Assyrian society were disastrous.

The continued expansion of the empire soon demanded a standing army that exceeded the numbers that could be provided by an even fully mobilized Assyrian population. Accordingly, it became necessary to conscript the subjects of conquered lands and vassal states into the army. However, the need to rely increasingly on alien elements to support the empire, at the same time that its economic base was going to ruin, soon began to sap its inner strength. The empire was therefore in a poor position to satisfactorily meet the challenges it confronted, as the conquered nations became restive under its rule. Thus, it transpired that at the very time that Assyria was at the height of its imperial power, it was faced with a renewal of problems on its eastern frontier that were to result in its collapse soon thereafter.

NOTES

1. Georges Roux, *Ancient Iraq*, p. 236.
2. Ibid., p. 237.
3. George Rawlinson, *The Seven Great Monarchies of the Ancient Eastern World*, Vol.1, p.386.
4. Roux, *Ancient Iraq*, p. 253.
5. Chaim Herzog and Mordechai Gichon, *Battles of the Bible*, p. 84.
6. 1 Kings 20:1.
7. M. Chahin, *The Kingdom of Armenia*, p. 53.
8. 2 Kings 17:4.
9. Isa. 36:6.
10. James B. Pritchard, ed., *Ancient Near Eastern Texts Relating to the Old Testament*, pp. 294–295.

4

The Rise and Fall
of Media

Reacting to the series of setbacks that Urartu had suffered at Assyrian hands, Rusas I (c. 735–714), the son and successor of Sarduris II who had been defeated by Tiglath-pileser III, sought to restore Urartu's fortunes. He banded together the small tribes of Medes scattered along his southern frontier into an anti-Assyrian alliance. The purpose of this alliance was twofold. Rusas needed allies not only against Assyria, but also, perhaps even more important, to assure the security of the trade route from the east that was critical to sustaining Urartu's economy.

During this period, the primary east-west trade route from Iran and points farther east, possibly including China and India, passed between the west bank of Lake Urmia and the east bank of Lake Van to the vicinity of modern Erzerum, and from there to Trebizond on the Black Sea. It seems reasonable to assume that some of the trade passing along this route through Urartu most probably had previously taken the more southerly route through Assyrian-held territory to ports on the Mediterranean, from which Assyria drew lucrative revenues. It therefore would have been in Assyria's interest to disrupt the Urartian route, forcing a diversion of the trade through territories under its full control. This would seem to be a plausible explanation for Sargon's repeated forays into the region. Rusas evidently succeeded in mobilizing the Median tribes on his southeastern flank into a defensive alliance, no doubt because the Assyrians were generally perceived as a common danger.

One of the Median chieftains, Daiukku or Deioces (c. 727–675), recognized that the Medes might forever remain at the mercy of powers like Assyria because of their fragmentation under dozens of autonomous tribal leaders. The solution was obvious, and he soon emerged as the preeminent advocate of merging the Median tribes into a coherent political and military force. Sargon was quick to react to this nascent threat to Assyria's regional hegemony and invaded Media once again, forcing twenty-eight tribal chiefs to acknowledge his suzerainty. Daiukku, however, remained loyal to his alliance with Rusas who continued to harass the Assyrian vassals along his frontiers.

In 714, after a period of careful preparation, Sargon launched a full-scale invasion of the region. The coalition of Urartu and the Medes under Daiukku was quickly smashed, enabling the Assyrians to march through Urartu virtually unopposed and leave behind them a wide trail of destruction, stretching as far as the region immediately north of Lake Van, before withdrawing. Daiukku was captured and deported with his family to Hama in Syria. Nonetheless, Daiukku had succeeded in triggering what became an irrepressible and growing movement for national unification of the Medes and their liberation from under the Assyrian yoke. The struggle of the Medes for independence continued after him under the leadership of his tribe, the Bit Daiukku. A renewed attempt to impose a coherent and integrated structure on the Median tribes brought Sargon back to Media in 713, when he again subdued some forty-two tribal chiefs.

The extreme pressure applied against the Medes by Sargon to prevent their unification was not sustained under his successor, Sennacherib, who was distracted by other conflicts in the southern and western reaches of the Assyrian Empire. As a result the Medes were encouraged once again to rally around the house of Daiukku. About the year 700 they finally succeeded in achieving *de facto* independence. Assyria, however, was unwilling to accept the diminution of its empire and continued to seek to reassert its control over Media, an effort that led to a prolonged conflict that fully engaged the attention of Daiukku's successors.

During this same period, Egypt also effectively freed itself from the Assyrian yoke, although it briefly allied itself with Assyria to block the advance of the hordes of Indo-Europeans that were now pouring into the region from the north. The Cimmerians and Scythians, closely related tribes of aggressive horsemen and warriors, came down in droves from the southern slopes of the Caucasus Mountains into Azerbaijan and Anatolia. Their point of entry into the region was Urartu. Although they were ultimately repulsed, they so laid waste the country that Rusas is reported to have committed suicide out of despair. According to Assyrian records, "When Ursa [Rusa], king of Urartu, heard that Musasir had been destroyed and his god Haldi carried away, then with his own hand . . . he put an end to his life."[1] However, it is possible that he actually died from wounds received in battle.

The Cimmerians were compelled to veer westward into Anatolia where they occupied the southern shore of the Black Sea. They settled near the mouth of the Halys River, and from this base periodically plundered the rich areas of Asia Minor. They subsequently destroyed the kingdom of Phrygia in northern Anatolia and attacked Lydia along with its Ionian Greek allies in the western part of the peninsula. About 679, a Cimmerian force crossed the Taurus into northern Syria, but was turned back by the Assyrians.

After crossing the Caucasus, the Scythians turned eastward and descended into northwestern Iran. It did not take long before they found themselves confronting the Assyrians who blocked their path at the frontier. To maintain relative stability on his northeastern flank, the Assyrian king Esarhaddon managed to establish friendly relations with the Scythian horde by offering an Assyrian princess in marriage to its chief, Bartatua. This political strategy worked well, transforming the Scythians into loyal allies of Assyria for some time. Most significantly, the Scythians served as Assyria's proxy in the ongoing struggles with Urartu that finally came to an end about 672. Both Assyria and Urartu came to recognize the folly of bleeding each other inconclusively while more serious threats to both were emerging in Iran to the east, where the Medes were actively engaged in consolidating their power.

Within a few years, under the leadership of Khshathrita (c. 674–653), also known as Phraortes or Fravartish, the Medes finally achieved the national unification of their numerous tribes. Khshathrita welded them into a formidable military power and enabled them to undertake their own program of territorial expansion. From their base in northwestern Iran the Medes soon conquered the central part of the country. Media now represented a major but loosely-knit kingdom whose territory stretched from the Caspian Sea south to Ecbatana (Hamadan) and eastward to the fringes of the Salt Desert. This development was contrary to the interests of Assyria, which did all it could short of a major war, including raids as far as the desert region east of Tehran, to prevent it from happening. Unsuccessful in preventing the consolidation of Median power in the north, Esarhaddon turned his attention to developing a buffer zone of small states between Mesopotamia and Elam.

The Elamite ruler Humban-haltash II (681–675), who came to the throne the same year as Esarhaddon, appears to have been generally favorably disposed toward maintaining peaceful relations with Assyria, as was his brother and successor Urtaki, who may have ascended the throne of Elam with Assyria's help. As a result, Mesopotamia's southeastern frontier remained relatively stable for more than a decade. Then, between 665 and 655, during the reign of Ashurbanipal, the security arrangements put in place by Esarhaddon began to fall apart and the Assyrians had to deal with a major crisis on their eastern frontier.

It seems that at about the same time that Ashurbanipal became king of Assyria, dynastic politics in Elam forced Urtaki into what amounted to co-regency with an ambitious cousin, Tempt-Humban-Inshushinak. Under

the influence of the latter, Urtaki abruptly changed his policy of accommodation with Assyria. In 665, at a time when Ashurbanipal was preoccupied
with campaigns far to the west in Egypt and Ethiopia, the Elamites
mounted an attack on Mesopotamia. When he received word in Nineveh of
what had occurred, Ashurbanipal claimed to have been stunned by what
he considered a crass act of ingratitude on the part of the Elamites. "When
hard times came upon Elam and famine filled the land, I sent him [Urtaki]
corn to keep his people alive. I was his support. Those of his people who
fled from the hard times, and had found refuge in Assuria till rain fell once
more and there was a harvest—I sent these people, who had kept themselves alive in my country, back to him. In my heart I should never have expected an attack from the Elamite, never suspected him of hatred." He
quickly dispatched someone to the south to observe what was happening
and to report directly back to him. The report stated, according to Ashurbanipal, that "the Elamites have overrun all Akkad like a swarm of locusts
and are proceeding towards Babylon."[2] Once Ashurbanipal mobilized a
force and began marching southward, Urtaki withdrew from Mesopotamia and conveniently died shortly thereafter, effectively forestalling an
Assyrian punitive expedition against Elam.

With Urtaki out of the way, Tempt-Humban (c. 663–653) usurped the
Elamite throne and forced Urtaki's sons and other Elamite nobles, some
sixty in all, to flee to safety in Nineveh. Ashurbanipal rejected Tempt-
Humban's request that they return to Elam and they were granted asylum
in Assyria. Unable to do anything about it at the time, Tempt-Humban
spent the next decade consolidating his control of Elam and neighboring
territories in Iran such as Luristan. Then, in the summer of 653, the Elamites
mounted a major assault on Akkad that was successfully repulsed. Once
again, Ashurbanipal mobilized an expeditionary force that marched into
Elam shortly thereafter forcing Tempt-Humban to retreat to Susa, where he
was trapped and slain.

Ashurbanipal then critically weakened the indigenous political authority in Elam, hoping thereby to seriously reduce its potential for mischief.
The eldest of Urtaki's sons who had taken refuge in Assyria, Humban-
nikash II, was made king of Elam, and another son, Tammaritu I, was made
ruler of Hidali (Behbehan). But, to preclude national cohesion, the throne of
Susa was given to Atta-hamiti-Inshushinak, the scion of a family related to
the usurper Tempt-Humban. For five years the Assyrian ploy seemed to
work. However, by 648, when Atta-hamiti died and was succeeded by his
son Humban-haltash III, Elamite power was once again concentrated in the
throne of Susa and the country again became involved in an anti-Assyrian
conspiracy.

This situation was intolerable to the Assyrians, and Ashurbanipal
launched a major invasion of Elam, the capital at Susa falling in 646. He
boasted of his destruction of Elam: "In the course of a march which lasted

fifty-five days, I transformed the land into a wilderness. I scattered salt and thistles on its meadows. The wives and daughters of the kings of Elam, of old and new family, the town governors, the commanders, the whole corps of officers including the engineers, all the inhabitants, whether male or female, old or young . . . all these I dragged back to Assyria."[3] It seems clear that Ashurbanipal was determined to uproot Elam in a manner that would eliminate it as a future threat to Assyrian interests.

The political vacuum created in Elam by Assyrian policy provided the opportunity for the Persians, who had settled in the region of Persis or Fars on the northeastern shores of the Persian Gulf, to occupy Susa and begin to develop their power base in southwestern Iran.

Around 653, the relative quiet on the Median-Assyrian frontier was shattered when Khshathrita attempted an assault on Nineveh, the Assyrian capital. This adventure turned into a debacle when his forces were attacked in the rear by the Scythians who, at the time, were still allied with Assyria. Khshathrita was defeated and killed, leading the Scythians to follow up on this reversal by invading Media and subjecting it to their control for the next twenty-eight years. Emboldened by their victory over the Medes, and now joined by the Cimmerians who had survived their defeat in Cilicia by Ashurbanipal, they established themselves in Azerbaijan, in the area south and southeast of Lake Urmia, effectively placing the territory outside the reach of Assyrian control. From their base in Azerbaijan the Scythians turned on their erstwhile Assyrian allies and penetrated deeply into the Assyrian Empire, raiding and sacking the cities of Asia Minor, northern Syria, Phoenicia, Damascus (southern Syria), and Palestine. It was this onslaught that turned Assyria and Egypt, long-standing enemies, into temporary allies. After withdrawing from the coastal region, the Scythians returned to their base in Azerbaijan from which they extended their sphere of control to the region of the Zagros Mountains and the territory of the Mannai, another Iranian tribal group.

During the period in which the Medes were forced to accept Scythian suzerainty, Cyaxares or Huvakshatara (c. 624–585), the successor of Khshathrita, managed to rebuild the Median army, probably adopting many of the tactics of the Scythians, who were masters of mobile warfare. He also used the time to consolidate his political control over a number of areas in the vicinity of Lake Urmia. In 625, Cyaxares was ready to throw off the Scythian yoke and apparently won a decisive victory over them. He quickly made himself overlord of the other Iranian tribal groups, the Persians and the Mannai, thereby unifying the entire western part of the Iranian plateau under his rule. Cyaxares now turned his attention to Assyria, determined to complete what Khshathrita had tried but failed to accomplish, namely its destruction as the dominant regional power. He was to be assisted in achieving this goal by events that were transpiring on Assyria's southern flank.

THE BABYLONIAN-MEDIAN ALLIANCE

Upon the death of Ashurbanipal in 626, Assyria underwent a series of internal crises that not only sapped some of its strength but also encouraged insurrection by those previously held in check by its awesome power. Assyrian control of Syria and Palestine became increasingly ineffective and the Phoenician cities appear to have severed their ties to Nineveh. In Judah, the prophet Zephaniah was able to predict with confidence that the Lord "will stretch out His hand against the north and destroy Assyria; and will make Nineveh a desolation, and dry like the wilderness."[4] However, the greatest imminent danger to the continued viability of the empire lay to Assyria's immediate south, in Babylonia, where the struggle for independence had resumed.

Nabopolassar (Nabu-apal-usur), the Chaldean governor of the Sealands, assumed leadership of the insurrection and launched a guerrilla war that the Assyrian troops garrisoned at Nippur were unable to contain. In late 626 Nabopolassar (626–605) placed himself on the Babylonian throne, triggering an eleven-year war with Assyria. The initial focus of his struggle was the liberation of southern Mesopotamia, Sumer and Akkad, from Assyrian domination, a struggle that he effectively won when he succeeded in seizing the ancient Mesopotamian religious center at Nippur. Nabopolassar then made an abortive attempt to invade Assyria itself by simultaneously marching up both the Euphrates and Tigris Valleys. Although this attempt was repulsed, by 615 the Assyrian king Sin-shar-ishkun (621–612) was clearly on the defensive, his empire in a process of disintegration.

Taking advantage of Assyria's preoccupation with the war in Babylonia, Cyaxares invaded Assyria in 615, took Arrapha, and marched on Nineveh. But, like Khshathrita before him, he was attacked in the rear by bands of Scythians still loyal to the alliance with Assyria. Cyaxares was forced to suspend his assault on Nineveh while he dealt with the Scythians, soon bringing their role in history to an end. He then continued his attack on Assyria, taking Ashur in 614 as Nabopolassar approached from the south. The following year, Nabopolassar and Cyaxares concluded a mutual friendship and peace treaty that was sealed by the marriage of Cyaxares' granddaughter Amytis to the Babylonian heir apparent, Nebuchadrezzar. Once the alliance went into effect, the decisive defeat of Assyria was only a matter of time.

In 612 the Medes and Babylonians placed Nineveh, considered to be virtually impregnable, under a siege that lasted only thirteen weeks, a relatively short period as sieges went in antiquity, before its walls were penetrated. It is suggested that this signal military accomplishment was in great measure the result of the deliberate diversion of the Khosr River, which undermined Nineveh's defenses and caused a flood in the city. The last real king of Assyria, Sin-shar-ishkun, perished in the flames that consumed his palace as the city fell to the invaders. His successor, Ashur-uballit (612–605), one of his officers who took the name of the ancient monarch who had liberated Assyria from the Hurrians in the thirteenth century, fled to Harran in northeastern Syria, the Assyrian administrative center for the western provinces of the empire. There he attempted to mobilize what was left of the army.

At this point, sensing an opportunity for Egypt to regain its traditional role as a major power in Asia, the pharaoh Necho II (609–594) entered into an alliance with Ashur-uballit and took the field against the Babylonian-Median entente. With Assyria no longer a threat to its security, Egypt was determined to try to prevent Babylonia from taking Assyria's place as the dominant regional power. Accordingly, it was prepared to join forces with its erstwhile enemy in an effort to tip the regional balance of power in its own favor.

However, for Josiah (637–607), king of the small state of Judah, as for the other small states of the region, relative territorial security and national independence were possible only when the regional balance of power was such that Egypt, Assyria, and Babylonia were in contention with one another. Josiah therefore interpreted the Egyptian-Assyrian alliance as a threat to Judah's independence and he attempted to prevent Necho from joining forces with Assyria against Babylonia. Judah, in effect, had made itself a de facto ally of Babylonia. Josiah rejected Egypt's offer of neutrality and confronted Necho's army at the strategic crossroads of Megiddo, but his forces were overwhelmed and he was killed in the ensuing battle. The combined Egyptian-Assyrian forces then marched eastward reaching Carchemish in 607, where they took control of the Euphrates crossing point.

As a practical matter, Babylonia was not in a position to replace the Assyrian Empire with its own. The rise of a powerful Median state on its eastern flank precluded this. As a result, control of the trade routes in the west became even more important to Babylonia than they had been to Assyria. Nebuchadrezzar, who succeeded to the throne of Babylonia, was determined to establish his absolute mastery of Syria and the eastern Mediterranean coastal region. Thus, while still the crown prince, Nebuchadrezzar undertook the task of re-conquering Syria for Babylonia in 607. For two years the Babylonian army struggled to establish bridgeheads at other Euphrates crossing points that would enable them to outflank the Egyptian-Assyrian forces, but to no avail. Finally, in 605 Nebuchadrezzar launched a successful frontal attack on Carchemish, taking the city.

With Carchemish in his hands, and the road to the west open before them, the Babylonian armies under Nebuchadrezzar swept through Syria and Palestine in the spring of 605. It was at this time that Judah, under Jehoiakim (607–597), was forced to become a reluctant vassal state of Babylonia. Nebuchadrezzar had advanced as far as Pelusium on the frontier of

Egypt when he received word of the death of his father. Concerned about the political risks involved in not being in the capital during a succession, which was rarely trouble-free, Nebuchadrezzar abruptly terminated his campaign and swiftly returned to Babylon by the end of the summer to mount the throne.

Nebuchadrezzar (605–562), like the Assyrian kings before him, soon discovered that it was relatively easy to conquer Syria and Palestine but very difficult to maintain Babylonian authority there and, more important, to collect the tribute that was levied on the Phoenicians, Philistines, and Jews of the coastal region. He was compelled to campaign in the region repeatedly to enforce his writ. Finally, in 601, he decided to march on Egypt once again. By this time, however, the Egyptians had been able to rebuild their forces to the extent that they were in a position to fight the Babylonians to a stalemate at the very gateway to the country.

Having incurred heavy losses, Nebuchadrezzar was forced to withdraw to Babylon to replenish his army. This reverse encouraged Jehoiakim and other minor kings of the region to reconsider their position regarding Babylonian suzerainty. In 597, Jehoiakim decided, against the advice of the prophet Jeremiah, to transfer Judah's allegiance to Egypt and to refuse to pay any further tribute to Nebuchadrezzar. The latter's response to this act of rebellion came swiftly. As Jehoiakim had been warned, the Egyptian alliance proved to be worthless. In March 597, Jerusalem was placed under siege by Nebuchadrezzar's forces. It was not long before Jehoiakim was forced to capitulate. His misjudgment resulted in the subsequent exile of thousands of Judah's leading families and military officers to Babylonia.

The immediate struggle for control of the Fertile Crescent had been decided decisively in favor of Babylonia. Egypt was effectively forced to remain behind its own traditional frontiers in Africa, and Assyria disappeared entirely from the stage of history.

The Assyrian Empire was divided among the victors, the southwestern part as far as the Egyptian frontier going to Babylonia, while the rest of Assyria as far north and west as the Halys in Anatolia was annexed by Media. Beyond the Halys lay the kingdom of Lydia, which had by this time already become a major center of international commerce. For the next five years, after having absorbed Urartu within his domains, Cyaxares attempted in vain to gain control of Lydia. The latter, however, proved to be quite formidable and the conflict was ultimately settled on the basis of the preservation of the status quo, with the Halys serving as the boundary between Media and Lydia. Once again, peace was to be assured by a royal marriage, this time between the daughter of the Lydian king and Astyages or Arshtivaiga (c. 584–549), who was to succeed Cyaxares as king of Media.

THE DECLINE OF MEDIA AND THE RISE OF
THE PERSIANS

The restored kingdom of Babylonia reached the height of its power and glory under Nebuchadrezzar. He had defeated the Egyptian-Assyrian coalition organized to block Babylonian expansion at Carchemish, and forced an Egyptian withdrawal from Asia to its own frontiers. Hophra (588–568), the new king of Egypt, decided to inaugurate his reign by contesting Nebuchadrezzar's control of Syria and Palestine. He marched up the coast and attacked Tyre and Sidon. At the same time, he encouraged Zedekiah (597–586), nominal king of Jerusalem by the pleasure of Nebuchadrezzar, to take advantage of the changing situation and join with Egypt in an anti-Babylonian coalition. Beguiled by the prospect of breaking loose from Nebuchadrezzar's grasp and contrary to the counsel of the prophet Jeremiah, Zedekiah revolted and joined an Egyptian alliance that also included the petty states of Edom, Ammon, Moab, Tyre, and Sidon.

Nebuchadrezzar soon responded by marching into Syria and Palestine once more, systematically subduing the states that had risen against him. He invaded Judah and destroyed Jerusalem in 586 after an eighteen-month siege, carrying the rest of the most potentially restive elements of the population off to exile in Babylonia. He also finally achieved the subjugation of the offshore city-state of Tyre in 572, after a record thirteen-year siege. However, despite Babylonia's own enormous strength, Nebuchadrezzar saw the growing power of Media as a serious threat to the ultimate security of his empire. In anticipation of a Median attack he began the intensive fortification of his northern frontiers.

At about the same time, the Lydians, their frontier with Media secured by treaty with Cyaxares' successor Astyages, and harboring imperial ambitions of their own, launched a campaign to drive the Greeks out of Asia Minor. Croesus (560–546), who had become king of Lydia, attacked and subdued the Ionian and Aeolian cities along the Aegean and Mediterranean coasts of Anatolia, except for Miletus with which his father Alyattes had signed a treaty. He also subjugated the Dorian state of Caria, thereby extending the bounds of Lydia from the Halys in the east to the Aegean Sea in the west. Croesus now began to think in terms of expanding his realm beyond the Aegean; that is, he considered transforming Lydia into a naval power so that he might undertake the conquest of the Greek islands. Croesus' plans were upset, however, by events taking place farther to the south that were to result in the overthrow of his brother-in-law, the king of Media, and bring an abrupt end to the presumed security of the frontier separating the two states.

As Nebuchadrezzar had suspected, it was not to be long before his former allies, the Medes, would attempt to conquer Babylonia. Astyages led the Median armies, augmented by levies from Urartu, the Mannai, and the Scythians, against the last prince of Babylonia, Nabonidus (555–539), at

Harran. Nabonidus, however, outmaneuvered Astyages by entering into an alliance with Cyrus II, the king of the Persians, who had imperial ambitions of his own and was at the time attempting to obtain control of the major trade route that passed through Ecbatana, the capital of Media.

The Persian tribes had for some time been settled at Parsumash, in the foothills of the Bakhtiari Mountains east of the large bend in the Karun River. From this position, Elam buffered them from Assyria and Babylonia, a situation that gave them a degree of isolation that permitted gradual consolidation and expansion. The clan of Achaemenes, or Hakhamanish, established its hegemony over the Persians sometime during the eighth century. In the second quarter of the seventh century, Teispes or Chishpish (c. 675–640), the successor to the eponymous head of the clan, was forced to recognize the suzerainty of the emerging Median state under Khshathrita. The latter was engaged at the time in forming a military coalition of the Median and Iranian tribes in order to attack Assyria. The subsequent defeat of the Medes in 653, followed by their subjection to the Scythians until 625, effectively freed the Persians from Median control. Teispes subsequently divided his realm between his two sons, Ariaramnes (c. 640–590), who became the king of Parsa (Fars), and Cyrus I (c. 640–600), the king of Parsumash. Both shrewdly avoided taking sides in any of the conflicts raging in the area, a policy that permitted them to concentrate on the expansion and consolidation of their respective kingdoms.

When the Assyrian king, Ashurbanipal, undertook to put an end once and for all to the troublesome kingdom of Elam in the last quarter of the seventh century, his forces drove eastward as far the western frontier of Parsumash. This brought the Persians into direct contact with the Assyrians for the first time. On this occasion, Cyrus pledged his loyalty to the Assyrian crown. However, with the dismantling of the Assyrian Empire only a few years later, and in recognition of the resurgence of Median power under Cyaxares, the two relatively small Persian kingdoms had little choice but to recognize Median hegemony once again.

The prestige of the branch of the Achaemenids presided over by Cambyses I (c. 600–560), successor to Cyrus, rose dramatically with his marriage to the daughter of Astyages, king of Media, which was arranged by the latter in the hope of thereby securing the loyalty of the Persians. On the basis of this direct connection to the throne of Media, Cambyses apparently was able to pressure Arsames, the heir of Ariaramnes, into abdicating the throne of Parsa in favor of the family of Cyrus, again unifying the Persians under a single head. Cambyses' son and successor as king of the Persians was Cyrus II (559–530), who was thus both grandson and vassal of Astyages.

Cyrus II (the Great) harbored substantial imperial ambitions of his own and established a new royal Achaemenid capital at Pasargadae in the territory of Fars. He also began to impose his control over the tribes on the periphery of the kingdom he inherited from his father. It was because of his recognition of Cyrus' ambitions with respect to Media that Nabonidus sought his help in about 553. Nabonidus wanted the Persians to create a diversion that would split the Median forces, thereby permitting the Babylonians to retake Harran from them, which was essential to the restoration of vital communications and trade links with Syria and the Mediterranean seaboard. Reassertion of control over the regional trade routes was considered imperative to help counter the high inflation that had hit Babylonia as a consequence of the expansionist policies pursued by Nebuchadrezzar and Nabonidus. Indeed, Babylonia's economic woes had reached the point where it appears that Nabonidus may have made a serious attempt to shift the center of the empire to the west as part of an effort to secure control of the trade routes coming from southern Arabia. He appointed his son Belshazzar as regent in Babylonia while he led an army through Syria to northwestern Arabia where he established a base for the next decade at Taima, a crossroads for the trade routes from Damascus, Egypt, and the Arabian Sea. He then struck southward another 250 miles as far as Yathrib (Medina) to secure the caravan route through the Hejaz. For Cyrus, the alliance was equally desirable because, with the Medes preoccupied with the Babylonians, he would have greater freedom of action in extending his sphere of control northward into Media.

Astyages soon learned of the Babylonian-Persian conspiracy and demanded that Cyrus appear before him in Ecbatana. Cyrus, well aware of the implications of the summons refused to comply, thereby placing himself in revolt against his grandfather. Although he suffered an early defeat, Cyrus was able to recoup and carry on the insurrection. With the help of the Parthians and Hyrcanians who pledged their allegiances to him, and the subsequent betrayal of Astyages by the Median aristocracy during the decisive battle, Cyrus emerged victorious. With the fall of Ecbatana in 550, Cyrus was able to unite the Medes and Persians under a single crown, as the different parts of the Median Empire submitted to him without further struggle. He now presided over a unified and powerful empire stretching from the frontiers of Lydia in the west to Bactria in the east, and from the Caspian Sea to the Persian Gulf, which he organized into provinces governed by a *kshathrapavan* (protector of the kingdom) or satrap.

NOTES

1. M. Chahin, *The Kingdom of Armenia*, p. 89.
2. Cited by Walther Hinz, *The Lost World of Elam*, pp. 152–153.
3. Ibid., p.158.
4. Zeph. 2:13.

5

The Empire of the Achaemenids

From the outset of his unification of the Persians and Medes into a single imperial state, Cyrus the Great appears to have pursued two fundamental geopolitical objectives. In the east, he sought to contain any spillover from the movement westward of numerous hordes of Central Asian peoples that might threaten the integrity of the empire. To achieve this, it was necessary to extend the northeastern frontier of Persia to the Syr Darya (Jaxartes) River. Cyrus' basic aim in that region was therefore primarily defensive in that he wanted to assure the security of his frontiers against encroachment. However, expansion eastward was not his highest immediate priority. The acknowledgment of his suzerainty by Hyrcania and Parthia in the region east of the Caspian Sea (Transcaspia) provided a degree of security on his eastern flank that permitted him to focus his initial efforts at imperial expansion in the west.

There his goal was conditioned by the prevailing geopolitical environment, which was far more complex than that which prevailed in the east. The situation that Cyrus found on his assumption of power was complicated and somewhat chaotic. For the preceding three centuries the Assyrians had managed, at considerable cost in blood and treasure, to keep open the mountain passes leading into Media, Armenia, and Cappadocia. After the fall of Nineveh (in 612 B.C.E.), the Medes had taken control of the eastern and northern passes, while those providing access to Anatolia to the northwest were under the effective control of the Lydians and Cilicians. Maritime traffic to and from the Phoenician ports was subject to depredations by pirates from the Lydian coast as well as by Greeks aligned with Egypt. At the same time, the Babylonians were doing what they could to maintain control of trade in the Persian Gulf region, and were aspiring to seize control of the increasingly prosperous trade of Southern Arabia and the Red Sea littoral.

Given this situation, Cyrus adopted a twofold approach to achieving his objectives in the west. First, he sought to obtain possession of the Mediterranean ports that were the terminals of the major trade routes crossing western Asia. Second, he wanted complete control of Anatolia, including Lydia and the Greek cities and the maritime bases located along the coasts. The latter were of great strategic as well as commercial importance, providing well-established trade connections with the Greek world in addition to containing a reserve corps of highly skilled technical and military manpower. It is worth noting that Cyrus was primarily interested in the political and strategic control of Anatolia, along with the economic benefits to be derived from such a position, but not necessarily in its conquest, which would have entailed a host of practical problems. It is quite likely that he would have been satisfied if his suzerainty were to have been acknowledged by the states of the region, accompanied by some payment of tribute.

However, the fast moving events transpiring to the east, the deposition of Astyages, and the unification of the Medes and Persians under Cyrus, were apparently misread by Croesus (560–546), the king of Lydia. The latter viewed the collapse of Media as an opportunity to pursue his own expansionist interests in the territories previously under its sway. According to Herodotus, Croesus inquired of the Delphic oracles as to whether he should go to war with Persia, and whether he should seek to do so in conjunction with allies to enhance his overall military strength. The responses he reportedly received were "in each case a prophecy that if Croesus attacked the Persians, he would destroy a mighty empire, and a recommendation to him to look and see who were the most powerful of the Greeks, and to make alliance with them."[1] We cannot know if the course of action he subsequently undertook was a direct consequence of this revelation. In any case, to bolster his position in preparation for a probable conflict with Persia, Croesus entered into mutual defense alliances with Nabonidus of Babylonia and Amasis (568–526) of Egypt. He also obtained a pledge of support from Sparta, which promised to make its fleet available for the defense of Lydia should it become necessary. Croesus was soon to discover that Cyrus had no intention of permitting any part of the former Median Empire to slip through his fingers.

Cyrus learned of the Lydian alliances and took decisive steps to prevent them from coalescing into a coherent challenge to his ambitions in the spring of 546. He decided to move the Persian army into position to attack Lydia. How to accomplish this was rather problematic. Basically, Cyrus had only two choices. He could march northward and then cross into eastern Anatolia through Armenia, or he could move west across Mesopotamia and enter central Anatolia through Syria and Cilicia. The northern route was clearly the safer since, for the most part, it passed through Persian-controlled territory. However, attempting to move a large army through the mountains of Armenia in the springtime, when the snows were melting, did not present an appealing prospect. The alternate route was far more dangerous because it would expose the left flank of the army to attack by Nabonidus. Cyrus ultimately decided to risk a Babylonian attack and took the route across northern Mesopotamia and Syria.

It may be that Cyrus concluded, notwithstanding the Babylonian alliance with Lydia, that Nabonidus was unlikely to take the risk of initiating hostilities without assurance of a simultaneous attack by Croesus from the west, something that was not very likely. If this was Cyrus' calculation, it was soon to be vindicated; the Babylonians did not take advantage of Cyrus' vulnerability to an assault on the flank of his forces from the south, and the Persian army reached Cilicia unchallenged. Once arrived, Cyrus quickly and peacefully established his suzerainty over the local rulers who were disinclined to run the risks that refusal would have incurred. This development had the immediate effect of cutting the overland lines of communication between Lydia and its Egyptian and Babylonian allies. While it was still possible to communicate with Egypt by ship, there was no practical way to do so with Babylonia. This effectively nullified any potential for coordinated military action by the anti-Persian alliance.

It seems, however, that the change in circumstances did not cause Croesus to reassess his strategy. Evidently still expecting his allies to come to his aid, Croesus crossed the Halys, the accepted frontier between Media and Lydia, with an army that included sizable contingents of Ionian Greeks, and seized Cappadocia. Presumably, if it were necessary to engage the Persian army, which was rapidly approaching, he preferred to do so on other than Lydian territory. Cyrus moved into central Anatolia to take up the Lydian challenge and confronted Croesus' forces for the first time at Pteria in the fall of 546. Before the armies clashed, Cyrus proposed to Croesus that Lydia be incorporated intact into the Persian Empire with Croesus remaining its ruler. It was an offer that Croesus could not accept but just as clearly should not have refused.

The outcome of the battle was indecisive, giving Croesus hope that he might fare even better the next time. He retreated across the Halys to Sardis, hoping to use the coming winter to regroup his forces and to call, once again, for assistance from Sparta and Egypt, the putative allies with whom he was able to maintain sea communications. Moreover, since Cyrus had just taken Harran, an important commercial and administrative center, from Babylonia, there was reason to believe that Nabonidus might now be induced to attack the Persian army in its rear. What Croesus did not anticipate was that, contrary to the typically seasonal conduct of war in the region, Cyrus would have no reluctance to continue the campaign into the winter. Having disbanded much of his army to await remobilization the following spring, Croesus was unable to stop the Persian onslaught and soon found himself bottled up in his capital at Sardis. He now pleaded with the Spartans for help. However, before that help could come, Sardis had fallen and with it the independent kingdom of Lydia.

Lydia had served as a very important strategic asset for the Greeks, providing a buffer zone between them and the empires of the east. It had kept Greece from coming into direct contact with Assyria, and for more than half a century separated the Ionians in Anatolia from Media. Now with Lydia gone, Cyrus demanded the complete surrender of the Ionian city-states. The Ionians rejected the demand, with the initial exception of Miletus which, rather than risk possibly irreparable damage to its trade interests, quickly submitted. The defection of Miletus precluded the possibility of a fully coordinated resistance to the Persians since it split the Ionian front. Cyrus' general, Harpagos, laid effective siege to the Ionian cities, most of which, either through force or treachery paid for with Persian gold, were soon forced to submit. Only the Lycians, it seems, barricaded themselves in their city of Xanthus and fought to the death. Within three years Cyrus had achieved what Croesus had so much desired but could never quite manage to bring about, the subjugation of all Asia Minor.

Cyrus turned next to the east where he successively added the territories of Drangiana, Arachosia, Margiana, and Bactria to his rapidly expanding Persian Empire. He crossed the Oxus (Amu Darya) and moved on to the Syr Darya, making the latter the northeastern limit of his control. He then built a series of fortified towns along the frontier to serve as a forward defense against depredations by the nomadic tribes of Central Asia.

It also soon became quite evident that Cyrus would no longer tolerate the continued independent existence of Babylonia on his southern flank, always in a position to split his empire in two by a northward thrust. The southern part of the country had already been invaded from Elam in 546, and a Persian governor ruled the region from Erech. Then, in the autumn of 539, a Persian army crossed the Diyala and, joined by the forces of Gubaru, the Assyrian governor of Gutium who had defected to the Persians, overwhelmed and destroyed the Babylonian army at Opis on the Tigris. Babylon itself was subsequently taken virtually without a struggle, only token resistance being offered by the forces in the citadel. Babylonia as an independent state simply ceased to exist. The fate of Nabonidus is uncertain. Some suggest that Cyrus appointed him to be governor of Carmania in central Iran, others that he died in Babylon the following year.

In addition to being a great general, Cyrus was also a masterful statesman. He went out of his way to show particular sensitivity to the religious traditions and practices of the peoples who had become subject to his rule. Rather than characterize his victory as a defeat of the enemy, he portrayed himself as the successor of the national rulers he had displaced, making appropriate gestures of affiliation to their gods. He made it appear that all that had happened was a change of dynasty, with social and economic life being restored to its traditional patterns. As a result of such policies, the Persians experienced a far greater degree of loyalty to the Achaemenids than might otherwise have been expected from the peoples conquered by them. Moreover, in sharp contrast with the legacies of the Assyrian and Babylonian kings, Cyrus neither decimated the conquered peoples nor deported their leaders. His policies of benevolence and reconciliation were clearly unprecedented in the tumultuous history of the region.

As successor to the throne of Babylonia, Cyrus also became ruler of its imperial dependencies, most notably Syria and Palestine. During his first year of rule at Babylon, Cyrus issued an edict authorizing the return of the Jews from their captivity in Babylonia and the restoration of their temple in Jerusalem. In 537, under the leadership of Zerubbabel, who became their governor, more than 40,000 Jews were permitted to leave their places of exile in Mesopotamia to return to their homeland in Palestine. This single act earned the undying gratitude and loyalty of the Jewish people to the House of Cyrus and the Persian state for the next two centuries. In this instance, Cyrus' basic inclinations to tolerance and generosity also served a broader geopolitical purpose. Palestine was on the road to Egypt, whose conquest remained to be accomplished. It was surely desirable to have the strong support of the indigenous population if Cyrus intended to use Palestine as his forward base for such a venture.

Although the conquest of Egypt might have been considered essential to assuring control of the Red Sea region and the Arabian Peninsula, it seems that Cyrus' desire to take it was less the result of primarily strategic or commercial imperatives and more that of an imperialist obsession. Egypt was the seat of the other great civilization of the ancient Middle East, and for Cyrus, conquering it in addition to Babylonia meant becoming undisputed master of the heartland of the entire extended region. Cyrus, however, never got to undertake this project himself. After his subjugation of Babylonia he became distracted by turbulence on his Central Asian frontiers and seems to have met his death while battling against the Massagetae, a nomadic horde that had crossed the Syr Darya into Sogdiana. It was therefore left to Cambyses II (530–522), his eldest son, to complete the conquest of the Middle East begun by his father.

After some three years during which he was preoccupied with resolving internal issues stemming from his succession, and during which his brother Bardiya, who was governor of the eastern provinces, was assassinated, Cambyses turned his attention to an invasion of Egypt. It has been suggested that one of the reasons why Cambyses considered it necessary to attack Egypt may be connected with the Egyptian claim to Cyprus which, if acted upon, would have destabilized the Phoenician cities that were economically linked to both Egypt and Cyprus.

Perhaps in anticipation of a Persian drive toward Egypt after the elimination of Lydia, the Egyptian king Amasis allied himself with Polycrates, the powerful tyrant of Samos, hoping thereby to have the capacity to thwart or deter such an invasion. However, by the time the Persian armies reached Gaza, Samos abandoned Egypt to its fate. Polycrates switched allegiances and sent forty galleys to join the Phoenician fleet, which had aligned with the Persians for a seaborne assault on Egypt. The Egyptians appeared immobilized, relying primarily on Ionian mercenaries, who were quite disheartened by the defeats inflicted on their countrymen in Asia Minor, to defend the country.

By the time Cambyses' army crossed the Sinai desert and arrived at Pelusium in 525, Amasis had already died. The defeat of the Egyptian forces under his successor, Psammetichus III, who ruled Egypt for only about six months, and the subsequent fall of Memphis, spelled the end of Egyptian independence. Egypt was transformed into the Persian satrapy of Mudraya. However, to demonstrate the legitimacy of Persian rule to the Egyptians, Cambyses adopted the approach of Cyrus and made obeisance to the gods of Egypt, proclaiming himself the son of Ra, and styling himself not as the king of Persia but as the pharaoh of Egypt. He thereby established a claim to the throne that was independent of the fact that he had mounted the throne as a consequence of military conquest.

Following the subjugation of Egypt, Cambyses conceived of a plan to further expand the Persian Empire into Africa and perhaps over the rest of the known world. First, he sought to launch a naval expedition against Carthage, which dominated the western Mediterranean. However, this project had to be abandoned because the Phoenicians, whose fleet was critical to the enterprise, refused to fight against a sister colony. Second, he planned a campaign against the oasis of Ammon, which controlled the coastal route to Cyrenaica. A large force was dispatched for the purpose but failed to achieve its objective when it was overwhelmed by a powerful sandstorm in the desert. Nonetheless, the very fact of the Persian attempt proved sufficient to induce the Greeks of Cyrenaica to submit to Cambyses voluntarily, thereby bringing a part of the Greek world under Persian domination. Finally, Cambyses was intent on restoring Nubia to Egypt and conquering and annexing Ethiopia to the Persian Empire. He failed to realize this ambition as well. It seems that the expedition ran out of supplies and was forced to turn back to Memphis.

At this point, Cambyses was compelled to abandon his African adventures to return to Persia in 522, where a major internal crisis had developed. It seems that a certain Gaumata, who had a strong resemblance to Cambyses' brother Bardiya who had been secretly assassinated, assumed the identity of the latter and proclaimed himself the legitimate ruler of the empire. He quickly bought the loyalty of the people by promising to remit their taxes for a period of three years, and obtained the recognition of most of the provincial satraps. Cambyses died on the way home, possibly by his own hand.

The pretender was subsequently overthrown and killed in a palace coup, after ruling for only eight months, by Darius I (522–486), the son of Hystaspis, satrap of Parthia. As usual, any sign of disarray in the imperial capital produced rebellion in the provinces, and the present crisis was no exception. A serious insurrection broke out in Babylonia under Nidintu-Bel, who claimed to be a descendant of Nabonidus and styled himself as Nebuchadrezzar III. Babylon underwent a long and wearying siege before the revolt was suppressed. Darius' dilemmas were compounded by revolts that also erupted simultaneously in Elam, Media, and Armenia. At the same time, the Persian satraps of the distant provinces of the empire such as Egypt began to assert their independence, creating a new explosive situation that threatened the cohesion of the empire.

It took Darius about two years and nineteen battles to deal with these challenges to his authority, and he resolved to take steps to preclude such from easily happening again. Darius concluded that part of the problem was a consequence of Cyrus' very liberal administrative policy that effectively granted a great deal of autonomous authority to the satraps. At the same time, he also recognized that it was impractical to attempt to rule the vast empire of diverse peoples, religions, and cultures directly from the imperial capital. He therefore reorganized the administrative structure of the empire to provide for a combination of local autonomy and devolution of power with unquestioned centralized authority and control.

Since the satraps had to be given a considerable degree of autonomy, he deemed it necessary to reduce the extent of their authority by increasing their number to twenty, hoping thereby to make it easier to control them from the capital. He also established a system of governance that provided for the diffusion of local authority to multiple officials as a constraint on the ambitions of the satraps. Parallel to each satrap, he designated a commander in chief of the army in the province who reported directly to the king, as well as a third independent official who was responsible for taxation and revenues. He also appointed inspectors who reported to the king independently on conditions in the provinces.

To tie the provinces more closely to the new capital he established at Susa, Darius built a network of roads throughout the empire that facilitated both trade and the movement of troops wherever they might be needed. Thus, the royal road extended from Sardis in western Anatolia to Susa, a 1,700 mile distance, and had staging posts established all along the route with men and horses ready to carry the royal mail from the capital to the farthest reaches of the empire in about a week.

Darius' organizational skills and administrative reforms gave the vast Persian Empire a degree of coherence unknown in the region before his time.

NOTE

1. Herodotus, *The Persian Wars*, I.53.

6

The Persian-Greek Wars

Once having reasserted control over the far-flung Persian imperial domains, Darius turned to pursue the aim of expanding the reach of the empire into Europe. It seems likely that his original plan was to conquer Thrace first to secure the northern approaches to the Bosphorus, and then to proceed to establish Persia's northern frontier at the Danube. This would be followed by a thrust westward to conquer Macedonia, thereby securing control of the entire Balkan Peninsula. Domination of the Balkans would have the immediate effect of cutting off Greece's main supply of timber, which was essential to its survival as a maritime power. Moreover, Greece had long imported most of the wheat it needed to feed its growing population from Egypt and Libya, which were now under Persian control. Seizure of the Bosphorus and the Turkish Straits would have cut off the import of grain from its last major source of supply, the markets along the northern littoral of the Black Sea. This combination of military and economic pressures could be expected to force the Greeks into submission. The strategic conception behind this plan was bold, to say the least.

The Thracians, who were to be targeted first, were closely related to tribes that were based north of the Danube between the Carpathian Mountains and the Pruth River, the region of modern Wallachia and Moldavia. Since the Danube froze in winter, it would be relatively easy for these tribes to cross the river and carry out raids in support of the Thracians, destabilizing the frontier and necessitating the maintenance of large forces to ensure its security. Darius therefore understood that it would be necessary to extend Persian control to the opposite bank of the Danube if the security of Thrace were to be assured. Indeed, a move beyond the Danube would also serve a broader strategic purpose. A thrust toward the Syr Darya from

Thrace through southern Russia would enable him to outflank and attack from behind the nomadic hordes of Scythians. The latter was the name applied by the Greeks to the variety of peoples living between the Carpathians and the Caucasus that were plaguing Darius' northern frontier in Asia. Furthermore, and perhaps even more important, Darius may have wished to gain control of the gold mines of Dacia and to establish secure lines of communication between Dacia and the Danube to facilitate export of the metal. Once having secured Thrace, as already noted, he would march westward into Macedonia, thereby effectively isolating Greece and denying it access to the timber so essential to its economic well-being.

Darius enlisted the support of the Ionian cities of Anatolia in this campaign. He was able to obtain the cooperation of the ruling tyrants against their mainland kinsmen because the retention of their positions of power was wholly contingent on the preservation of Persian suzerainty. Given the trends toward democratization in the Greek world at the time, a Persian defeat would also have probably meant revolution throughout the Ionian cities. Accordingly, they cooperated in the construction of a boat bridge across the Bosphorus to facilitate the crossing of the Persian army into Europe.

The invasion of Europe began in about 512 with a thrust into Thrace in the direction of the Danube. To assist further in the implementation of Darius' plan, the Ionian fleet sailed up the Danube to build another boat bridge that permitted the Persian army to cross the river in what appears to have been a futile attempt to catch the Scythian ruler, Idanthyrsos, in the Russian steppes. The Scythians, however, were more resilient than Darius anticipated. They harassed the Persian forces and, applying a "scorched earth" policy, forced Darius to abandon the campaign because of the difficulties encountered in keeping the army supplied with essential provisions. Although the Scythian phase of the campaign was without clear result, the Scythians did avoid crossing the Danube as long as Thrace was under Persian control.

Upon Darius' return to Anatolia, he left part of his army in Europe under the command of Megabazos, the satrap of Dascylium, who soon completed the subjugation of Thrace. Then, following Darius' grand strategy, Megabazos marched westward along the coast to Macedonia. His advance envoys were met at Amphaxitis in 510 by Amyntas (d.–c. 495), the king of Macedonia, who acknowledged Persian suzerainty to avoid a war he could not have won. Amyntas, who provided important military services to the Persians by protecting the strategic crossing of the Axius near Ichnae and by securing the passage through the Iron Gates, was permitted to remain on his throne as a vassal of Darius. In the meanwhile, Darius appointed Otanes as the new satrap of Ionia with his headquarters at Byzantium on the European side of the Bosphorus, where he was better positioned to control maritime traffic through the straits.

The powerful Persian presence on both shores of the Bosphorus soon had the effect of drawing Darius into the politics of the Greek city-states. Thus, when Athens came under attack by Sparta in 507, in a desperate attempt to preserve the democracy that was coming into being under Cleisthenes the Athenians sent a delegation to Artaphernes at Sardis inviting Persian intervention in the conflict on their behalf. The Persian terms for rendering such assistance were steep. They asked for no less than Athenian acceptance of Persian suzerainty and the surrender to Persia of all Athenian-held territories. The Athenian delegation reluctantly agreed to these terms, but by the time they arrived back in Athens the crisis had passed and their agreement was repudiated, a development that left Darius angry and perhaps determined to make Athens pay a steep price for this slight.

It was not long before the Ionian cities became disgruntled over the financial losses they were incurring as a result of Persian control of the Bosphorus traffic, as well as the tyrants imposed on them by the satraps. Ionian discontent with Persian suzerainty and taxation erupted in a revolt in 499 under the leadership of Aristagoras, the tyrant of Miletus. Aristagoras approached Athens and Sparta for help against Persia. Sparta was uncertain of its ability to obtain the support of the other members of the Peloponnesian alliance, especially Aegina and Corinth, whose navies would be essential in a campaign against the Persians, and therefore declined to get involved in the conflict. Athens, on the other hand, angered by Darius' recognition of the deposed tyrant Hippias as the legitimate ruler of Athens, agreed to send twenty ships to Ionia in support of the struggle. The Athenian naval contingent was bolstered by another five ships sent by Athens' ally Eretria.

The Persian satrap of Lydia, Artaphernes, marched on Miletus with the troops he had on hand, while the Ionians and their allies grouped at Ephesus and, pushing inland, were able to outflank Artaphernes and capture Sardis behind him. During the ensuing melee, the city caught fire and was virtually destroyed in 498, making the Lydians extremely hostile to the Ionian occupation. This, coupled with the fact that the Persian army was now marching on Sardis, forced the Ionians to withdraw. The Ionian forces were subsequently overtaken near Ephesus, where they were defeated after suffering heavy losses. At this point in the Ionian revolt a war broke out between Athens and Aegina that caused the Athenian and Eretrian fleets to abandon the Ionians and return to Greece. Notwithstanding the withdrawal of Athenian support, which virtually assured the failure of the uprising, the revolt soon spread northward to the Propontis, across the water to Thrace and Macedonia, and southward to Caria and Cyprus.

Darius reacted strongly to this challenge and soon retook Cyprus and the towns of the Hellespont. The re-conquest of Caria was more troublesome and cost Darius the loss of an army. Once the rebellion in Asia was completely suppressed, Darius decided to do three things. He undertook the reorganization of the Ionian cities, eliminating the tyrannies that had proved ineffective in preventing rebellion, and permitting the establishment of democracies in their place. Second, he was determined to reassert Persian authority and control in Thrace and Macedonia. Finally, he would punish those Greek city-states that had supported the Ionian rebellion and participated in the occupation and destruction of Sardis. However, the fates of Eretria and Athens were to be different. Eretria was to be destroyed, but not Athens. The army's mission there was to seize the city and restore the deposed tyrant Hippias, who had been living in exile in Persia for the past twenty years, to power. Presumably, the re-imposition of his rule was considered to be sufficient punishment for the Athenians.

Darius dispatched his son-in-law Mardonius to reestablish Persian supremacy in Thrace and Macedonia, following which he was to proceed south through Macedonia to attack Athens and Eretria. Mardonius marched through Thrace in 492 and promptly received the submission of Macedonia once again from Alexander I (c. 495–452), the successor of Amyntas, and launched a combined land and sea attack against Athens. The assault had to be called off, however, because a good part of the Persian fleet was destroyed by a storm off the dangerous promontory of Mount Athos, forcing Mardonius to return to Asia. Darius soon ordered a second invasion by way of the Aegean and the Greek islands, which seemed far more promising than another attempt through Macedonia. Setting sail from Samos with a large fleet in 490, the Persians headed first for Naxos and the Cyclades, which were quickly subdued. The fleet then made its way up the channel between Euboea and Attica and attacked Eretria. However, the Persian forces made no attempt to occupy Eretria. This was a purely punitive campaign and not a war of conquest. The city was sacked and its population enslaved and shipped off to servitude in Persia.

In retrospect, the harsh treatment accorded Eretria turned out to be a serious political blunder. The Greeks were divided among themselves and it might have been possible to reach a political settlement under which Athens would acknowledge Persian suzerainty. However, instead of promoting accommodation, the destruction of Eretria all but eliminated such a possibility. If Athens had to pay the price for the earlier destruction of Sardis, it would have to be extracted from it by force.

The Athenians met the Persians as they landed on the sea-plain of Marathon in 490 and engaged them in what was to prove to be a decisive battle. The Athenians had positioned themselves to attack the Persian flank as it tried to move down the coast toward Athens. The Persians therefore sent an advance force to block the Athenians, leaving the bulk of the Persian army free to move on Athens with its flank protected. The Athenians proceeded to attack the Persian blocking force, thereby disrupting the Persian operation. The Persians were shaken by the ferocity of the Greek assault and their lines quickly collapsed, resulting in a disorderly withdrawal and a slaughter of their forward troops, once again leaving the flank of the main force exposed. Seeing their operational plan nullified, the main Persian force embarked and withdrew from Marathon, and after exploring other sea approaches to Athens abandoned the enterprise.

The Greek victory at Marathon was unquestionably an event of supreme importance for the history of Greece and the Western world. By preventing the fall of Greece to Persia, the history of Europe, and consequently of much of the rest of the world, took a rather different course from what probably would have been the case had the Persians won the battle. Nonetheless, at the time, the Persians saw the defeat as a matter of little consequence. It was considered a comparatively minor military operation, the failure of which was simply attributed to the incompetence of the commanders of the relatively small force that actually engaged the Athenians. That Darius did not see Marathon as a decisive defeat is clearly reflected in the fact that he immediately began preparations to lead a great army and fleet to Greece with the intent of destroying Athens. Fortunately for the latter, the new invasion was deferred as a consequence of the revolt that broke out unexpectedly in Egypt in 486, which forced Darius to divert his attention away from Greece. He died the following year while preparing to lead the strike at Egypt personally.

Xerxes I (485–465) who had served as viceroy of Babylonia for a dozen years was chosen by Darius to be his successor, and it was he who finally subdued the Egyptian uprising in 484 with great brutality. However, before he could redirect his attention back to Athens another revolt broke out in Babylonia, causing a further delay in the Greek campaign, which had to wait until the rebellion was stamped out. Xerxes' policy in dealing with the restive peoples under Persian rule differed substantially from that of his predecessors. He went out of his way to humiliate the defeated. He not only tore down the walls of Babylon but also destroyed the temples and melted down the golden statue of the god Bel. This approach to dealing with the various subject peoples was to contribute significantly to the vulnerability and chronic instability of the empire in the years to come.

The unanticipated delay of four years in the start of the Persian attack gave the Greeks ample opportunity to prepare for the expected onslaught. They organized a confederation or league of Hellenic states, which was for all practical purposes a military alliance of Sparta and the Peloponnesian League, Athens, and a number of the other Greek city-states who agreed to join forces in resisting the invaders. There was general agreement that the defense of the country against the Persians should be led by the Spartans.

The long-awaited campaign began in the spring of 480 as Xerxes began his march from Sardis to the Hellespont with an army composed of contingents from forty-six nations and commanded by twenty-nine Persian generals. It took seven days for the force to cross the straits over the boat bridge constructed for it by the Phoenicians. Xerxes then made his way to Thessaly which, along with Boeotia, had decided to submit to the Persians without a fight. The army marched as far as Thermopylae, a narrow pass between the sea and the mountains that was the gateway to central Greece. The Persian fleet reached Artemisium, where it encountered the combined forces of the Greek states that had refused to submit to Xerxes and thereby placed themselves in a precarious situation in the event of a Persian victory over the Athenians. The ensuing naval battle was indecisive, shifting the principal burden of the battle to the land forces at Thermopylae.

Despite the heroic resistance put up by the Spartans to block the Persian advance at the strategically important pass, after several days the attacking forces broke through the Greek defenses and marched on toward Athens. The Persians took the city with little difficulty. With winter approaching and the main Greek armies still intact and well entrenched, Xerxes sought to outflank them from the sea with the fleet that had shadowed the progress of his land forces. At Salamis in 480, the Persian and Greek fleets subsequently engaged in what was surely the greatest sea battle known up to that point. In a remarkable upset, the Persian fleet met disaster as Xerxes watched.

Xerxes feared that the news of the defeat might precipitate another revolt by the Ionians in Anatolia, possibly cutting off his line of retreat. Accordingly, he immediately sent the remainder of the Persian fleet to the Hellespont to guard the boat bridge in order to ensure the security of his lines of communication to the coast. However, by the time Xerxes arrived there, the bridge had been destroyed by a storm and he had to be ferried across to Abydos.

The defeat at Salamis had left the Persian land forces fully intact. The problem, however, was how to keep them supplied without having control of the sea. Since cold weather was approaching rapidly, it was decided to defer restarting the campaign until the following spring. Xerxes left the bulk of the Persian army under Mardonius, perhaps some 90,000 men or more, to spend the winter in Thessaly while he withdrew to Sardis with a contingent of 60,000 troops to await the renewal of hostilities.

In the spring of 479, Artazabus and the troops that had accompanied Xerxes the previous winter returned to join forces with Mardonius who, in the words of one writer, "was charged with finishing off the war, downgraded from a royal expedition to a frontier operation."[1] To split the Greek alliance and perhaps to get Athens to withdraw from the Hellenic league, Mardonius offered exceptionally generous terms to Athens through Alexander, the king of Macedonia, who urged their acceptance. According to Herodotus, Xerxes had instructed Mardonius as follows: "All the trespasses which the Athenians have committed against me I freely forgive. Now then, Mardonius, thus act towards them. Restore to them their territory; and let them choose for themselves whatever land they like besides, and let them dwell therein as a free people. Build up likewise all their temples which I burned, if on these terms they will consent to enter into a league with me."[2]

Fearing the possible strategic consequences of a defection by Athens for the defense of the Pelopennesus, Sparta appealed to the pan-Hellenic sentiments of the Athenians and made a counteroffer to compensate Athens for the heavy economic losses it had sustained over the past two years. "We offer you, therefore, on the part of the Lacedaemonians and the allies, sustenance for your women and for the unwarlike portion of your households, so long as the war endures."[3] Pan-Hellenism, supplemented by an economic incentive, prevailed and Athens rejected the Persian offer.

Mardonius forced the evacuation of Athens once again in 479 and then withdrew to Plataea, where he set up defensive positions and deliberately avoided taking any offensive action. It was his expectation that the longer a major confrontation was avoided the more likely it was that the shaky coalition of Greek states would disintegrate. His strategy seemed to be working for a time, but ultimately Sparta joined with Athens, together fielding a military force that though smaller than the opposing Persian army was quite formidable. As it turned out, Mardonius soon abandoned his strategy of delay, perhaps because of a conflict with his second in command, Artazabus, and took to the offensive. The initiative misfired when Artazabus refused to commit the 40,000 or more troops still under his command to the fight. As a result, the Persian forces were thrown back in disarray by the Spartans, with Mardonius being killed in the battle, further reducing the morale of his army. At the same time, a newly arrived Greek fleet destroyed the Persian ships that had taken shelter near Samos. After the death of Mardonius, Artazabus retreated to the Hellespont with the remainder of the Persian army. Following this debacle, Xerxes appears to have accepted the reality of his inability to maintain a Persian presence in Europe and returned from Sardis to his capital at Susa.

The struggle between Greeks and Persians continued for some years, albeit at a generally low level of conflict. Some of the Ionians, exhibiting renewed confidence in their ability to throw off Persian rule, joined the Hellenic confederation, which now moved from defensive to offensive operations. As the leading power in the Aegean region, Athens organized an alliance of the island and city-states and then assumed the leadership of the Delian League, each of whose members made a commitment to carry on the struggle against Persia. The Greek fleet under the command of Cimon soon made itself felt along the periphery of Anatolia. The coastal towns of Caria were freed from Persian rule and the Lycians were pressured into joining the league. Finally, in 466, on the banks of the Eurymedon in Pamphylia, the league decisively defeated the Persian army and fleet in a combined land-sea operation. In addition to the earlier Greek gains in the Ionian Islands, this defeat cost Persia control of the southern Anatolian coast from Caria to

Pamphylia, effectively eliminating any potential Persian threat against Greece.

The failure of the Persian campaign in Greece, as important as it was for Europe, had little noticeable impact on the vast Persian Empire in Asia. The Greeks were never sufficiently united to follow up their victories against Persian arms with an invasion of the Anatolian heartland, and the Bosphorus therefore became the de facto military frontier between the Greek and Persian worlds. However, the geographical divide could not prevent Greek cultural penetration into the frontier regions, particularly Anatolia where Hellenic influences became especially prominent. At the same time, Persian political influence continued to be felt in Greece as Persian gold was used adroitly to deepen the rifts between the city-states, helping to prevent the unity that might have posed a security threat to the empire.

Xerxes was assassinated in 465 and was succeeded by Artaxerxes I Longimanus (464–424). The succession did not go uncontested, and a rebellion by his brother, the satrap of Bactria, was the first of many that the new ruler had to deal with. More significant for the future of the empire was the revolt that broke out in Egypt in 460. Inaros, a Libyan chief, had stirred up the territories of the lower Nile region and appealed to the commanders of the Athenian and confederation fleets that were operating in the waters off Cyprus for assistance in expelling the Persians. The potential benefits of such intervention were quite appealing to the Athenians. Not only did the expulsion of the Persians offer the prospect of an assured supply of grain from Egypt, supplies that had become difficult for Greece to obtain because of the breakdown in the normal trade links with Anatolia, but also it raised the possibility of Athenian control of the entire trade of the Nile Valley as well as the establishment of an Athenian naval base on the Egyptian coast. Athens stood to gain significant advantages over its rival Greek cities from an Egyptian connection. Such an expedition, however, was a radical departure from the character of previous campaigns against the Persians, all of which could be rationalized as defensive in nature or for the purpose of restoring freedom to Greek territories or colonies. An Athenian invasion of Egypt would be a purely imperialist adventure. Nonetheless, the temptation proved too great to resist and Athens took the step to build an empire of its own at Persia's expense.

In the meanwhile, a Persian army was dispatched to Egypt to suppress the revolt but failed to accomplish this goal. By the time the Athenian fleet reached the Nile it found that the Persians had already been defeated in the delta by the forces of Inaros. Nonetheless, the Athenians sailed farther up the river and took Memphis, except for the citadel where the Persian garrison held out for more than two years. Artaxerxes responded to the Athenian action by attempting to bribe Sparta into attacking Attica, forcing a withdrawal of the Athenian forces from Egypt to defend their homeland. This effort ultimately failed and Artaxerxes sent a large army to Egypt under Megabyzus, supported by a Phoenician fleet, to expel the Athenians and suppress the revolt. The Athenians were forced out of Memphis in 456 and their ships were then bottled up at Prosopitis, an island formed by a canal that intersected the Canopic and Sebennytic Channels of the Nile. Here Megabyzus kept the fleet blockaded for a year and a half until he drained the canal and grounded the fleet on dry land. The Athenians burned their ships and retreated to Byblos where, having no viable alternative, they capitulated. They were subsequently permitted to leave for Cyrenaica where they found transportation back to Greece. In the interim, an Athenian relief fleet had arrived but was trapped and attacked by the powerful Phoenician fleet that virtually destroyed it in the Mendesian Channel of the Nile Delta.

Notwithstanding the successful restoration of Persian control in Egypt, the tide of affairs clearly was turning against the Persian Empire. The Phoenician fleet, representing Persia's primary remaining naval forces, was sent by Artaxerxes to restore Persian authority in Cyprus. This development virtually coincided with the agreement reached in 452 between Athens and Sparta for a joint effort against Persia. Thus, Cimon, commander of the combined Hellenic forces, arrived off Cyprus with a substantial fleet and defeated the Phoenicians at Cypriot Salamis, effectively destroying Persia's existing naval capability. Nonetheless, at this point the success of Greek arms no longer served as a spur to continuing the seemingly interminable war with Persia. It became apparent to the Athenian leaders, particularly Pericles, that they could not successfully prosecute a war against Persia and deal with the internal conflicts of Greece at the same time. According higher priority to sorting out the rivalries that were plaguing Greece, they showed interest in arriving at a peace agreement with Persia. Artaxerxes, who was now confronted by the rebellion of Megabyzus, his general who had just suppressed the Egyptian revolt, was also anxious to be able to concentrate his energies on holding the core of the empire together and was therefore quite amenable to a peace treaty with Athens.

Although it is unclear, and probably unlikely, that a formal treaty was ever negotiated and signed, a tacit agreement between Athens and Persia, the Peace of Callias, was concluded about 448. Under the terms of the agreement, Artaxerxes relinquished his claims on the Ionian cities that were members of the Delian League. He also agreed to restrict the movement of Persian troops across the Halys in Anatolia and to refrain from sending warships into the Aegean. Athens, on the other hand, undertook to assure the security of the coasts of the Persian Empire from attack.

As a practical matter, the Athenian-Persian accord was not observed very scrupulously or for very long. Such restraint as was displayed by the parties was more a consequence of expediency than principle. Artaxerxes, as well as his successor, Darius II Nothus (423–404), was lavish in his use of gold for purposes of intervention in Greek affairs, particularly with inciting Athens against Sparta during the Peloponnesian War. Ever keen to find a weakness that would permit the reduction of Athenian influence in Asia, the Persians once again found an opportunity to intervene in Greek affairs following the disaster of the Athenian expedition against Syracuse in Sicily. The Athenians had given support to a Persian rebel and Darius apparently regarded this as an irreparable breach of the Peace of Callias. He subsequently urged his satraps in Ionia and Phrygia to resume the collection of tribute from the Greek cities in Asia. Tissaphernes, the satrap of Sardis, saw the moment as ripe to incite a rebellion of the Ionian cities against Athens, to be reinforced by a close alliance between Persia and Sparta.

The revolt against Athens began in Chios in the summer of 412 and soon spread, with the support of Sparta, to a number of other cities. The initial success of the venture quickly led to the Treaty of Miletus between Persia and Sparta, which provided:

Whatever country or cities the king [Darius] has, or the king's ancestors had, shall be the king's; and whatever came in to the Athenians from these cities, either money or any other thing, the king and the Lacedaemonians and their allies shall jointly hinder the Athenians from receiving either money or any other thing.

The war with the Athenians shall be carried on jointly by the king and by the Lacedaemonians and their allies; and it shall not be lawful to make peace with the Athenians except both agree, the king on his side and the Lacedaemonians and their allies on theirs.

If any revolt from the king they shall be the enemies of the Lacedaemonians and their allies. And if any revolt from the Lacedaemonians and their allies they shall be the enemies of the king in like manner.[4]

The treaty was subsequently revised at the insistence of the Spartans, who felt that their interests were not sufficiently provided for under the agreement as it stood. The revised treaty basically added the following financial and mutual security provisions:

The expense of all troops in the king's country, sent for by the king, shall be borne by the king.

If any of the states comprised in this convention with the king attack the king's country, the rest shall stop them and aid the king to the best of their power. And if any in the king's country or in the countries under the king's rule attack the country of the Lacedaemonians or their allies, the king shall stop it and help them to the best of his power.[5]

In essence, in return for Persian financial subsidies, Sparta recognized the right of the Persian king to those Greek cities in Asia that had been usurped by Athens, and to the arrears in tribute that they long owed the Persian crown. This amounted to a de facto recognition of Darius' sovereignty over the Greeks in Asia. It appears that Persian gold was now a more effective instrument of imperial policy than Persian arms. The Sparta-Persia alignment facilitated the blockade of the straits, denying Athens access to the wheat of northern Anatolia. This further compounded Athens' problems and contributed directly to its capitulation to Sparta in 404.

The accession to the throne of Persia that same year of Darius' son and successor, Artaxerxes II Mnemon (404–358), was marred by a succession crisis more serious than that experienced by any of his predecessors. His brother Cyrus, who as satrap of Lydia, Phrygia, and Cappadocia had virtually all the military forces in Anatolia at his disposal, contested the succession. Although Cyrus' bid for power was subsequently quashed at the battle of Cunaxa near Babylon in 401, it had consequences that bode ill for the stability of the empire. For one thing, Cyrus' army included a contingent of some 10,000 Greek mercenaries that remained a viable fighting force after Cyrus was killed and his Asiatic forces were dispersed. Instead of surrendering, the Greek troops decided to make their way home as a cohesive force. In a trek that was immortalized in the writings of Xenophon, they marched up along the Tigris and fought their way through Kurdistan, where they suffered greater losses than they had at the hands of the regular armies of Persia. They then made their way through Armenia into Anatolia eventually reaching the Greek colony at Trebizond on the southern shore of the Black Sea in the spring of 400. Although Persian forces continually harassed them, the Greeks were able to maintain their integrity as an army in retreat and there was little the Persians were able to do about it.

Sensing Persia's relative weakness, exacerbated by the palace intrigues of the queen mother Parysatis, Sparta hired the surviving two-thirds of the "Ten Thousand." Along with a Spartan army under Agesilaus, they invaded Anatolia in 399, where the Persian satraps who were busy quarreling among themselves were unable to put up a common defense against the Spartan plunder of the wealth of Asia Minor. Ironically, at this point, Athens, whose hatred for Sparta exceeded that which it had for Persia, came to Artaxerxes' aid. Through the judicious distribution of largesse, the Persians succeeded in forging an anti-Spartan alliance of Athens, Thebes, Corinth, and Argos, which was later augmented by other cities, thereby triggering the Corinthian War (395–387). By raising a new challenge to Sparta while it was engaged with the Persians, Athens compelled Sparta to withdraw from Anatolia in order to deal with the threat in Greece. Sparta's withdrawal cost it hegemony in Ionia, which was now reasserted there by Persia. The Persian alliance with Athens, however, was to prove a merely temporary marriage of convenience. In fact, there was a basic divergence of interests between the two states, each of which aspired to uncontested supremacy in the Aegean and eastern Mediterranean.

As Athens regained its strength, it sought to resurrect its maritime empire and reestablish its influence along the coasts of Asia Minor. At the same time, Persia aspired to reassert its control over Egypt, which had taken advantage of Artaxerxes' preoccupation with Anatolian affairs to declare its independence once again. These conflicting interests helped nurture a new alliance between Athens and Egypt, with the latter providing Athens with a large amount of money to spur its challenge to Persian supremacy in the region, thereby forcing Artaxerxes to divert his attention from his campaign against Egypt. In addition, aid from Athens, bolstered by supplementary support from Egypt, encouraged Evagoras, the king of Cypriot Salamis, to overrun Cyprus and to extend his reach to the coasts of Cilicia and Phoenicia. According to Diodorus: "Evagoras made an alliance with Acoris, the king of the Egyptians, who was an enemy of the Persians, and received a strong force from him."[6] This had the effect of disrupting Persia's lines of supply to its army in Egypt and ultimately resulted in the forced withdrawal of the Persian forces from the country in 387.

As a consequence of these developments, Artaxerxes reversed alliances and threw his support to Sparta in the ongoing Corinthian War. By playing Athens against Sparta, Artaxerxes succeeded in contributing significantly to the exhaustion of both. When the two crippled rivals ultimately decided to call an end to their struggle in late 387, the terms of the settlement, the Peace of Antalcidas, were dictated by Artaxerxes. As recorded by Xenophon:

King Artaxerxes thinks it just that the cities in Asia should belong to him, as well as Clazomenae [an Ionian city based on an inshore isle] and Cyprus among the islands, and the other Greek cities, both small and great, should be independent, except Lemnos, Imbros and Scyros; and these should belong, as of old, to the Athenians. But whichever of the two parties does not accept this peace, upon them I will make war, in company with those who desire this arrangement, both by land and by sea, with ships and with money.[7]

When Sparta subsequently began its recovery, Artaxerxes came to the support of Thebes and encouraged it to attack and complete the effective elimination of Sparta as a contender for imperial power. This was essentially achieved by the Theban victory at the battle of Leuctra in 371. The ascendancy of Thebes now caused Athens to align itself with Sparta in an effort to offset it. This imposed the requirement on the Theban leader Epaminondas to build a fleet to offset the naval power of Athens; and for this he needed Persian gold, which Artaxerxes willingly supplied. After Epaminondas was killed in a final battle with Sparta at Mantinea in 362, it was not long before there was a collapse of Theban supremacy without any of the other Greek city-states being strong enough to assume its place. As a practical matter, the power of the Greek city-states had been destroyed for all time. Once again, Persian gold proved to be a more powerful instrument of foreign policy than Persian arms.

From the chaos of Greek politics Persia now reemerged, at least for the moment, as the uncontested master of Asia Minor, including the Ionian cities. However, it was to be for but a relatively brief moment as the strength of the Persian Empire was sapped by internal problems that the series of ineffective rulers who followed Artaxerxes II failed to resolve.

NOTES

1. A. R. Burn, *Persia and the Greeks*, p. 492.
2. Herodotus, *The Persian Wars*, V.140.
3. Ibid., V.142.
4. Thucydides, *The Peloponnesian War*, VIII.xxiv.18.
5. Ibid., viii.xxiv.37.
6. Diodorus, 15.2.3.
7. Xenophon, *Hellenica*, V.i.31.

7

The Macedonian Conquest

The organization of the Persian Empire under Artaxerxes II was no longer as Darius I had left it. Without an overpowering personality at the helm of the state in Susa, the imperial satraps saw little reason for them not to reassert virtually autonomous control over both the army and financial matters in their respective provinces.

The Egyptian ruler Achoris (394–381) had aided the Greeks in their struggle against Persia through the supply of grain and ships, and had encouraged the ambitions of Evagoras in Cyprus and along the eastern Mediterranean littoral to disrupt the Persian campaign to restore control over Egypt. In the process, Achoris also built a substantial army composed primarily of Greek mercenaries. His successor, Nekhtnebf (381–363), ascended the Egyptian throne just about the time that the Persians were preparing a new campaign to suppress the revolt. By 380, Artaxerxes had reestablished Persian control over Cilicia and Phoenicia, had driven Evagoras back to his enclave at Cypriot Salamis, and, under the direction of Pharnabazus, the former satrap of Hellespontine Phrygia, had begun preparations for an assault on Egypt. The campaign was delayed until 373, however, because of a conflict that broke out with the Cadusians in the interim. Although the Egyptians suffered an initial reverse, the indecisiveness of the Persian commander Pharnabazus permitted them to reconstitute their forces and, subsequently, fight the Persian army to a stalemate, making it necessary for the latter to withdraw. This time, however, Artaxerxes could not muster the resources necessary to send yet another army to attempt to suppress the rebellion.

By default, Egypt had finally regained its independence, even though Artaxerxes understood that with the loss of Egypt it would not be long before the other western dependencies also tried to throw off the Persian yoke. Indeed, it was just at the moment when he had finally reached the point where he was able to dictate policy to the Greek cities of Asia Minor that the consequences of Egypt's successful rebellion began to be felt throughout the empire, but most especially in its western part. Following Egypt's lead, the satraps of Cyprus, Phoenicia, and Syria soon declared their independence, followed by those of Bithynia, Caria, Lydia, Mysia, Lycia, Pisidia, Pamphylia, and Cilicia.

The rebellious satraps formed an alliance for the purpose of challenging the authority of the central government in all the territories west of the Euphrates. One critical outcome of this was the denial to the Persian treasury of half its total revenues. However, it also produced a good deal of chaos in the region as plots and counterplots began to be put into operation. The non-Persian satrap of Cappadocia, Datames, seized control of Paphlagonia and began attacking the Greek cities along the northern Anatolian coast. Because Cappadocia straddled the major land route connecting Asia Minor to the rest of the empire, the possibility of a revolt by Datames bore serious geostrategic consequences and Artaxerxes ordered the satrap of Lydia, Autophrades, to mount a major offensive against him in 370/369. The army put in the field to deal with Datames outnumbered his by twenty to one. Nonetheless, Datames succeeded in exploiting the difficult terrain of eastern Anatolia to his advantage and inflicted so many casualties on the Persian army under Autophrades that the campaign was called off after Datames promised to reconcile with Artaxerxes.

The losses sustained by the Persian army in this campaign, forces that were being readied in Syria for an invasion of Egypt, encouraged the Egyptians to take the initiative with their own assault into Asia. Nekhtnebf's successor as king of Egypt, Takhos (363–361), in alliance with Agesilaus, king of Sparta, invaded Syria in 362. Although the prospects of success were reasonably good considering the disarray in the Persian camp, the effort came to nothing. One reason was that Takhos had apparently offended Agesilaus by not designating him as supreme commander of the allied Egyptian-Spartan forces. Agesilaus retaliated for this slight by supporting a military coup by the Egyptian king's cousin Nekhtharheb, who seized the throne. This caused Takhos to surrender to Artaxerxes along with the forces still under his command, thereby serving to reassert some central Persian authority in the western provinces of the empire. Perhaps the most significant outcome of the episode was what did not happen—the opportunity of possibly rendering a decisive blow against Persia was squandered. Shortly afterwards, the alliance of the rebellious satraps was dissolved, and most of them either surrendered or were betrayed and murdered. Although there were continuing political problems with the provinces, exacerbated by civil disturbances and lawlessness when Artaxerxes II died, the empire had been saved, at least for the time being.

The decline of Persia appeared to go into remission with the accession to the throne of Artaxerxes III Ochus (358–338) amid a bloodbath that engulfed virtually the entire royal family. He completed the suppression of the revolt of the satraps, ordering the dissolution of their autonomous military forces in 356. Artaxerxes then committed himself to the re-conquest of Egypt, although his first attempt to do so met with failure and precipitated another series of satrapal revolts. Ervand, the hereditary satrap of Armenia and ruler of Mysia and much of western Anatolia, including Pergamum, established an independent relationship with Athens around 355, and with the latter's support led a revolt against Susa that lasted five years. However, Athens ultimately withdrew its support for the insurrection under a Persian threat of war, and it came to an end.

With this crisis resolved, Artaxerxes was free to return to the project of re-conquering Egypt. To clear the land route along the Fertile Crescent, he first had to deal with rebellious Phoenicia, which had sought to interfere with the Persian war effort by destroying the supplies that had been amassed there to support the planned campaign against Egypt. As a result, Sidon was sacked and burned as punishment in 345, thereby eliminating the last impediment to Artaxerxes' goal. The mercenary forces of Persia, which included some 14,000 troops from Thebes, Argos, and the Greek cities of Asia, swept into Egypt and defeated the mercenary armies of the pharaoh, which also included a large number of Greeks. Nekhtharheb was forced to flee to safety in Ethiopia as the Persian armies laid waste a good part of the country. Persian rule was finally reinstituted in Lower Egypt in 341, and the remaining western satraps quickly reaffirmed their loyalty to the throne.

The Greek leaders perceived the sudden resurgence of Persian power in the region as a new and significant challenge to their interests. To gain support for an activist policy, some attempted to redefine the nature of the Greek-Persian conflict from one of straightforward geopolitics to the more emotional issue of pan-Hellenism. For such proponents of a continuation of the struggle the issue was no longer merely the matter of the defense of the Greek city-states. The Persian challenge was now characterized as a conflict of principle, of Hellenic culture and civilization against Asiatic barbarism in an unrelenting struggle for survival. They advocated a crusade to be carried out by a unified Greek nation that was to include all that partook of Greek civilization. However, the traditional leadership of Athens and the other prominent city-states, exhausted by the long external and internal wars, were unable to mobilize the support necessary for an effective response to the Persian challenge. Nonetheless, the pan-Hellenic crusade was soon to be undertaken, but not by Athens. It was Macedonia that was to impose its own leadership on Greece and undertake the renewed struggle against Persia in the name of the Hellenes.

THE RISE OF MACEDONIA

Since it had come under the dynamic rule of Philip II (360–336), Macedonia had been expanding its control in the region east and north of the Pelopennesus. Within three years after coming into power, Philip virtually doubled the territory of the state. After successfully annexing Thessaly and Thrace, Philip was widely acknowledged as the natural leader of a Hellenic alliance. The venerable Isocrates saw Philip as the man that Greece needed to deal with a chronic demographic problem that menaced its future. He argued that Greece was plagued by overpopulation, which produced large numbers of men suitable for military service who wandered about, without loyalty to any city, selling their services to anyone who could pay for them and thereby posing a constant menace to the stability of the country. What was needed, he suggested, was a new country that might be colonized by Greece's surplus population. This new land would have to be conquered from Persia, and Philip of Macedon, who was already successfully challenging the Persians in a contest for control of the European shores of the Hellespont, was clearly the only one who might be able to annex all Anatolia to the Hellenic world. Isocrates asserted, "I found that on no other condition could Athens remain at peace, unless the greatest states of Hellas should resolve to put an end to their mutual quarrels and carry the war beyond our borders into Asia, and should determine to wrest from the barbarians the advantages which they now think it proper to get for themselves at the expense of the Hellenes."[1]

Notwithstanding the logic of his argument, in Athens, the idea of Greek subservience to the Macedonian king did not sit well with many. Demosthenes, for example, raised his influential voice against Macedonian leadership and argued instead that an alliance with Persia was the only means by which to prevent the subjugation of Athens to Philip.[2] This viewpoint prevailed and Athens sent a diplomatic mission to Persia where a new alliance was concluded. Philip recognized the dangerous ramifications of the Athenian-Persian pact for Macedonian security and resolved to subjugate Greece, by force if necessary. It became necessary and, at the battle of Chaeronea in 338, Athens and its ally Thebes were decisively beaten. Philip then convened a meeting of the Greek city-states at Corinth where the league against Persia was revived under the rubric of the "Greeks of the Common Peace." Not surprisingly, Philip was unanimously elected commander of its armed forces in 337. This move effectively put an end to the independence of the Greek city-states, all of which were now brought within the Macedonian imperial embrace.

Philip had no illusions about the stability of the Common Peace, given the turbulent history of the Greek city-states, their competitiveness, and their general reluctance to sacrifice their freedom of action even for the common good. Moreover, he was a Macedonian, from the backwater of the Greek world. The instruments that Philip employed to overcome these problems were religion and culture. He made it a point to characterize his campaigns as fought in the name of Apollo. He depicted the war against the Persians as a crusade against their profanation of the temples of the Greek gods, as well as to free the Greeks of Asia from the yoke of the enemies of Hellenic culture and beliefs. The Common Peace that he established was predicated on the oath taken by all, except for Sparta and Epirus, in the name of the Greek pantheon, to maintain the peace among the members of the alliance and to provide for their collective security. Philip found the blending of religion and politics to be a potent means for forging a military power that could confront the powerful Persian army in its native territories in Asia.

Fortuitously, in 338, at about the same time that Philip was mobilizing his forces for the forthcoming struggle for empire, Artaxerxes III, who might have been able to contain the power of Macedonia within Europe, was assassinated by his grand vizier Bagoas, the true power behind the Persian throne. To ensure his control of the court, he contrived to have Artaxerxes' youngest son, Arses (338–336), succeed to the throne, only to poison him as well after a two-year reign. During this period the Persians were left without a leader capable of dealing with the looming threat of a united Greece under Macedonian leadership as instability mounted throughout the empire. Egypt took advantage of the power vacuum to declare its independence once again and an insurrection broke out in Babylonia. With the death of Arses, the crown was taken by Darius III Codomannus (336–330), an outstanding soldier who had been rewarded for his service with the satrapy of Armenia, succeeding Ervand I upon his retirement from that post in 344. (When Codomannus left Armenia in 336 to mount the Persian throne, the satrapy was awarded to Ervand II [336–325], who would play an important role there later.) He immediately removed Bagoas and moved decisively to restore Persian control in Egypt and Babylonia. Within a year, he managed to restore a semblance of order in the provinces that permitted him to begin to prepare to cope with the major threat that was looming in the western part of the empire. He refitted the primarily Phoenician and Cypriot fleet that had been used to subdue Egypt and, by 334, was ready to challenge the Macedonian-Greek alliance for control of the Aegean. However, although the new Persian king was a man of considerable competence, he was no match for Philip.

In 336, the same year that Darius Codomannus mounted the Persian throne, Philip dispatched an advance force of Macedonians and Greek mercenaries into Asia Minor to prepare the ground for a full-scale invasion that was to follow. This expeditionary force quickly conquered the western coastal region as far south as Ephesus, liberating a number of Greek cities in the process. Philip's immediate purpose was to seize control of the Hellespont and establish a beachhead in the Troad and Bithynia in preparation for the arrival of the main Macedonian army under his personal command.

Philip, however, was soon assassinated, probably with Persian complicity, leaving his dream of empire to be realized by his successor, his exceptionally capable son Alexander.

THE END OF THE ACHAEMENID EMPIRE

Alexander's succession to the Macedonian throne at the age of twenty was greeted by a swarm of conspiracies aiming to dissolve the Macedonian suzerainty imposed on the Greeks by Philip. Once again, the hand of Persia could be seen behind the scene in many of these. The new Persian king Darius had come to see Macedonia as a serious potential threat and wished to do whatever was necessary to keep Alexander from crossing into Anatolia in force. The advance of the troops that had been sent there by Philip in 336 had ground to a halt the following year as the Persian forces began to counterattack. The Macedonians were pushed back to the shores of the Hellespont, but they managed to maintain a grip on the crossing points. The satraps of Anatolia pooled their resources and concentrated them in a blocking position to prevent a breakout from the beachhead held by the Macedonians.

The Persians, however, did not rely on military strength alone to achieve their objectives. They were also expert at the tactical use of gold as a weapon to create dissension in the enemy camp. Accordingly, Persian subsidies were offered to the Greek states to help foment rebellions. Although only Sparta, which was not a member of the Common Peace, openly accepted Persian gold, it seems quite evident that others did so covertly as well. A Persian offer of 300 talents was privately accepted by Demosthenes, who employed it for purposes compatible with mutual Athenian-Persian interests in thwarting Macedonian ascendancy. This included the purchase of arms for a group of Theban exiles that would soon succeed in precipitating an open rebellion by the city against the league, which meant, in effect, against Alexander who was its supreme commander. However, to the chagrin of many and the surprise of most, Alexander was soon able to overcome the numerous rebellions and defections that had taken place and firmly establish his position as leader of the Greeks. In the process, Alexander captured and completely destroyed the ancient city of Thebes. This sent an unmistakable message to the other Greek states that he would brook no opposition.

Having consolidated his control in Greece, Alexander was now ready for the implementation of the project originally planned by his father, the invasion of Asia. The Greek states contributed some small contingents to his army; and Athens, a fleet that was too small to be of any real consequence in denying the Persians virtually uncontested control of the sea. To maintain the security of Macedonia against the unreliable Greek states during his absence, Alexander left a substantial portion of his troops behind under the command of Antipater. In 334 Alexander crossed the Hellespont and proceeded to lead his army of some 50,000 strong, of which about a third were Macedonians, into Asia to challenge the Persian Empire.

Darius apparently did not take this challenge too seriously. The situation was quite different from that which prevailed two years earlier when he was caught unprepared for a Macedonian attack. This time his troops were ready and in a tactically advantageous position to confront the invaders. He expected to defeat Alexander rather handily with an army, made up of indigenous soldiers, Persian cavalry, and Greek mercenaries, that was about the same size as the Macedonian expeditionary force. Indeed, Darius was so certain of the outcome that he gave instructions that Alexander was to be brought to Susa after his capture. However, at the first full-scale battle between the armies of Alexander and Darius at the River Granicus, the forces amassed by the satraps of western Anatolia were quickly defeated by the tactically superior Macedonians. This left the Persian defense of the region in disarray as Alexander continued his march southward taking the principal cities one by one, Sardis surrendering without a fight. It was not long before all of western Anatolia was under Macedonian control.

The treatment of the captured Greek mercenaries who served in Darius' army was harsh. They were viewed as traitors to the Hellenic cause, having violated the decrees of the Common Peace, and were sent back to Macedonia as slaves, to redeem themselves through hard labor. By contrast, the surviving Persian and indigenous soldiers were treated with uncommon generosity, being released and permitted to return to their homes.

Alexander's treatment of the defeated Persian troops at the Granicus was a remarkably shrewd political gesture that signaled the policy that Alexander would pursue in consolidating his control of the empire he intended to create. He seems to have concluded from the outset that his power base in Macedonia was simply too limited to support the conquest and absorption of an empire that covered all of southwestern Asia and Egypt. He would never have enough Macedonian troops to police such an empire, and like Philip before him he had few illusions about the reliability of the Greeks that he had coerced into following him. The solution he adopted was to follow the same basic approach taken two centuries earlier by the great Persian conqueror Cyrus, who had a comparable dilemma. The answer was to have his legitimacy accepted by the numerous peoples that made up the Persian Empire. He therefore made it his policy from the first to be perceived as their liberator from Persian despotism, hoping thereby to gain their loyalty by his generosity and respect for their beliefs and customs. In effect, he promoted pan-Hellenism to satisfy his Greek constituents at the same time that he demonstrated a broad tolerance of the varied cultures of the peoples who would come under his sway. As one writer put it, "For the Macedonians and the Greeks the message was that Zeus was ruling over Asia. . . . For the Asians the emphasis was on continuity with their earlier traditions."[3]

Although Alexander expected all the Ionian cities to welcome their liberation, such was not the case. Some, like Miletus and Halicarnassus, preferred to maintain their effective autonomy under nominal Persian rule. These had to be placed under siege and compelled to surrender to their nominal liberators. With the capture of Miletus on the Aegean coast, Alexander was able to open a secondary line of communication with Greece through the intermediary islands of Samos, Icaria, Myconos, Tenos, and Andros. He thereby reduced somewhat the threat to his lines of communication posed by the prevailing Persian domination of the sea-lanes in the region.

Although the Persian fleet was still in effective control of the Mediterranean, it had thus far failed in several efforts to cut off the maritime links between Alexander's forces in Asia and their supply bases in Europe. For the time being, Alexander chose to ignore the continuing naval threat to his rear, going so far as to disband the Athenian fleet, which he held to be too small and too unreliable to be of any consequence; it mainly served as a drain on his limited financial resources. He was also convinced that the punishment he had earlier meted out to Thebes would prevent the Persians from successfully inciting rebellions against him while he was absent from Greece. He had instilled sufficient fear of him to nullify the value of Persian gold. Confident that his rear was secure, Alexander marched eastward, following the route earlier taken by the famous "Ten Thousand." He soon safely passed through the Cilician Gates, which had earlier been secured by an advance force, where he confronted the main army of Persia under the personal command of Darius near the Gulf of Issus in 333. The Macedonians took the initiative and mounted an offensive that quickly broke the Persian lines and precipitated a disorderly retreat, leaving the royal family behind to be captured. The retreat did not stop until the Persian forces had crossed the Euphrates. At the same time, one wing of the Macedonian army under Parmenion struck southward with great rapidity and trapped the Persian supply train in Damascus, yielding a great amount of booty that offered immediate relief for Alexander's continuing concern about how to finance the extensive military campaign he had undertaken.

At the same time, news of the Persian defeat at Issus interrupted the ongoing negotiations between the Persian satrap Pharnabazus and the Spartan king Agis regarding a joint plan for the liberation of Greece from Macedonian control. It also precipitated the slow but steady disintegration of the Persian fleet as the various national components began to give serious consideration to their need to reach an accommodation with Alexander, who was clearly emerging as the victor from the contest with Darius. The erosion of Persian naval supremacy reduced the threat to Alexander's lines of communication to Europe, and enabled him to proceed with the campaign with even greater confidence.

Darius saw no realistic alternative other than to sue for peace. He sent a letter to Alexander proposing the ransom of the royal family for a very large sum of money. He also sought an alliance with Macedonia that would make the Halys the boundary between their empires, conceding all of Asia Minor west of the river to Macedonia. Alexander rejected the offer. He rationalized the continuance of the conflict by insisting that it was Persia that had initiated the war by its earlier invasions of Greece and its continual attempts to influence Greek politics through the corruption of officials. He declared his mission as being the rectification of past wrongs. However, he also portrayed himself, somewhat prematurely, and with no little arrogance, as the lord of Asia, and invited Darius to meet him on the battlefield to resolve the issue between them decisively if he was not prepared to capitulate at once.

Perhaps for the first time, it was now evident to Darius, and possibly to Alexander's generals as well, that Alexander harbored ambitions that went much further than merely righting a past wrong, liberating the Greek cities of Asia Minor, or establishing Macedonian rule over its western portion. He clearly appeared to have decided to undertake the conquest of the entire Persian Empire.

Alexander declined to follow up on his victory at Issus and pursue Darius immediately. He was shrewd enough to realize that he dare not penetrate too deeply into Asia without first dealing with the Persian fleet, which was predominantly Phoenician, that still dominated the Mediterranean behind him and remained a threat to his lines of communication to Greece. His strategy for resolving this problem was elegantly simple. He would conquer the rimlands of the Mediterranean and thereby deny the Phoenician ships access to their home ports. He assumed quite correctly that the Phoenician sailors and oarsmen would abandon their commitment to the Persians if the price they had to pay for their loyalty were the forfeit of any further connection with their families and homeland. Accordingly, Alexander delayed further movement eastward for the moment, and instead swung his armies southward along the eastern littoral of the Mediterranean to capture all the Phoenician ports along the route, particularly Tyre, which was the most strategically important Phoenician base. Its loss would effectively doom the Persian fleet, while without its submission it would be too dangerous to proceed either to Egypt or to Mesopotamia.

Alexander presented his strategic perceptions to his generals at the time in a rather remarkable exposition that is worth quoting in full, assuming that we are dealing with a reliable record:

My friends and allies, so long as Persia is supreme at sea I cannot see how we can march in safety to Egypt. Nor again, is it safe to pursue Dareius, leaving in our rear the city of Tyre, of doubtful allegiance, and Egypt and Cyprus still in Persia's hands, especially in view of the state of Greek affairs. There is a fear lest the Persians, again seizing the coast places, when we have gone in full force toward Babylon and Dareius, should with a larger army transfer the war into Greece, where the Lacedaemonians are at the moment fighting us; and Athens is kept in its place for the present by fear rather than goodwill toward us. But with Tyre once destroyed, Phoenicia could all be held, and the best and strongest part of the Persian navy, the Phoenician element, would most probably come over to us. For neither the rowers nor the marines of Phoenicia will have the courage, if their cities are in our hands, to sail the sea and run its dangers for the sake of others. After this, Cyprus, moreover, will either come readily to our side or be captured easily by a naval raid. Then if we hold the sea with our Macedonian ships, and the Phoenician navy too, and with Cyprus ours, we should firmly hold the sea-power, and in virtue thereof our expedition to Egypt would be easy. Then, when we have possession of Egypt, we shall have no cause for uneasiness for Greece and our own home, and we shall make the expedition to Babylon, with security at home, and with our enhanced prestige, with the whole sea cut off from Persia and all the country this side of Euphrates.[4]

Alexander attempted to gain the submission of Tyre without a battle, but his overtures were rejected. Tyre, which considered itself to be virtually impregnable if not unassailable, had a well-established privileged position within the Persian Empire that it was loathe to surrender. As a consequence, according to Diodorus, Alexander "threatened to use force, but the Tyrians cheerfully faced the prospect of a siege. They wanted to gratify Dareius and keep unimpaired their loyalty to him, and thought also that they would receive great gifts from the king in return for such a favour. They would draw Alexander into a protracted and difficult siege and give Dareius time for his military preparations, and at the same time they had confidence in the strength of their island and the military forces in it. They also hoped for help from their colonists, the Carthaginians."[5]

At the time, Tyre was an island about a half mile off the shore and was indeed virtually impregnable. Alexander had to build a causeway from the shore to the island before it could be successfully attacked. This proved a most difficult task, but it was done and Tyre was conquered in the summer of 332, after a grueling seven-month siege that gave Darius the breathing spell he needed to prepare the defense of the Persian heartland.

While Alexander was occupied in the siege of Tyre, Darius tried once more to stop the Macedonian advance by diplomacy. He offered his daughter in marriage to Alexander along with all the land west of the Euphrates, which would now be the boundary between Persia and Macedonia, as a dowry. In addition, according to Arrian, he was prepared to pay the handsome ransom of 10,000 talents for the release of his family.[6] Once again, Alexander rejected his offer. The issue between them could only be resolved on the battlefield.

As Alexander anticipated, the fall of Tyre caused much of the Phoenician fleet to abandon the Persians and join him at Sidon. This was followed by a rapid sweep south through Palestine, at least as far as Gaza where Alexander encountered fierce resistance that stalled his advance toward Egypt for two months. Once he reduced Gaza, the capitulation of Egypt took place upon his entry into the country in 332. With Egypt in his hands, the remainder of the Persian fleet was denied all contact with its bases and home ports and soon dissolved and scattered. Alexandria, which was established the following year, replaced Tyre as the principal port of the Mediterranean and the Greeks became the dominant maritime power of the region.

Having disposed of the threat to his rear, Alexander now turned toward Mesopotamia, building bridges across the Euphrates and Tigris without significant opposition. For reasons that are unknown, Darius did not attempt to defend the river crossings. Instead, he sought to stop Alexander near the ruins of ancient Nineveh. There, at Gaugamela, with the Assyrian highlands to his rear, Darius massed his armies for a decisive stand against the Macedonians in 331. Although the Persians significantly outnumbered the Macedonians, it was the latter that carried the day, primarily through the use of superior tactics and discipline. The Persian army was crushed and Darius fled eastward across the Zagros Mountains to the former Median capital, Ecbatana. Instead of pursuing Darius immediately, Alexander moved first to take Babylon and Susa, which, to his surprise, surrendered without a fight. For many, Darius' desertion from his army was tantamount to abdication and they accepted Alexander as the legitimate successor to the Persian throne. As already noted, Alexander was astute enough to recognize that it would not be possible to govern the Persian Empire with only a relative handful of Macedonians. It would be necessary to co-opt the Persian leaders into willing cooperation in order to sustain the empire. Accordingly, he left the Persian satraps of Babylon and Susa in place, and began the integration of Persians and Macedonians in his army. Alexander then moved into the heart of Persia seeking to prevent Darius, who was already in Parthia beyond the Caspian Gates (a complex of defiles separating Media from the eastern satrapies) from forming a new army in more tactically advantageous territory.

Darius, however, now discovered that his authority was no longer considered paramount by the satraps of the eastern marches of the empire. They were displeased with his handling of the war and were reluctant to follow him to further military debacles. As a result of these problems within the Persian camp, the army began to disintegrate. As Alexander approached, Darius was seized and subsequently murdered in 330 by Bessus, the satrap of Bactria, in conjunction with Nabarzanes of Hyrcania and Satibarzanes of Areia, who were determined to prevent having him fall into Macedonian hands and possibly becoming a vassal of Alexander. They intended to defend their lands and did not want Darius interfering with their efforts.

With the death of Darius, Ervand II, the satrap of Armenia, who had been with him at Gaugamela and had managed to escape, abandoned the fiction of the satrapy and declared himself the independent king of Armenia. His successors were generally able to maintain this status for more than a century. Thus, although Mithranes (c. 325–317), Ervand's son and successor, was nominally a vassal of Alexander, he in fact ruled as king of Armenia and was not challenged in this regard by the Macedonian leader even when he failed to make the expected payments of tribute. Armenia was apparently too inaccessible to bother about for the purposes of enforcing the payment of tribute, although at least one serious but unsuccessful attempt to do so was made. Alexander, who at the moment was interested more in the expansion than in the consolidation of his empire, had more significant concerns to attend to.

It took several years for Alexander to completely conquer and pacify the eastern marches of the Persian Empire: Hyrcania, Areia, Carmania, Bactria, Sogdiana, Arachosia, Drangiana, and Gedrosia. Nonetheless, less than five years after first crossing into Asia, Alexander had made himself undisputed master of the entire Middle East. After establishing an administration for the empire, he took an army and moved beyond the imperial frontiers deeper into the heart of Asia, building cities named after him at strategic points along the way, and finally stopping on the eastern bank of the Indus. After an absence of seven years, Alexander returned to Babylon in 323 and began preparation of an expedition to conquer the Arabian Peninsula. It was Alexander's grand vision to transform the littoral of the Persian Gulf into a second Phoenicia. He envisioned the establishment of a major trade route from the Indus to the Tigris and Euphrates and from there to the canals that linked the Nile to the Red Sea. It was his intention to make Babylon the capital of his empire and to transform the city into a center of maritime trade and power. However, Alexander soon died of apparently natural causes at the age of thirty-three. With him died his vision of an integrated Greek-Persian Empire reaching from the Mediterranean to India.

NOTES

1. Isocrates, V.9.
2. Demosthenes, Fourth Philippic, 31–34.
3. N.G.L. Hammond, *The Macedonian State*, p. 207.
4. Arrian, *Anabasis Alexandri*, II, xvii.
5. Diodorus, XVII.40.3.
6. Arrian, *Anabasis Alexandri*, II, xxv.

8

The Dissolution of
Alexander's Empire

Alexander's untimely demise in June 323 left his principal generals and commanders in a quandary. Without a clear plan regarding what to do with the vast empire they had helped create, they convened a Council of Friends in Babylon to decide on a course of action. Even though some of them harbored expansive ambitions, no one expressed any interest in seeing the empire dissolved into smaller chunks of territory. Two schools of thought seem to have emerged. One, espoused by Ptolemy, was that the empire should remain intact but that the imperial sovereignty should reside in a council of the chief satraps, who would convene periodically. In effect, this would give the satraps virtually undisputed control of their provinces, but would also keep them united in the common Macedonian interest. The second school of thought, which had the strong support of Perdiccas, held that the empire should remain a unitary state under the rule of Alexander's heirs. It was the latter view that prevailed. Notwithstanding the opinions of their generals, the armies were fiercely loyal to Alexander and proud of their unprecedented achievements under his leadership, and they were expected to remain as loyal to his heirs.

Perdiccas was given overall command of the army and, along with Alexander's other senior commanders, Leonnatus, Craterus, and Antipater, was named co-regent for Alexander's as yet unborn child by his Bactrian wife. The child, who would become Alexander IV Aegos, was to rule jointly with Alexander's stepbrother, the mentally impaired Philip Arrhidaeus. However, the prospect of being ruled by either an incompetent or the son of a non-Hellenic woman had little appeal to many of the battle-hardened Macedonians. As it turned out, Alexander's mother Olympias murdered

Arrhidaeus in 317, while Alexander Aegos met a similar fate about 310 at the hands of Cassander, the son of Antipater.

It was decided at the council meeting in Babylon to entrust most of the satrapies of the empire to the officers who were in control of them at the time. However, some of the larger and wealthier provinces, such as Egypt and Syria, were awarded to the highest political and military officers. Macedonia and Greece, where a secessionist war broke out as soon as word was received of Alexander's death, were left in the charge of Antipater, whom Alexander had entrusted with their care while he was still alive. As the principal regent, or chiliarch, it became Perdiccas' goal to keep the vast empire intact under a central authority, ostensibly on behalf of Alexander's heirs but perhaps also, as many suspected, for himself. He met with little success in this regard. Two decades of incessant wars had produced some very hardened military leaders, and without a Philip or Alexander to keep them under control, it did not take long before each pursued his own interests and purposes, leading to the eventual disintegration of the Macedonian empire.

In Asia Minor, the political situation had been unstable since the Macedonian conquest began, with large areas such as Bithynia, Paphlagonia, Cappadocia, and what would become known later as Pontus, having been bypassed by Alexander during his initial thrust into Asia and his pursuit after Darius. These provinces had never been brought under effective Macedonian control. Indeed, even in some of the satrapies that were under nominal Macedonian domination the need for ongoing pacification efforts remained high. Cappadocia was a case in point where Macedonian authority did not extend beyond the Halys.

Antigonus Cyclops (so named because he had lost an eye in battle) had been appointed satrap of Greater Phrygia, Lycia, and Pamphylia. However, he soon incurred the enmity of Perdiccas when he refused to assist the latter in the conquest of Cappadocia. From Antigonus' standpoint, it was not worth the effort since that province had been assigned to Eumenes, Alexander's secretary and a protégé of Perdiccas. As a result, it became necessary for Antigonus to leave Anatolia for his own safety. He went to Greece where he joined forces with Antipater, Craterus, and a number of Alexander's other generals who were opposed to Perdiccas' attempts to concentrate all power in his hands as imperial regent.

Although Perdiccas was justifiably wary of Ptolemy, he needed the latter's political support if he was to succeed in positioning himself as the central authority in the Macedonian Empire. Accordingly, Perdiccas appears to have struck a bargain with Ptolemy, who had imperial ambitions of his own, which resulted in his obtaining formal appointment as satrap of Egypt. Even before his own appointment Ptolemy had already assumed effective control of the rich province by contriving to eliminate Cleomenes, the financial controller who had been appointed as overseer of Egypt by Alexander and who also was Perdiccas' original choice as satrap.

It soon became evident, as Ptolemy's separatist aims took on practical political dimensions, that Perdiccas had gotten the short end of the arrangement. For one thing, Ptolemy took immediate advantage of an opportunity to annex Cyrenaica to the satrapy of Egypt. Although this move ostensibly enhanced the Macedonian Empire, it antagonized Perdiccas who did not want any of Alexander's generals to accumulate enough power to challenge his own leadership aspirations. To make matters worse, one of the concessions Ptolemy wrung from Perdiccas as the price of his support was the appointment of a trusted officer named Arrhidaeus to be responsible for Alexander's funeral arrangements. It was assumed that Alexander would be returned to Macedonia for burial, and that the choice of whom to place in charge of the arrangements had little political significance. This proved to be a mistake.

The relations between Perdiccas and Ptolemy reached a critical point when Ptolemy contrived to have Arrhidaeus bring Alexander's body to Memphis, where it was to remain until a suitable tomb could be prepared for it in Alexandria, the new city that Alexander had built in Egypt. Ptolemy was understood by Perdiccas to be sending the unmistakable message that, at least as far as he was concerned, it was Egypt rather than Macedonia or Babylonia that was henceforth to be considered the center of the empire. This led to an open rupture between the two generals. Perdiccas was determined to prevent the disintegration of the empire into autonomous power centers, and was prepared to go to war for that end. Ptolemy now joined Antipater and Antigonus in the coalition of Macedonian generals who opposed Perdiccas and his ally Eumenes.

Perdiccas moved first with an assault on Egypt that was intended to crush Ptolemy. His Egyptian campaign, however, turned into a debacle from which he was unable to recover. His repeated attempts to break through the Egyptian defenses at Pelusium failed and he suffered heavy losses as he tried unsuccessfully to cross the Nile farther south. The failure to impose his will on Ptolemy undermined his ability to keep the rest of the empire under his control.

Antigonus, who was given command of the coalition forces that were dispatched to defeat Eumenes, landed at Ephesus and began driving across Anatolia, while Antipater crossed the Hellespont and was marching on Cilicia in order to come up behind the army of Perdiccas facing Egypt. In 320, once it became evident that Perdiccas had no realistic possibility of recouping his losses, the highly ambitious Seleucus and another of his senior officers murdered him.

Upon the elimination of Perdiccas, a second council of the principal satraps was convened at Triparadisus in northern Syria for the purpose of redistributing the satrapies among the members of the victorious coalition against Perdiccas and Eumenes. The regency was awarded to Antipater, who was given charge of the two kings (the child Alexander Aegos and Philip Arrhidaeus), moving the nominal center of the empire back to Macedonia from Asia. The choice, however, did not assure stability for very long since Antipater was already seventy-six years old and not in the best of health. He was to persevere in office for only two years before he died of illness, leaving the regency to Polyperchon rather than to his own son Cassander. Antipater did this because he believed it would help stabilize the situation in Macedonia and Greece where Cassander was not very popular. Cassander, however, was unwilling to accept the situation and became determined to rectify it to his satisfaction at all costs, creating the very instability that Antipater had hoped to prevent.

The situation was very different in Africa, where Ptolemy was solidly entrenched. To no one's surprise he was reconfirmed as satrap of Egypt, perhaps the most stable province of the empire. It was in Asia, however, where some complex and unpredictable developments began to take place. The most important of these concerned Antigonus, who retained the satrapies of Greater Phrygia, Lycia, and Pamphylia, but was also made supreme commander of the armies in Asia, and Seleucus, who was designated satrap of Babylonia, perhaps as his reward for doing away with Perdiccas.

Antigonus proceeded with the conquest of the remainder of Asia Minor, which was completed for practical purposes by the spring of 319. The struggle with Eumenes was concluded two years later. In the meantime, the imperial treasury in Susa had been relocated to Cyinda in Cilicia, placing substantial wealth within Antigonus' grasp. Moreover, the death of Antipater removed any qualms Antigonus may have had about repudiating the general agreement to preserve the empire intact for the two kings in Macedonia. Finding himself in command of both the armies and the wealth of the empire in Asia, the temptation to arrogate absolute power in Asia to himself became too great to resist. Antigonus decided to declare himself lord of all Alexandrian Asia, and he began to impose his direct control over the satraps of the eastern reaches of the empire. In 316 he entered Babylon, effectively forcing Seleucus to flee for safety to Egypt.

The fact that Antigonus had unilaterally deposed Seleucus was hardly a matter of any great concern to Ptolemy and his allies. Such was the nature of power politics. However, the reports, now confirmed by Seleucus, that Antigonus was marching westward with a powerful army and was intent on imposing his control over the entire empire, were quite another matter. With his access to the treasures of Persia to finance his expansionist aims, Antigonus' ambitions were viewed by Ptolemy as a direct threat to his own interests, a perception that was shared by Lysimachus, the satrap of Thrace, and Cassander, who had just come into power in Macedonia. The three constituted a coalition to thwart Antigonus' aims. The coalition was bolstered a bit later by the adherence to it of Asandros, the disaffected satrap of Caria.

Unwilling or perhaps unable to conduct and sustain major military campaigns on two fronts simultaneously, Antigonus seems to have planned to confront Lysimachus and Cassander first, anxious to extend his reach to Thrace and especially to Macedonia, the common motherland. Once having dealt with them he would turn south to deal with Ptolemy and Egypt. However, before he crossed the Taurus into Anatolia in 315, Antigonus received an ultimatum from the coalition that caused him to stop in Cilicia and wheel around to challenge Ptolemy, who now appeared to be the more immediate threat to his ambitions. The coalition demanded no less than that Babylonia be ceded to Seleucus; Hellespontine Phrygia to Lysimachus, giving him control of the straits; Lycia and Cappadocia to Cassander, encircling Antigonus' main Anatolian base in Phrygia; and that Syria from Phoenicia north to the Taurus be turned over to Ptolemy. It is not clear what purpose the ultimatum was intended to serve other than possibly to intimidate Antigonus, since it effectively called for his surrender and the dismemberment of his empire. Not surprisingly, Antigonus rejected these demands out of hand and a war for the control of the region ensued.

Ptolemy, whose primary goal became that of securing his position of independence in Egypt, nonetheless represented a foreign element in the land and saw no alternative to relying on a steady supply of Greek and Balkan mercenaries to maintain control of the country. This meant that he had to achieve mastery over the eastern Mediterranean in order to assure the security of his lines of communication to Greece. Toward this end, he directed particular attention to assuring his control over the Greek settlements along the Mediterranean coast in Cyrenaica. For the same reason he transferred the capital of Egypt from Memphis to Alexandria, the great port that Alexander had built in the western Nile Delta. From there he was in a better position to project power and maintain control over the maritime routes through the region. With the subsequent establishment of a protectorate in Cyprus in 318, Ptolemy transformed the entire eastern Mediterranean into an Egyptian lake for nearly a century. At the same time, to guard the land approaches to Egypt from Asia, and to provide additional strategic depth for the Nile delta region, which was relatively close to the frontier along the Mediterranean coast, he also seized Palestine and southern Syria.

When the war broke out in 315, Antigonus found himself on the defensive, faced by enemies coming at him from several directions at once. His immediate concern was to prevent the coalition forces from acting in concert. To achieve this, Antigonus sent an army north to seize the shores of the Hellespont to prevent an invasion by Cassander. This was a costly but necessary move for him. He then sent agents abroad with enough bribe money to cause considerable dissension in the enemy camp. As a result, Ptolemy seemed likely to lose control of Cyprus, which was important for his continued maritime control of the eastern Mediterranean. Antigonus also managed to conclude an alliance with Rhodes that further threatened to disrupt Egyptian domination of the sea. While most of the coalition was distracted by these moves, Antigonus led the rest of his armies against Ptolemy, forcing the latter to withdraw from Phoenicia and Palestine. Antigonus' immediate objective there was less to regain territory than to harvest the lumber with which to build a navy. Ptolemy was in control of the sea, and Antigonus was determined to wrest it from him.

Notwithstanding the soundness of Antigonus' strategy, he could not carry it out successfully because of the lack of adequate resources. The conflict was being transformed into a war of attrition that was exhausting all the belligerents. Ptolemy reestablished his dominance over Cyprus in 313, and in the following year, in alliance with Seleucus, invaded Palestine and defeated Demetrius, the son of Antigonus, in a major battle at Gaza. He reoccupied Palestine but was forced to abandon it again a few months later when Antigonus arrived there with a powerful force. Although Antigonus seemed to be gaining the upper hand, he had poor prospects for a conclusive victory and was as anxious as Ptolemy and his allies to find a way to end the conflict, even if only for a short while. Negotiations led to an armistice among the several belligerents in 311.

As expected, with none of the issues that caused the war in the first place having been resolved, it was not long before fighting broke out once again. In 309, Ptolemy personally commanded a naval force that attacked Anatolia and succeeded in detaching the coastal territories of Lycia and Caria from Antigonus' control. He also crossed to Greece, where he captured Corinth, Sicyon, and Megara in the following year. Ptolemy's campaign of territorial aggrandizement suffered a setback in 306 when a large fleet under Demetrius, son of Antigonus, attacked and retook Cyprus, and also wrested part of Greece from Cassander, who had made himself master of Macedonia. Antigonus tried to follow up on his son's success in Cyprus with an invasion of Egypt, but Ptolemy was able to successfully block his advance at the frontier. At that point, Antigonus and Demetrius declared themselves to be kings in Asia Minor and Greece, respectively. They were followed in this by the other major contenders for the empire—Ptolemy, Seleucus, Cassander, and Lysimachus—who declared themselves monarchs in the lands under their control.

The success of Demetrius' counteroffensive in Greece raised the concern that, with Antigonus already controlling most of the empire in Asia, they might have the momentum to soon dominate the entire Macedonian Empire, picking off their opponents one at a time. To prevent this from happening, Cassander succeeded in reviving the coalition against Antigonus in 302. Lysimachus, the first of the coalition members to be ready to move, promptly crossed the Hellespont and invaded Seleucid-held Phrygia, bolstered by a contingent of Cassander's forces. Antigonus, who was at his new capital in Syria, moved across the Taurus to meet the challenge and recalled Demetrius from Greece to assist him. This forced Demetrius to abandon Greece and Macedonia to Cassander. The arrival of Demetrius and his army at Ephesus, on Lysimachus' flank, compelled the latter to retreat to Heracleia for the winter to await the arrival of Seleucus from Mesopotamia.

The earlier defeat of Demetrius' forces at Gaza by Ptolemy in 312 had made it possible for Seleucus to return to Babylonia, from which he began to extend his sway over what had been most of Alexander's empire in Asia as far east as the Jaxartes and Indus Rivers. During the course of the following decade, he managed to establish his dominance first over the neighboring satrapies of Persis, Susiana, and Media, and then over the lands beyond the Elburz Mountains, Hyrcania, Parthia, Aria, Margiana, Bactria, Sogdiana, Drangiana, and Arachosia in southern Afghanistan. By the time the conflict with Antigonus was resolved, he was also master of Armenia and southern Cappadocia, which gave him effective control of the major trade routes across Anatolia. Seleucus also sought to regain those parts of Alexander's empire that lay beyond the Indus. However, he found himself faced with a new bid for power by Antigonus in the west, which reopened the war with the coalition. In 302, Seleucus found it necessary to settle for a peace treaty with Chandragupta, the king of the Maurya and ruler of western India, in order to enable him to move his forces from the Punjab to far distant Anatolia where Lysimachus awaited him. Under the terms of the agreement with Chandragupta, Seleucus received 500 elephants in exchange for which he ceded the eastern marches in Arachosia and Gedrosia. Seleucus subsequently used the elephants he obtained from India to good effect at the battle of Issus in 301, in which he and Lysimachus jointly challenged Antigonus, after the latter failed to prevent the linking of their forces.

In the meantime, Ptolemy invaded Palestine once more, presumably to be able to attack Antigonus' rear. However, the always-cautious Ptolemy evacuated Palestine for a third time when he received a report that Antigonus had won a decisive victory over Lysimachus in Asia Minor. The report, of course, was false. Antigonus had in fact been defeated and slain at the battle of Ipsus by the combined forces of Lysimachus and Seleucus. As a result of the victory, Lysimachus extended his realm from southern Thrace to most of Anatolia while Seleucus annexed Syria and consolidated his position as the paramount Macedonian ruler in the rest of Asia.

When Ptolemy learned the truth of what had occurred at Issus, he quickly reoccupied Palestine for the fourth time, even though the coalition had decided to reassign the territory to Seleucus because of Ptolemy's defection from the alliance at a time of crisis. Although Seleucus refused to acknowledge the legitimacy of Ptolemy's claim to the territory, he was not prepared to go to war with his former ally over it at the time. However, because of the conflicting claims to Palestine, domination of the strategically important strip of land became a matter of ongoing contention between the Ptolemies and the Seleucids for the next century. Once again, as in more ancient times, control of the narrow land bridge between Africa and Asia became an important question in the geopolitics of the region.

With the struggle against Antigonus at an end, Ptolemy was able to direct his attention to quelling a series of rebellions against his authority that had broken out in the North African province of Cyrenaica. The territory was finally brought under control about 300, and was assigned by Ptolemy to his stepson Magas. It took several more years before he was able to reestablish his earlier dominance in the eastern Mediterranean, because Demetrius, who failed to come to Antigonus' aid at Issus, continued to challenge Egyptian control of the sea-lanes. It was not until about 295 that Ptolemy was able to dislodge Demetrius from Cyprus. By the time Ptolemy abdicated in favor of his son Ptolemy II Philadelphus (284–245), he left behind a relatively secure realm that stretched from Cyrenaica to the Cyclades and a good part of the Mediterranean coastal areas of Anatolia from Caria to Cilicia.

In Macedonia, Cassander died in about 296 without leaving a strong successor. Instead, his two sons Antipater and Alexander jointly sat on the throne, creating an inherently unstable situation of which the ever-resourceful Demetrius was quick to take advantage. Demetrius began to intervene in the country once more and, in 293, seized the throne of Macedonia. This was seen as a threat to the interests of the three remaining principal Macedonian kings, Seleucus, Ptolemy, and Lysimachus, who formed an alliance against him. As Ptolemy moved his fleet to the waters of Greece, Lysimachus and Pyrrhus of Epirus invaded Macedonia on behalf of the coalition. Plagued by desertions in his army, Demetrius was forced to abandon Macedonia. It was divided initially between Pyrrhus and Lysimachus in 287, but was subsequently annexed to Thrace along with Thessaly by Lysimachus in 285. As a result of these events, the Macedonian Empire was now subdivided among Lysimachus, Ptolemy, and Seleucus.

In Asia, with his eastern frontier under relatively firm control, Seleucus appointed his son governor of the provinces east of the Euphrates about 293, and began to direct his own attention to the western reaches of the empire in Europe. It appears that Seleucus also aspired to that which Antigonus failed to achieve, dominance over the entirety of what had been Alexander's empire. And, as occurred with Antigonus and Perdiccas before him, this ambition constituted a clear threat to the interests of his colleagues. Accordingly, Ptolemy and Lysimachus now formed an alliance against him. Seleucus was eventually murdered in 281 while attempting to take over Macedonia. His last major rival in Asia, Lysimachus, was defeated and killed earlier that same year at the battle of Corupedion in Lydia, by Seleucus' own hand. With the elimination of Lysimachus, Seleucus' son and successor Antiochus I Soter (281–262) was able to firmly establish his rule over northern Syria and most of Asia Minor.

SELEUCIDS, PTOLEMAIDS, AND ANTIGONIDS

Although Seleucus and his successors ultimately fell heirs to the largest segment of Alexander's empire, they found themselves in a comparatively weaker position than the new rulers of Egypt. For the most part, the limits of their territories, stretching from the Aegean to the Indus, were not fixed by natural boundaries, and the relative vastness of the lands involved made effective control of them very difficult. In fact, many territories that were part of Alexander's empire eluded Seleucus' grasp. For example, it appears that the Seleucid writ did not extend to Armenia, Azerbaijan, Gilan, or Mazanderan, all of which asserted their independence under indigenous rulers. Similarly, in Asia Minor, two Persian houses that were remnants of the Achaemenian aristocracy managed to carve out independent principalities: Arariathes (c. 302–281) became the founder of the autonomous kingdom of Cappadocia, and Mithradates (281–266), of the new kingdom of Pontus.

Seleucus was compelled to adopt a policy of military colonization along the main lines of communication traversing the region and along the northern rim of the Persian Gulf, in order to bolster his ability to control the far-flung territories that had come into his grasp. Like the Ptolemaids, the Seleucids needed to depend on Greece for the supply of trade, troops, and colonists. However, their access to Greece was significantly restricted by Egyptian control of the seas. This had the effect of hindering the commercial development and prosperity of their Asian Empire. To offset the growing power of Egypt, their primary contender for dominance of the region, the Seleucids concentrated their attention on the development of Syria in the region between the Mediterranean and the Euphrates, and in western Anatolia, or Ionia, which was an important source of Greek colonists. Seleucus founded his western capital on the lower Orontes, naming it Antioch (after his father Antiochus), while in the east the capital was established at Seleucia, on the Tigris in Babylonia.

Antioch ultimately became an effective commercial rival of Alexandria and the hub of trade in the northeastern Mediterranean. In contrast to the traditional pharaonic form of government that emerged in Egypt, Seleucus adopted a style of government that was closer to the hybrid Graeco-Persian model adopted by Alexander. Under this scheme, the Greek settlements that dotted the country along the main communications routes were given local autonomy and self-government as republics in return for the payment of tribute and homage. The latter was to be in the form of reverence and obedience to the Seleucid ruler, who was to be considered and treated as a divine personage, as a god-king. As a practical matter, however, the Seleucids were able to rule only where their strategic settlements could ensure control of the countryside.

When Ptolemy Philadelphus ascended the throne of Egypt in 284, his half-brother Ptolemy Ceraunus took refuge first at the court of Lysimachus,

who had become king of Macedonia. After the latter's death, Ptolemy
Ceraunus was welcomed by Seleucus, who became his sponsor and principal supporter of his claim to the Egyptian throne, a move that was done for
the obviously political purpose of promoting instability in Egypt. This
proved to be a serious mistake. Thus, when Lysimachus was killed by Seleucus in 281, and the Macedonian throne became vacant, it appeared that
Seleucus was finally in a position to fulfill his ambition to become master of
the entire Alexandrian Empire. However, there clearly was no place in this
scheme for anyone else with imperial ambitions in the region. As a result,
Ptolemy Ceraunus assassinated Seleucus and contrived to seize the throne
of Macedonia himself. However, his reign there was to be very brief. Whatever plans Ptolemy Ceraunus may have had with regard to either Egypt or
Asia were quashed in 280 by the sudden invasion of the Gauls or Galatians,
who poured across the Balkans from the north and devastated Macedonia
and parts of Greece before being driven back. Ptolemy Ceraunus fell an
early victim to this onslaught and, in 277, after a period of some chaos, Antigonus II Gonatus, the grandson of Antigonus Cyclops, took the crown, finally bringing Macedonia under the Antigonid house.

Antigonus Gonatus sought to impose his control over Greece, but was
hampered in this effort by the Egyptian fleet, which completely dominated
the Aegean at the time. Since the Egyptian fleet was also a thorn in the side
of the Seleucids, Antigonus formed an anti-Egyptian alliance with Antiochus Soter. Antigonus built a large fleet and, in a protracted naval war with
Egypt that went on intermittently for about fifteen years, managed to create
a new naval balance of power in the Aegean. The resulting decline in Egyptian dominance of the regional sea-lanes necessarily placed new constraints on Ptolemy Philadelphus' ambitions in Asia, thereby offering some
welcome relief to the beleaguered Seleucids.

The death of Seleucus had triggered a series of revolts that shook the empire, and Antiochus Soter proved unable to maintain effective control over
the vast territories that he had inherited. It was during his tenure that major
segments of Persia broke away from the Seleucid Empire and asserted their
independence. Ptolemy Philadelphus took advantage of Antiochus' problems to invade Palestine and Syria in about 276. Preoccupied with trying to
maintain order in Asia Minor and elsewhere in the empire, Antiochus was
in no position to wage a full-scale campaign against Ptolemy to regain Palestine. A peace treaty concluded between them in about 272 confirmed
Egyptian control of the territory. An attempt was subsequently made by
Antiochus II Theos (261–246) to force the Egyptians to withdraw from Palestine and the coastal areas of southern Syria, but it proved unsuccessful. A
new peace agreement that was finally concluded in about 252 essentially
confirmed the existing situation between the two kingdoms.

It was during the reign of Antiochus Theos that the remainder of the Seleucid Empire to the east of the Euphrates began to disintegrate. The major

factor contributing to this development was the emergence of a new and formidable power in the region, the Parthians, who are believed to have originated from the Parni, a member of the Dahae coalition of Scythian tribes that roamed the steppe between the Caspian and Aral Seas. They are thought to have moved south to occupy the region of the upper Tejen about the year 250. From there, they soon moved into the Transcaspian frontier region that became known as Parthia, which placed them in position to begin to push the Seleucids westward out of the region.

With the sudden death of Antiochus Theos in 246, possibly at the hands of his former queen, a major crisis developed in connection with the succession to the throne. His wife Berenice, who was a sister of the new Egyptian king Ptolemy III Euergetes (246–221), was murdered along with her infant son by Antiochus' former wife, Laodice, who wanted to secure the throne for her own son, Seleucus II Callinicus (246–227). Ptolemy Euergetes used the occasion to launch a major invasion of the weakened Seleucid Empire, advancing as far as Babylonia before being forced to withdraw in 243 in order to deal with internal disturbances that had broken out in Egypt. In the process, he took control of the entire Mediterranean coastal strip. However, once Ptolemy returned to Egypt, Seleucus Callinicus was able to emerge from Anatolia, where he had taken refuge, and recover northern Syria and the territories farther east from the Egyptians.

Seizing the opportunity provided by the Seleucid preoccupation with the internal crisis in the kingdom and the war with Egypt, Andragoras, the Greek satrap of Parthia, followed by the satrap of Hyrcania, rebelled against Seleucid rule in 245. At about the same time, Arsaces, leader of the Transcaspian Parni, took advantage of the chaotic situation in the east to eject Andragoras and occupy the province of Parthia. Simultaneously, a movement to break away from Seleucid rule was also taking definite form in Bactria, perhaps the most important of the eastern provinces. Bactria provided the trade link between southwestern Asia and China on the one hand, and with gold-rich Siberia, as well as southern Russia, on the other. Bactria was also essential for the security of the empire in Asia because it constituted the frontier against invasions from Central Asia. As a consequence, some 20,000 former Greek soldiers had been settled there by Alexander, making Bactria a truly Graeco-Iranian province guarding the empire's most vulnerable flank.

With the accession of Seleucus Callinicus to the throne, the Greek satrap of Bactria, Diodotus, began to assert his independence and finally revolted in about 239, taking with him the province of Sogdiana (Samarkand). Seleucus moved aggressively to restore his control over the eastern provinces, entering the region with a large army the following year. He forced Tiridates (246–212), the brother and successor of Arsaces, and his Parni tribesmen out of Parthia and back into the Central Asian steppes. However, the campaign had to be abandoned in midcourse because of a challenge to Seleucus' rule in Asia Minor raised by his brother, Antiochus Hierax, with the support of their mother Laodice, who aspired to rule the region through her teenage younger son. The subsequent defeat of Seleucus' forces at Ancyra (Ankara) in 238 by Antiochus Hierax, supported by a coalition of enemies of the Seleucid Empire that included Bithynia, Pontus, Pergamum, and Egypt, forced him to abandon all the territory north of the Taurus Mountains to his brother. Within a decade, Antiochus Hierax was himself driven across the strait to Thrace, where he perished in obscurity, as Pergamum, under Attalus I (241–197), became for a brief moment in the long history of Asia Minor its preeminent state.

Struggling to maintain his grip on the shrinking empire, Seleucus Callinicus became preoccupied with trying to complete the pacification of the rebellious eastern provinces. However, before he could accomplish this, he was killed in an accident in 227, leaving the Seleucid Empire in political disarray. Taking advantage of the situation, the deposed satrap Tiridates returned to take control of Parthia once again, while Bactria exploited the period of instability accompanying the change of ruler to secede from the empire some two years later. Seleucus III Soter (227–223) made a valiant but unsuccessful attempt to re-conquer the territory north of the Taurus from the Pergamenes, devoting his brief reign, which was ended by assassination, to the task. By the time of his death, the eastern frontier of the diminishing Seleucid Empire had receded from the Indus, where it was originally set by Alexander, as far west as Media, while the western frontier had moved eastward from the Aegean to the Taurus Mountains.

However, Seleucid fortunes soon took a turn for the better, for a while at least, with the accession of Antiochus III the Great (223–187) to the imperial throne. He suppressed a revolt by the satraps of Media and Persis and, in 217, attempted to drive the Egyptians out of southern Syria and Palestine. The latter effort turned into a debacle when he was stopped by the forces of Ptolemy IV Philopator (221–204) at the battle of Rafah, at the gateway to the Sinai, and was forced to withdraw to the north of Lebanon. The treaty that was subsequently negotiated between Ptolemy and Antiochus provided for the cession to Egypt of Coele-Syria, thereby reconstituting most of the earlier Ptolemaid Empire in Asia.

Antiochus was effectively compelled to make this concession because he was confronted by an even greater threat to the cohesion of his realm in the north. Achaeus, the able commander of the Seleucid army in Asia Minor, succeeded in turning back the expansionism of Attalus and the Pergamenes, and was able to restore much of the region to Seleucid control. However, Achaeus was also very ambitious and therefore politically unreliable. Not surprisingly, he soon revolted and declared himself the independent king of the territories under his control, with the covert support of Egypt. To deal with this challenge, Antiochus was forced to reach an accommodation with Attalus that provided for the territorial expansion of Pergamum in return for its support in suppressing Achaeus' insurrection. The latter soon found himself caught between the Pergamenes on one side and the army of Antiochus on the other. It was not long before Achaeus was defeated on the battlefield and forced to take refuge in Sardis, which was placed under siege by Antiochus and taken by him in 213.

Having restored Seleucid control of much of Asia Minor except for Pontus, Pergamum, Bithynia, and Cappadocia, Antiochus marched eastward on a campaign of re-conquest that lasted eight years. He invaded Armenia, whose king Xerxes (228–212) was compelled to acknowledge Seleucid suzerainty in 212. During the reign of Xerxes' successor Ervand IV (212–200), Antiochus appears to have instigated a revolt by two royal princes, Artashes and Zareh, the net result of which was to make Armenia easier to control. Ervand was overthrown and the country partitioned into two tribute-paying provinces: Greater Armenia, which included all the northern Armenian lands east of the Euphrates almost as far as the Caspian; and Sophene, the region around Diyarbekir and Edessa.

By 209, Antiochus had re-conquered Hyrcania, which had been annexed in 217 by Tiridates of Parthia. He then fought his way into Parthia, occupying the capital at Hecatompylus. With its domination of the southeastern coast of the Caspian, Parthia had become a significant force straddling the major trade routes from the west to Bactria. Now, Artabanus I (211–190), who succeeded Tiridates, was forced to accept Seleucid suzerainty over Parthia and to pay tribute to Antiochus. The latter then moved against Bactria, where Euthydemus had replaced the dynasty established by Diodotus. After a difficult struggle, from which he emerged essentially victorious, Antiochus acknowledged that he could not maintain effective direct Seleucid control of the remote region and decided to recognize it as an autonomous client state. The conflict ended with a treaty of friendship, sealed by the marriage of Euthydemus' son Demetrius to the daughter of the Seleucid king. Antiochus then crossed the Hindu Kush, meeting and reaffirming the peace with the Indian king Sophagasensus, and then returned to Seleucia in 205 after a wide triumphal tour through the imperial domains. Buoyed by his successes in the east, Antiochus soon decided to try his hand at territorial expansion in the west once again, a decision that was to have fateful consequences.

The incessant feuding between the heirs of Alexander continued until the beginning of the second century, with Egypt, under Ptolemy V Epiphanes (203–181), reaching the point of exhaustion first. The new Egyptian ruler was only five years old when he mounted the throne, and he immediately came under the control of corrupt and unpopular regents. The moment seemed ripe for a move by both Seleucids and Antigonids to regain those territories in their traditional spheres of control that were now in the possession of the Ptolemaids.

In the winter of 203–202, Antiochus entered into an alliance with Philip
V (220–179) of Macedonia that called for a general division between them
of the Ptolemaid possessions outside of Egypt proper. Ptolemaid holdings
in Syria and Palestine were to be returned to Antiochus, while the territories under Egyptian control in the Aegean region, including the Ionian seaboard, were to be absorbed by Philip. It seems clear that both parties
probably considered this alliance to be a temporary marriage of convenience. Antiochus surely had no serious intention of allowing Philip to annex territories in Asia Minor that had been claimed by the Seleucids for a
century. It is far more likely that Antiochus hoped that an invasion of Asia
Minor by Philip would engage him in an exhausting war with Pergamum,
providing an opportunity for Antiochus to dispatch both at a later time. In
the meanwhile, such an assault on Egyptian interests in the Aegean and in
Asia Minor would facilitate Antiochus' campaign to re-conquer Coele-
Syria and Palestine. While it is less clear what Philip stood to gain by such
an alliance, at a minimum, a simultaneous Seleucid campaign against
Egypt would facilitate his elimination of Ptolemaid influence in the Aegean.

Antiochus launched his campaign of re-conquest in the spring of 202
and subsequently defeated the Egyptians decisively at the battle of Panium
(Panias) in northern Palestine in 198, driving them back behind their own
African frontier. From this point on, Palestine reverted to Seleucid control.
At the same time, Philip attacked the Ptolemaid holdings in Thrace and
along the Asiatic shores of the Hellespont. Within a year he had driven the
Egyptians out of Samos and had landed his forces on the Pergamene coast.
By 200, he completed the conquest of the coast of Thrace and crossed into
Asia Minor from the north, placing Abydos under siege. However, as an
unintended consequence of these advances at Egypt's expense, a new and
critical geopolitical factor was to intrude into the regional power equation,
namely, the interests of distant Rome.

9

Reconfiguration of the Middle East

When the long and difficult Punic Wars between Rome and Carthage finally came to an end in 202, the Roman Senate took special note of the fact that the Carthaginian general Hannibal had induced Macedonia to take Carthage's side in the conflict. Philip V had signed a treaty of alliance with Hannibal in 215, and after the latter's decisive defeat by the Romans at the battle of Zama he was welcomed in Macedonia. Although the practical import of Philip's support of the Carthaginian cause was inconsequential, the fact of Hannibal's presence in Macedonia caused Rome to view Philip's new alliance with Antiochus with some suspicion, since Philip had already acted against Rome's interests.

Roman concern was further heightened when the alliance was characterized to the Senate by the envoys of Rhodes and Pergamum, which were at war with Macedonia, as a direct threat to Rome itself. Antiochus was described as a self-styled second Alexander who had an insatiable appetite for conquest. Note was also taken of the fact that Philip had recently rebuilt his fleet, giving him the capacity to project power abroad. This could be interpreted as suggesting, even though it didn't seem very likely, that Antiochus and Philip might be planning a joint invasion of Italy. However, such speculation, unsupported by some more definitive evidence despite the belligerent sentiments of some of the senators, was not considered sufficient to obtain a decision of the Senate in favor of a preventative war against the alliance. A commission was therefore sent to Greece and Asia in 200 to find out just what Philip and Antiochus had in mind. The commission was also empowered to seek out prospective allies in the region, particularly among the Greeks for whom they felt a cultural affinity, in the event of a conflict with the Antigonid and Seleucid kings.

To assist in identifying potential allies, the Roman commissioners came armed with a policy statement from the Senate insisting that Macedonia desist from making war against any Greek state, and that its ongoing conflict with Pergamum be submitted to an impartial international tribunal for peaceful resolution.

However, by the time the Roman commissioners reached Athens, the latter had already declared war on Macedonia and Philip had sent an army under Nicanor to ravage Attica. The commissioners were still in Athens when Nicanor arrived at the city. On their own initiative, they presented him with the Senate's policy statement in the form of an ultimatum. That is, should Philip reject the Senate's terms he could consider himself at war with Rome. Philip, who was presiding over the siege of Abydos at the time, was furious and rejected the ultimatum out of hand, ordering a renewal of the attacks on Attica.

Although the commissioners had not been authorized to issue such an ultimatum, they nonetheless had effectively committed the prestige of Rome to it. Philip's vehement reaction was sufficient to swing the Senate to a decision in favor of war, and Philip was soon faced with a Roman army bent on his defeat.

Notwithstanding their alliance, Antiochus was too preoccupied with the re-conquest of southern Syria and Palestine from Egypt and too uninterested in Philip's fate to come to his aid. In fact, he exploited the opportunity presented by Philip's struggle with Rome to advance his own interests in Asia Minor. The Romans crushed Philip's army at Cynoscephalae in Thessaly in 197, and he was forced to sue for peace.

Antiochus sought to capitalize on Philip's defeat, and the resulting power vacuum in the Aegean region that it created, by trying to seize some of the Greek cities in Asia Minor that had been under Macedonian control and that Rome had since declared to be free. Smyrna and Lampsacus appealed to Rome for help, and the Senate sent another commission to Antiochus to discuss the matter. This was seen by Eumenes II (197–159), who had succeeded Attalus as king of Pergamum, as an opportunity to manipulate Rome into serving as an instrument of his own foreign policy, and he attempted to influence the commissioners in favor of a Roman intervention. According to Livy:

Eumenes was anxious for war against Antiochus, believing that a king so much more powerful than himself was a dangerous neighbor, if there was peace, and also that, if war should be provoked, he was no more likely to be a match for the Romans than Philip had been, and that either he would be utterly destroyed or, if peace were granted him after he had been defeated, much that was taken from Antiochus would fall to his own lot, so that thenceforth he could easily defend himself against Antiochus without any Roman aid. Even if some misfortune should befall, it was better, he thought, to endure whatever fate with the Romans as allies than by himself either to submit to the sovereignty of Antiochus or, if he refused, to be compelled to do so by force of arms; for these reasons he urged the Romans to war.[1]

Although there was a growing sentiment for war against Antiochus in Rome, no tangible preparations for the conflict had as yet been undertaken. Nonetheless, it was already quite clear that the Seleucid Empire and Rome were on a collision course. Relations between the two powers deteriorated sharply when Antiochus crossed the Bosphorus in 196 and established a foothold in Thrace. But matters reached the point of explosion when, at the urging of Hannibal who had become an adviser to Antiochus after the defeat of Philip, the Seleucid ruler invaded Greece in 192 in the wake of the Roman evacuation of the country. Rome declared war in 191 and, joined by the forces of Philip who had his own score to settle with Antiochus as a result of the latter's earlier abandonment of him in his hour of need, soon routed the Seleucid army at Thermopylae. Antiochus was forced to flee from Greece back to Asia Minor where he hoped to rebuild his army and prepare for a new confrontation with Rome in Europe.

The Romans, however, had no intention of allowing Antiochus to recover from his defeat to the extent that he might again pose a threat to their interests. There could be little doubt that they would pursue him into Asia once they disposed of the Aetolian Confederation, which had gone to war with Rome in support of the Seleucids. And indeed, it was not long before an armistice ending the Aetolian War permitted the Roman commander L. Cornelius Scipio, assisted by his brother, the illustrious general Scipio Africanus, to give his undivided attention to dealing with Antiochus.

Having decided to go after Antiochus on the latter's territory, the Romans were confronted by a major logistical problem, namely, how to get their legions to Asia. Even with the assistance of the Pergamene and Rhodian fleets, the Romans still had not established naval supremacy in the Aegean, which made it very dangerous to attempt to bring an invasion force across the open sea from Greece to Asia Minor. Given the risks of not being able to assure the security of the sea-lanes for their troop transports, Scipio elected to adopt the more difficult tactical alternative open to him, which entailed a march of several weeks duration through northern Greece and across Thrace to the Hellespont. At the same time, a major naval campaign was initiated for the purpose of wresting dominance of the sea from the Seleucids and their allies and assuring control of the shores of the Hellespont, which was essential to the safe crossing of the Roman army into Asia.

The success of Scipio's strategy far exceeded his expectations. After Roman naval supremacy was established in the region, Antiochus precipitously withdrew his forces from both sides of the Hellespont, abandoning Thrace without a struggle. It seems that the Seleucid king's impulse was to draw all the forces he could muster for a major battle in which he apparently hoped either to defeat the Romans decisively, or at least to fight them to a standstill. As a result, the Roman legions were permitted to cross unimpeded into Asia Minor. By late summer 189 the Scipios were ready to challenge Antiochus on his own territory.

Antiochus seems to have tried to induce the Romans to forego the coming battle by offering a number of concessions that he believed would eliminate the justification for any further hostilities. As far as he was concerned, the question of Thrace was already made moot by his unilateral withdrawal. He also proposed to renounce any claims to the Greek cities of the Ionian coast and to recognize their independence. Finally, he offered to pay an indemnity amounting to half the cost of the war. However, Antiochus' offer was too little too late. Once having committed their forces, the Romans would accept nothing less than a complete Seleucid evacuation of all of Asia Minor north of the Taurus and the payment of all the costs of the conflict. Unwilling to concede so much, Antiochus elected to settle the matter on the battlefield. He took up a position near Magnesia in the plain close to Smyrna, where he awaited the Roman assault.

His decision to face the Roman legions in a pitched battle soon proved to have been a horrendous mistake. The Seleucid army was almost annihilated as Antiochus fled eastward to Syria, the cities of Asia Minor capitulating in rapid order in the wake of the Roman victory. Antiochus had gambled and lost. As a result, the long struggle of the Seleucids for dominance in Asia Minor was brought to an ignominious end. Moreover, unwittingly to be sure, Antiochus had drawn the Romans into Asia. From this point on, they would increasingly become involved in the affairs of the region that now constituted the eastern marches of their growing empire.

Under the Peace of Apamea that was concluded in 188, the Romans extracted from Antiochus the identical concessions that they had demanded before the battle of Magnesia. The Taurus was to be the northwestern frontier of the Seleucid Empire and all claims and ambitions in Europe were to be forsworn. An indemnity covering the entire cost of the war, some 15,000 talents of silver, was to be paid to Rome, one fifth initially and the remainder over a twelve-year period. An additional indemnity of 400 talents was to be paid to Eumenes of Pergamum.

The payment of this heavy debt was to have significant economic and political impact on the empire as the Seleucid government scrambled to garner the wealth required. Since Antiochus had no legitimate means of generating the necessary levels of revenue, he as well as his successors resorted to plundering the temples of the various religions and cults that existed within the Seleucid Empire. This was done in recognition of the fact that the temples also served as safe depositories for their worshippers, particularly after the invention of coinage, with much of the wealth of the empire being contained in their treasuries. Antiochus ultimately met his death in 187 as a consequence of his attempt to plunder the temple of Bel in Elam, an act that touched off a rebellion.

DECLINE OF THE SELEUCID EMPIRE

Taking advantage of Antiochus' discomfiture at the hands of the Romans, the two vassal states that he had helped establish to better control Armenia revolted. Artashes (188–159) declared himself king of Greater Armenia and marched south to occupy the ancient lands of Urartu (Media Atropatene) between Lake Urmia and the Caspian. His brother Zareh also declared his independence as king of Sophene and immediately adopted an expansionist policy that sent his armies marching westward across the Euphrates into Cataonia. At the same time, Arsaces IV Priapatius (c. 190–175), who succeeded to the Parthian throne, and his successor Phraates I (c. 175–170), took advantage of the Seleucid problems with the Romans and launched an extended campaign to re-conquer the provinces south of the Caspian. Phraates ultimately retook Hyrcania and pushed to the Parthian frontier west of the Caspian Gates. The framework of the Seleucid Empire seemed to be coming apart at its seams.

By the time of the accession of Seleucus IV Philopator (187–176) to the throne, a year after the Peace of Apamea, the once vast Seleucid Empire that reached from the frontiers of Central Asia to Europe had been reduced to Syria (including Cilicia), Palestine, Mesopotamia, Babylonia, Media, and Persis. It was also on the verge of bankruptcy. Pressed by the rise of indigenous tribal powers in the east and by Rome in the west, Seleucus saw no realistic alternative to accepting the reduced state of the empire. He adopted a policy of retrenchment, which soon led to his being viewed as a weak ruler, a perception that ultimately brought about his assassination by Heliodorus, who attempted to seize power while Seleucus' son and heir Demetrius was still being held as a hostage in Rome. However, Heliodorus' ascendancy was short-lived as Seleucus' younger brother Antiochus IV Epiphanes soon dispatched him and seized the throne in 175.

These developments, and their possible implications for Egypt, proved to be of some concern to Rome. Ever since the original alliance between Antiochus III and Philip V, Rome had taken a direct interest in the security of Egypt and this intensified significantly after the Peace of Apamea. Accordingly, in 173, a Roman embassy arrived in Egypt to renew the "friendship" between Rome and the young Egyptian king Ptolemy VI Philometor (181–145). However, neither Ptolemy nor Antiochus Epiphanes were entirely clear about what this Roman friendship entailed, and both were cautious about any moves they might make that would run afoul of Rome's interests.

When Antiochus Epiphanes first mounted the Seleucid throne, he had little concern about stability on his southern frontier with Egypt. His sister Cleopatra was the widow of Ptolemy Epiphanes and had been ruling Egypt, as regent for her son, since her husband's death in 182. Ptolemy Philometor, who was only five or six at the time. The situation changed with the death of Cleopatra in 173. The regents who subsequently ran the coun-

try in the name of the young king were still smarting over the earlier loss of
Palestine to the Seleucids, and they apparently were convinced that the
time was ripe for an attempt to regain control of the territory. Antiochus,
who was well aware of Egypt's preparation for an attack, contemplated a
preemptive strike. Wary of what Rome's reaction might be to an outbreak of
fighting in an area that it considered to be within its sphere of interest, both
parties sent embassies to the Senate to present their cases. At the time, however, Rome was engaged in a war in Macedonia and was not prepared to intervene in the quarrel between Ptolemy and Antiochus.

In 170, the Egyptians attempted an invasion of Palestine for which
Antiochus was well prepared. Launching their attack without the element
of surprise, the Egyptian assault turned into a debacle as Antiochus defeated their army before it could even cross the Sinai desert. Ptolemy Philometor subsequently tried to flee the country but fell into Antiochus' hands.
His younger brother, Ptolemy Euergetes, was named king in Alexandria in
his place. This provided Antiochus with a plausible pretext for invading
Egypt, namely, to place the legitimate king of the country back on the
throne. Left without an effective defense, Egypt lay open to Antiochus who
seized Pelusium and proceeded up the Nile to Memphis to reinstall Ptolemy Philometor as king. Antiochus Epiphanes had done what Perdiccas,
Antigonus, and Antiochus the Great failed to accomplish. For the first time
since Alexander the Great, Egypt was successfully invaded from Palestine.

However, having defeated and conquered Egypt, Antiochus did not
quite know what to do with it. The Alexandrines insisted upon the legitimacy of Ptolemy Euergetes and prepared the city's defenses against a possible Seleucid attack. Although Antiochus initially placed Alexandria
under siege, for reasons that remain unclear he decided to abandon the effort to force the city into submission. Moreover, since he was not in a position to occupy the country permanently, and had no desire to get overly
involved in the squabble that was taking place between the supporters of
the rival claimants to the throne, he decided to withdraw from the country.
He did, however, publicly announce his position on the succession question. He formally recognized his older nephew Ptolemy Philometor as the
legitimate king of Egypt in Memphis, and insisted that Alexandria should
acknowledge him as such, notwithstanding the fact that because of Alexandria's greater accessibility to the outside world, Ptolemy Euergetes was
gaining international recognition as the king of Egypt. Antiochus withdrew from Egypt in 169, but left a garrison at Pelusium to keep the door to
the country open to him should he decide to intervene again at some later
time.

That occasion presented itself within a few months after Antiochus'
withdrawal. Contrary to his announced policy regarding the succession to
the Egyptian throne, an agreement was reached that the two brothers
should jointly rule the country from Alexandria. Since he had already de-

clared in favor of Ptolemy Philometor, Antiochus decided to intervene on his behalf, although uninvited to do so, and invaded Egypt again in the spring of 168, returning first to Memphis and then marching on Alexandria. At this time, however, Rome had just successfully concluded the war in Macedonia, which wiped out the latter's independence as a state, and was now free to direct its attention to the cries for assistance that it had been receiving from Alexandria. To his chagrin, Antiochus was met at Eleusis near Alexandria by an embassy from the Senate, headed by the Roman consul Gaius Popilius Laenas. The latter advised him, in effect, that Rome had already established a de facto protectorate over Egypt and that Antiochus must withdraw from the country at once.

In the course of his confrontation with Popilius, Antiochus was publicly humiliated by the Roman and compelled to acknowledge tacitly that the Seleucid Empire was henceforth to be considered a client state of Rome. According to Livy:

Popilius handed him the tablets containing the decree of the senate in writing, and bade him read this first of all. On reading the decree, he said that he would call in his friends and consider what he should do; Popilius, in accordance with the usual harshness of his temper, drew a circle around the king with a rod that he carried in his hand, and said, "Before you step out of this circle, give me an answer which I may take back to the senate." After the king had hesitated a moment, struck dumb by so violent an order, he replied, "I shall do what the senate decrees." Only then did Popilius extend his hand to the king as to an ally and friend.[2]

Word of Antiochus' discomfiture at the hands of Rome soon precipitated an open civil conflict in Judaea between the pro-Ptolemaid former high priest Jason and the pro-Seleucid party of the incumbent high priest Menelaus. The roots of this conflict lay in a dynastic struggle over control of the sacred office, which also served as the central political authority in the country. The struggle threatened to undermine the Seleucid position in the country that now had enhanced importance to Antiochus. With the establishment of a de facto Roman protectorate over Egypt, Palestine became the southern Seleucid frontier with the Roman zone of influence in the eastern Mediterranean. Antiochus decided that direct intervention was necessary to secure the Seleucid position in the country, and in 168 he sent an army to invest Jerusalem. To prevent any challenge to Seleucid authority, the walls of Jerusalem were razed, leaving the city defenseless. The Temple treasury was seized, and a permanent garrison was established in the city in a newly built and virtually impregnable fort, the Acra, which remained in Seleucid hands until 141.

Antiochus was justifiably concerned about the country's traditional vulnerability to attack from the south, and he took steps to consolidate his position in Palestine against a resurgent Roman-backed Egypt. Since it was impractical to fortify the entire country, he needed to have assurance of the loyalty of its peoples. He sought to achieve this through the imposition of an essentially totalitarian regime, in conjunction with a broader bold but miscalculated attempt to weld together the diverse populations of his empire into a single people that would be supportive of the Seleucid dynasty. This was to be achieved by forcing the various indigenous peoples to abandon their distinctive cultures and religious practices in favor of a more homogeneous imperial culture that was rooted in Greek civilization. Only in this way, he believed, would it be possible for him to resist the inexorable pressures that he was under from Rome, which appeared determined to bring the Seleucid state to its knees. Accordingly, Antiochus launched an intensive program of Hellenization and insisted upon the universal adoption within the empire of a common core religion, the worship of Zeus Olympius.

In the pagan world, such a demand was not entirely unrealistic since it merely meant according special significance to one particular god out of the many that existed in the polytheistic pantheon. However, Antiochus could hardly comprehend that such a demand could be anathema to committed monotheists, given that the very notion of monotheism was alien to him. In Palestine, his policy precipitated an open rebellion in Judaea under the leadership of the Hasmoneans that ultimately destroyed the Seleucid position in the country. Under Judah Maccabee (165–160) and his successors, the Judaean struggle for political autonomy took on a serious military dimension that generated interest in Rome. If the Judaeans were to succeed in regaining independent control of the African-Asian land bridge, a Roman-Judaean alliance could prove to be of considerable strategic value to Rome. At the same time, Roman support might prove invaluable for the Hasmoneans in fending off the Seleucids.

Judah Maccabee took the initiative in this regard and sent an embassy to Rome in 161 to seek its support in the ongoing struggle for independence from Demetrius I Soter (162–150). The latter was the son of Seleucus IV, who had been held hostage in Rome but escaped after the death of Antiochus Epiphanes and had recently mounted the Seleucid throne. The Senate reportedly accepted the proposal of an alliance between Rome and Judaea, although there does not appear to be any evidence that Rome actually ever did anything in support of the Hasmonean struggle. The text of the treaty is contained in the following letter purportedly sent by Rome to Jerusalem in confirmation of the pact:

Forever may there be peace between the Romans and the nation of the Jews on sea and land. May sword and enmity be far from them. If any aggressor wages war upon the Romans or upon any of their allies throughout their empire, the nation of the Jews shall give aid wholeheartedly, as circumstances indicate, and to those at war with them the Jews shall not give or supply food, arms, money, or ships, as was agreed at Rome. In the same manner, if any aggressor wages war upon the nation of the Jews, the Romans shall give aid wholeheartedly, as circumstances indicate, and to those at war with them there shall not be given food, arms, money, or ships, as was agreed at Rome. The Romans shall carry out these obligations without deceit. On the foregoing terms have the Romans made a treaty with the Jewish People. If hereafter both sides shall agree to add or subtract anything, they shall act according to their decision, and any such addition or subtraction shall be valid. As for the misdeed which King Demetrius is perpetrating against you, we have written as follows: "Why have you made your yoke weigh heavy upon our friends, our allies, the Jews? If they make any further complaint against you, we shall get justice for them by waging war on you by sea and by land."[3]

Notwithstanding his problems in Palestine at the time, Antiochus Epiphanes had left Syria in 166 to attempt the re-conquest of the former Seleucid provinces in the east, where he had greater freedom of action from Roman intervention. He launched an invasion of Armenia in 165 and captured its king, Artaxias (Artashes), who was compelled to acknowledge Seleucid suzerainty over the country. From there Antiochus moved on to Persia where he was actively campaigning when he died in 163 at Gabae (Isfahan). With his death, the process of disintegration of the Seleucid Empire increased in tempo. The attempt of his successor Demetrius to suppress the rebellion of the satrap Timarchus in Media was preempted by an invasion of that country by the Parthians under Mithradates I (170–138), who is generally considered to have been the founder of the new and formidable Parthian Empire. Media fell to the invaders in 155, after a struggle that lasted some six years. The conquest of Media opened the door to Mesopotamia, which was soon lost to the Parthians as well.

The decline of Seleucid power seemed irreversible. Its brief resurgence in the west under Demetrius was soon brought to an end by a coalition of Egypt, Pergamum, and Cappadocia. In Palestine, Demetrius II Nicator (145–139 and 129–125) was forced to accept the independence of Judaea in 142. Three years later Rome renewed its treaty with the Hasmoneans, and reportedly sent a letter about it to Demetrius, Ptolemy VIII of Egypt, Attalus II of Pergamum, Ariarathes V of Cappadocia, Mithradates I of Parthia, and the rulers of the other states of the region. The letter is purported to have stated: "Ambassadors of our friends and allies the Jews, commissioned by the High Priest Simon and by the People of the Jews, came to us to renew their long-standing relations of friendship and alliance. They brought a gold shield of one thousand minas. Accordingly, we resolved to write to you kings and countries to refrain from attempting to harm them and from making war upon them, their towns, and their territory and from acting in alliance with those at war with them."[4] Once again, there is no evidence that this letter had any practical effect beyond demonstrating Rome's continuing if not growing interest in the region.

In the east, the various Seleucid satraps declared their independence and a host of petty states soon arose. These states all subsequently fell easy prey to Parthia. Between 160 and 140, Mithradates annexed the provinces of Media, Elymais, Persis, Characene, Babylonia, Assyria, and Gedrosia, and possibly also Herat and Sistan. The Parthians then established their capital at Ctesiphon on the east bank of the Tigris, directly opposite Seleucia and in easy striking distance of the Euphrates. Demetrius Nicator made a serious bid to reverse the Seleucid decline by attempting to re-conquer the eastern provinces. And for a while it appeared that his efforts might be rewarded as he received the willing support of the various Greek cities that had come under Parthian rule. In the end, however, Mithradates prevailed and Demetrius was taken captive and sent into honorable confinement in Hyrcania. When Mithradates died in 138, he left his son Phraates II (138–127) an empire that stretched from the Euphrates to Herat, putting Parthia well on the road to restoring the pre-Alexandrine Empire of the Achaemenids.

A final attempt to restore the vanishing Seleucid Empire was undertaken by Antiochus VII Sidetes (138–129), who moved first against Judaea, taking Jerusalem and subjugating the country once again, before marching against the Parthians in Media and Babylonia with a powerful and well-disciplined army in 129. The Parthians were defeated in three successive battles, and Phraates was on the verge of being forced to accept Antiochus' terms, which included the evacuation of all the eastern provinces other than Parthia itself, in addition to the payment of tribute. However, although Phraates had been defeated on the battlefield, he exploited other means to avoid the anticipated consequences of that defeat and to transform it into a Parthian victory.

Antiochus had reached Ecbatana by the time winter was setting in and halted operations to wait until the weather permitted resumption of the campaign. His army was quartered in the surrounding towns and villages, where they made themselves a heavy burden on the residents. Parthian agents therefore found the ground fertile for fomenting an uprising against the occupying force. At the same time, Demetrius Nicator was released from his confinement in Hyrcania and permitted to return to the west to create dissension in the enemy ranks by laying claim to the Seleucid throne. By the following spring, the situation had become sufficiently volatile for the outbreak of an insurrection against the Seleucids that apparently was timed to coincide with a surprise attack by Phraates. The disruptions behind the Seleucid lines coupled with the Parthian counteroffensive produced the desired result, chaos in the Seleucid camp. Antiochus was killed in the confusion, as part of his army was captured and then incorporated within the Parthian forces. Henceforth, the Seleucid Empire was effectively and irrevocably reduced to Syria alone.

Although the moment seemed right for a Parthian assault on Syria, it did not happen. At the moment that Phraates was completing his victory over Antiochus Sidetes at Ecbatana, a new and dangerous challenge to the Parthians arose on their own eastern flank. A vast movement of tribes of

Scythian origin coming from Chinese Turkestan, the Sakae, had advanced to the frontiers of Parthia, one wing heading west and another south in the direction of Sistan. Phraates moved to engage them in 128. However, the Seleucid troops that he had incorporated into his army turned on him at their first contact with the Sakaean forces, resulting in his defeat and death. His uncle and successor Artabanus II (c. 127–124) realized the same fate four years later. While this was happening, the governor of Babylonia revolted, and Hyspaosines, the ruler of Characene, at the head of the Persian Gulf, declared his independence and subsequently seized a good part of Babylonia. Thus, when Mithradates II the Great (124–88) became king of Parthia, he was faced with invasion in the east and rebellion in the west. Nonetheless, he soon succeeded in quelling the rebellions in the west and then turned east to drive the invaders out. He retook Merv, pushing the frontier back to the Oxus, subjugated Sistan, and advanced to Herat. Mithradates then reached an understanding with the Scythians who served as a buffer between Parthia and their kinsmen, the Sakae, who had settled in the plains of the middle Oxus in Bactria. In Mesopotamia, Mithradates extended the Parthian Empire to embrace the petty kingdoms of Adiabene (Mosul), Corduene (Kurdistan), and Osrhoene (Edessa), setting his western frontier at the Euphrates.

It was during the reign of Mithradates II that Parthia became a major regional power, largely because of the wealth it had accumulated from international trade by consolidating its control of the territories along the trade route from the Roman frontier to the outer fringes of the Chinese Empire. A Chinese embassy was sent to the Parthian capital by the Han emperor around 120, and a Parthian embassy accompanied them on their return to China.

Mithradates also attacked Artavasdes I (159–95) of Armenia and took the latter's son Tigranes hostage, ultimately making him his protégé. When the issue of the Armenian succession arose upon the death of Artavasdes, Mithradates intervened and saw to it that Tigranes (95–55) was placed on the throne, exacting from him in payment the return of some seventy valleys in Media Atropatene that had been seized earlier by Artaxias. Although Mithradates may have thought that Tigranes would continue in his earlier role of protégé, he was to be sorely disappointed. It turned out that Tigranes had expansive ambitions of his own. He subsequently split from Mithradates and asserted Armenia's independence from Parthia. At the same time, however, he managed to maintain cordial relations with his Parthian benefactor. Under Tigranes, Armenia and Sophene were quickly reunited into a single powerful state that enabled him to pursue a program of territorial expansion.

Tigranes allied himself closely to Mithradates VI Eupator (120–63) of Pontus, marrying his daughter Cleopatra. It seems likely that at least an implicit agreement was struck between Tigranes and Mithradates Eupator to carve up much of southwest Asia between them. Tigranes would be given a free hand in Syria and the interior of Asia, while Mithradates Eupator would have a free hand in Asia Minor and along the coasts of the Black Sea. In effect, such an agreement would have afforded each party the support of a powerful ally as well as protection from attack from behind as they expanded their separate spheres of control.

With Parthia in temporary disarray as a result of both external pressures and internal dissension, Tigranes moved in to fill the power vacuum that existed in the borderlands between Armenia, Mesopotamia, and Persia. Corduene (Kurdistan) and Media Atropatene (Azerbaijan) were transformed into Armenian fiefdoms, and the nearby kingdom of Adiabene became an Armenian dependency. Tigranes also extended his rule to the region of Nisibis in northern Mesopotamia. While he did not get a firm grip on southern Mesopotamia, which was mostly desert, he did manage to make effective use of the Bedouin tribes that roamed the region. He transplanted the tribe of the Mardani to the north where he gave its sheikh, Abgar I (94–68), control of Osrhoene. His purpose in this was to have the Bedouin dominate the trade route that crossed the Euphrates in the region, on his behalf. Tigranes also moved westward into Cappadocia, detaching its eastern province of Melitene, which he united with Sophene on the other side of the Euphrates. This gave him control of the major trade routes passing between Armenia and Anatolia.

Farther south, the Seleucid kingdom was in the process of disintegration following the assassination of Antiochus VIII Grypus (125–96) at the hands of one of his generals, which created anarchy in the country. Given this situation, there was no effective opposition to Armenian penetration into Syria. Indeed, according to the Roman historian Justinus, Tigranes was invited to intervene.

After the kings and kingdom of Syria had been exhausted by intermitting wars, occasioned by mutual animosities of brothers, and by some succeeding to the quarrels of their father, the people began to look for relief from foreign parts, and to think of choosing a king from among the sovereigns of other nations. Some therefore advised that they should take Mithradates of Pontus, others Ptolemy of Egypt, but it being considered that Mithradates was engaged in war with the Romans, and that Ptolemy had always been an enemy to Syria, the thoughts of all were directed to Tigranes, king of Armenia, who, in addition to the strength of his own kingdom, was supported by an alliance with Parthia and by a matrimonial connection with Mithradates. Tigranes, accordingly, was invited to the throne of Syria . . . where he reigned for eighteen years [83–69].[5]

In any case, Tigranes quickly occupied eastern Cilicia and northern Syria as well as most of the Phoenician coast. From this latter position he also posed a direct threat to the expanding kingdom of Judaea which, taking advantage of the situation in Syria, had extended its sway northward to Damascus.

Although there were to be several more Seleucid rulers in Syria, none were independent. As a practical matter, the Seleucid era had come to an end.

NOTES

1. Livy, XXXV.xii.

2. Ibid., LV.xii.

3. 1 Macc., XVII, 8:23–32.

4. Ibid., XXXV, 15:17–19.

5. M. Junianus Justinus, *Justini Epitoma Historiarum Philippicarum Pompei Trogi*, XL.1.1–4.

10

Rome Enters the Middle East

Although its specter had hovered over western Anatolia since the Peace of Apamea in 188, Rome had made no tangible moves to incorporate the territory into its empire. This was a reflection of the fact that there was still substantial opposition in the Senate to Roman expansion into Asia. The issue was brought to a head, however, when the king of Pergamum, Attalus III (138–133), faced by social unrest and the lack of an heir, decided to minimize the risks of political and social upheaval after his death by making Rome his legal heir.

When Attalus died in 133 the Senate, without great enthusiasm, decided to accept the legacy and take over most of the rich country. This promptly led to a revolt by Aristonicus, the illegitimate son of Attalus' predecessor. A Roman army under the consul Crassus was sent to suppress the revolt in 131, but met with defeat. A second attempt the following year under the consul Perperna proved more successful, with Aristonicus being taken captive. Nonetheless, the conflict continued for another year before a third commander, Aquilius, finally brought it to an end. The principal part of the territory of Pergamum was annexed to Rome as the new province of Asia. Some of the less fertile and therefore less valuable districts of the country such as Phrygia and Lycaonia, even though of strategic significance, were turned over to the kings of Pontus and Cappadocia, respectively, as rewards for their loyalty to Rome in the recent conflict. Although Rome had no expansionist objectives in Asia at the time, as evidenced by its voluntary cession of territory to some of the local rulers, the acquisition of Pergamum necessarily increased the direct stake of Rome in the turbulent region and inevitably involved it in political developments there.

Mithradates Eupator (120–63) of Pontus had inherited a relatively small state on the northeastern coast of Asia Minor, bounded inland by Paphlagonia and Galatia in the west, Cappadocia in the south, and Lesser Armenia in the east. He was, however, a man of considerable ambition, and when the Greek cities of the Crimea appealed to him for help against the Scythians and the Sarmatian tribes that were descending on them from southern Russia, he took on the role of their champion. He dispatched an army under his general Diophantus to assist them. Diophantus eventually defeated the Scythians and took possession of the entire Crimea. As a result, Mithradates became master of most of the northern coast of the Black Sea, control of which was vested in the newly founded Kingdom of the Bosphorus. At the same time, he expanded eastward along the southern shore of the Black Sea as far as the Caucasus, annexing Lesser Armenia, that is, Armenia west of the Euphrates, and the province of Colchis in the Caucasus. These conquests yielded immense supplies of grain, men, and money that enabled Mithradates to build a formidable military and naval force. Colchis was especially important in this regard because it provided Pontus with a major source of shipbuilding materials. Moreover, it was situated on the Transcaucasian trade route that linked the countries of the east with the Black Sea basin.

Not satisfied with merely filling such power vacuums as existed in the region, Mithradates Eupator also aspired to an expanded empire in western Anatolia, an ambition that would inevitably place him on a collision course with Rome. Between 112 and 93 he had managed to build a kingdom so powerful that Rome soon felt the need to take action against what it correctly perceived to be a threat to its position in Asia Minor.

Concerned about but not deterred by the power of Rome, which was preoccupied at the time in the protracted Jugurthine War, Mithradates shrewdly tried to expand his realm further without forcing an open break with the superpower to the west. Accordingly, in about 108 he invited Nicomedes III Euergetes (127–91), king of neighboring Bithynia, to join with him in carving up the territory of Paphlagonia, which lay between them. Presumably, Mithradates may have reasoned that Rome would be less concerned about Paphlagonia if its dismemberment were not seen as a unilateral action on the part of Pontus. Nicomedes may also have had some reservations about the proposal out of concern about how it might be viewed in Rome. But he was in no position to antagonize Mithradates by rejecting the invitation to become an ally of Pontus, since the latter was clearly capable of swallowing up Bithynia whenever it so chose. Accordingly, Nicomedes joined Mithradates in the dismemberment of Paphlagonia.

The Paphlagonians managed to send a deputation to Rome seeking its intervention on their behalf. The Senate responded favorably to their request and dispatched a mission to the area demanding that Mithradates and Nicomedes withdraw from Paphlagonia. Nicomedes attempted to convince the Romans that he was merely restoring Paphlagonia to its legitimate king, having changed the name of his son to Pylaemenes, a Paphlagonian royal name. It is not known whether the Romans were taken in by this ruse. It has also been suggested that Mithradates was able to forestall a strong reaction from Rome through the judicious use of bribery. In any case, it does not seem that the Senate was prepared at this time to enforce its demands, and nothing was done to compel the two kings to comply with them.

The prospects of a confrontation with Rome increased markedly, however, when Mithradates began intervening in Cappadocia. Touching both the Halys and Euphrates Rivers and reaching to the Taurus Mountains, Cappadocia was a land of significant strategic value, interposed as it was as a buffer zone between Pontus and the areas under direct Roman control in Asia Minor. It therefore represented a substantial territorial prize to anyone with imperial ambitions in Asia Minor.

Mithradates Eupator's father and predecessor, Mithradates V Euergetes, had marched into Cappadocia some years earlier to help ensure the enthronement of Ariarathes VI (125–111), who subsequently married Euergetes' daughter, and thereby achieved considerable influence there. Mithradates Eupator, however, wanted more direct control over the country and instigated the assassination of Ariarathes VI around 111, leaving the country to the queen regent, his sister Laodice, and her minor son Ariarathes VII Philometor (111– c. 100). However, to Mithradates' surprise, Nicomedes of Bithynia preempted his arrangements there by invading Cappadocia and marrying the queen regent, effectively placing himself on its throne. Since Nicomedes was in no position to challenge Mithradates in a contest of arms, it seemed to have been a rather imprudent move on his part. And, indeed, it was not long before Mithradates drove Nicomedes and his wife, the queen regent, out of the country and reinstalled his nephew Ariarathes Philometor on the throne of Cappadocia. About a decade later, after Ariarathes attempted to assert independence from his uncle, Mithradates murdered him with his own hands.

At this point, developments in Cappadocia became a matter of grave concern to Nicomedes, who came to believe that Mithradates now intended to wrest Bithynia itself from him. Since Bithynia was not powerful enough to prevail in a conflict with Pontus, Nicomedes contrived to involve Rome in the matter in order to place constraints on Mithradates' freedom of action. After the elimination of Ariarathes VII by Mithradates, Nicomedes produced another son of Laodice to claim the Cappadocian throne in his place. The latter ruled the country briefly as Ariarathes VIII with the support of the Cappadocian aristocracy.

Mithradates, however, was unwilling to allow himself to be outmaneuvered by Nicomedes and soon eliminated Ariarathes VIII as well, placing one of his own sons on the Cappadocian throne under the assumed name of Ariarathes IX Eusebes, which was intended to give him some superficial legitimacy. Nicomedes retaliated by producing yet another son of Laodice as a claimant to the throne and appealed to the Roman Senate to support his claim. This effectively forced Mithradates to do likewise. But, presented with what appeared to be a hopelessly complicated succession problem, the Senate declined to make a choice between the claimants and decided that the selection of who should sit on the throne should be left to the nobles of Cappadocia. As it turned out, the nobles preferred to be free of the influence of both Mithradates and Nicomedes and therefore selected a third party, Ariobarzanes, to rule the country. The choice of the nobles was subsequently confirmed in 96 by the Senate, which assigned the task of installing Ariobarzanes on the throne to Lucius Cornelius Sulla, at the time proconsul of Cilicia. For the moment, Mithradates' ambitions in Asia Minor had been checked. He had been denied control of a strategic region that dominated the northern approaches to the Taurus range.

Given his recent negative experience with Rome in regard to Cappadocia, Mithradates decided to bide his time and await an opportune moment to pursue his expansionist ambitions in Asia Minor, hopefully without provoking any further Roman intervention. He saw such an opportunity soon after Nicomedes III died in 91, leaving Bithynia to his son Nicomedes IV Philopator (90–74) who was recognized by the Senate as the legitimate ruler of the kingdom. Fortuitously, the transition period generally coincided with the eruption of the Social War in Italy in 90. As soon as Rome appeared to be sufficiently preoccupied with its internal problems, Mithradates, with the assistance of Tigranes of Armenia, seized both Bithynia and Cappadocia. He placed the pretenders Socrates Chrestus, a brother of Nicomedes, and Ariarathes IX on the respective thrones of the two countries. In 89, however, with the Social War coming to an end, Rome insisted that Mithradates withdraw from both kingdoms and restore Nicomedes Philopator and Ariobarzanes to the thrones of Bithynia and Cappadocia. Mithradates, ever cautious about openly confronting Rome, felt compelled to comply with its demands and to defer the pursuit of his imperial ambitions until a more opportune moment.

Nonetheless, as it turned out, officials who acted beyond the scope of their legitimate authority once again manipulated Rome's foreign policy, and thereby provoked an apparently unnecessary war with Mithradates. It appears that Nicomedes Philopator, in an effort to make certain that Rome did not waver in its determination to return him to the throne of Bithynia, had signed promissory notes for large payments to be made to the pertinent Roman commanders and other officials. The most notable of these were Manius Aquilius and Gaius Cassius who had been sent to the region by Rome to resolve the complex succession crisis. Naturally, now that Nicomedes had regained his throne he was expected to make good on these financial obligations, but was in fact unable to do so. As one historian observed, "it was coming to be an expensive business to be restored to one's throne by Romans."[1]

Unwilling to write off the bankrupt Nicomedes' financial obligations as a bad debt, Aquilius became determined to find a means of generating sufficient income for Nicomedes so that he would, in fact, be able to liquidate his debts. According to Appian, he urged Nicomedes and Ariobarzanes, "as they were neighbours of Mithradates, to make incursions into his territory and stir up a war, promising them the assistance of the Romans. Both of them hesitated to begin so important a war on their own border, because they feared the power of Mithradates. When the ambassadors insisted, Nicomedes . . . reluctantly made an attack on the territory of Mithradates and plundered it as far as the city of Amastris, meeting no resistance. For Mithradates, although he had his forces in readiness, retreated because he wanted to have good and sufficient cause for war."[2] When Mithradates protested to Aquilius about these raids, the latter responded that, although the Romans did not wish to see Mithradates harmed by Nicomedes, they would also not permit Mithradates to take any retaliatory action. That is, Mithradates would have to swallow his losses without any expectation of reparations. The unbalanced position taken by Aquilius in this situation is assumed by some historians to have been a reflection of his desire to precipitate a crisis that would justify a Roman intervention in Pontus without having to refer the matter to Rome.

The reaction of Mithradates, who consistently preferred to achieve his aims through diplomacy and subversion rather than war, but now found himself caught in a Roman vise that could destroy him, was swift and violent. If such provocation of Mithradates were indeed Aquilius' purpose, he evidently was quite successful. If this were not his intent, and he merely wanted to intimidate Mithradates and use Pontus as a cow to be milked, then he overplayed his hand, particularly since there was only one Roman legion in Asia Minor at the time. Rome clearly had not authorized Aquilius' actions and now found itself in a war for which it was not prepared.

Mithradates bolstered his alliance with Armenia, sought support from Greece, Crete, and Egypt, and recruited a substantial foreign legion made up primarily of Romans and others expatriated as a consequence of the recent civil war in the Italian peninsula. Although Parthia would not enter the conflict on the side of Pontus, it would not do anything to help Rome either. In the spring of 88, before Rome could land reinforcements, Mithradates struck, overrunning Bithynia and invading long-coveted Cappadocia. The Roman forces and their indigenous levies were severely mauled and Aquilius was captured and executed. Mithradates then overran almost all of western Anatolia, where most of the Greek cities opened their gates to him, ordering the wholesale simultaneous massacre of all Romans and their families and the confiscation of their properties.

Encouraged by his relatively easy successes in Asia Minor, Mithradates next turned his attention to Europe, apparently determined to resolve the issue of whether Rome or Pontus would dominate Asia on the battlefield in Greece. This was a shrewd decision on his part, since fighting the Romans outside of Asia would minimize the defections of his allies in Asia Minor once the pressure of the war was felt in their territories. Moreover, if the war there went well, he would be in a position to negotiate a new arrangement with Rome regarding the balance of power in the Aegean and eastern Mediterranean. Athens, under Athenion, had already taken his side in the war, and Mithradates had reason to believe that he soon would pick up additional Greek allies who wished to rid themselves of the Roman yoke. In essence, he had much to gain and little to lose by moving the conflict to Europe.

The Pontic forces crossed into Thrace and then struck into weakly defended Macedonia, where preparations were made for a further thrust southward into Greece. At the same time, Mithradates dispatched his fleet into the Aegean where, under his best general Archelaus the islands off the Greek coast were systematically conquered. Then, at the invitation of Aristion, who replaced Athenion as the tyrant of Athens, Mithradates landed a force on the Greek mainland, threatening to attack the Roman forces there simultaneously from opposite directions.

Rome had only a few troops in Greece, but with the help of the governor of Macedonia it managed to contain the Pontic army within Attica. In 87 Sulla finally arrived at Epirus with a Roman army of some 30,000 men and marched on Athens, laying siege to the city. Archelaus, however, was able to hold out in Piraeus where he was supplied by sea. Sulla finally took Athens in 86, an event that was soon followed by the collapse of resistance in Piraeus, as Archelaus was ordered to Boeotia to join forces with the main Pontic army. Shortly thereafter, following at least two major battles with the Pontic reinforcements that had arrived in Thessaly, the remnants of Mithradates' army were forced out of Greece. Mithradates, however, still retained command of the sea, and without an adequate fleet at his disposal Sulla was unable to follow up immediately on his victory in Europe by taking his offensive into Asia, although this was to take place soon enough.

Mithradates' heavy hand in the Graeco-Roman cities of Asia Minor caused some, such as Smyrna, Ephesus, and Sardis, to defect to the Roman army that landed in Anatolia later that same year and began to push him back toward Pontus. After several further setbacks Mithradates concluded that the tide of events was against him and, in 85, he decided to sue for peace. Sulla was anxious to return to Rome and was concerned that the war might go on for years because the Roman forces at his disposal were not sufficient to achieve a quick and decisive victory. He therefore was only too pleased to conclude a peace agreement that was readily acceptable to Mithradates. The resulting Treaty of Dardanus essentially restored the situation to that which had prevailed before the conflict broke out. That is, Nicomedes and Ariobarzanes were reseated on the thrones of Bithynia and Cappadocia, while Mithradates was recognized as king of Pontus and as an ally and client of Rome.

The Senate, however, had not formally ratified the treaty, partly as a result of the confusion that reigned after the resignation of Sulla from the dictatorship in 79. Mithradates, with some justification, suspected that Rome did not intend to abide by the agreement and began to mobilize his resources for another major conflict. Roman-Pontic relations deteriorated significantly over the next several years and reached the point of explosion in 74 when Nicomedes Philopator bequeathed his kingdom of Bithynia to Rome, which declared it to be one of its provinces.

Mithradates was simply not prepared to accept the fundamental change in the regional balance of power that would result from direct Roman control of Bithynia, which would give Rome unrestricted access to the Black Sea, and he invaded the country. The Roman consul responsible for Cilicia and Asia, Licinius Lucullus, raised five legions and marched against Mithradates through Phrygia. By 73, Lucullus had succeeded in defeating Mithradates in the field, principally by taking advantage of the major tactical blunder committed by the latter when he engaged most of his army in a fruitless attempt to take the city of Cyzicus by siege. Having sapped the effective strength of his forces, Mithradates was forced to retreat back into Pontus, which subsequently was taken by the Romans toward the end of 70.

Unable to stop the Roman advance, Mithradates abandoned Pontus and fled to safety in Armenia where he found refuge with his son-in-law Tigranes, who refused to turn him over to Lucullus. The Roman commander, however, soon concluded that it would be necessary to invade Armenia if he were to prevent Mithradates from launching yet another costly war against Rome. At this point, Tigranes, who initially had little interest in providing any tangible support for Mithradates' ongoing struggle with Rome, joined forces with the latter and pleaded with Phraates III (70–58), who had just become king of Parthia, for help in their struggle against Rome. As an inducement, they offered him seventy valleys, Adiabene, and northern Mesopotamia. Their plan was that Phraates should attack Mesopotamia, disrupting Lucullus' supply lines while the Pontic-Armenian forces engaged him in battle in Armenia. Lucullus, however, had learned that such negotiations were taking place and promptly initiated direct negotiations with Parthia in an effort to secure its support of Rome rather than Pontus in the conflict.

Lucullus succeeded in convincing Phraates that it was not in his interest to make an enemy of Rome for the sake of Mithradates, and Parthia agreed to remain neutral in the conflict. No longer concerned about the exposure of his forces to attack from behind from Mesopotamia, Lucullus proceeded to invade Armenia. This forced Tigranes to abort his campaign of conquest in northern Palestine and to return to defend his homeland. As Josephus noted: "News came to Tigranes, that Lucullus, in his pursuit of Mithradates, could not light upon him, who was fled into Iberia, but was laying waste Armenia and besieging its cities. Now, when Tigranes knew this, he returned home."[3] Lucullus captured the Armenian capital of Tigranocerta in 69, but Tigranes and Mithradates withdrew into the mountains and continued the struggle. Indeed, while Lucullus was tied up by Tigranes in Armenia, Mithradates slipped away and managed to march back to Pontus where he inflicted a serious defeat on the occupying Roman troops in 67 and once again regained control of the country.

Dissatisfied with Lucullus' conduct of the campaign against Mithradates, in 66 the Senate turned over responsibility for the war to Pompeius, who had just finished clearing the eastern Mediterranean of the pirates that had been plying the maritime trade routes in the region. Pompeius, who was in Cilicia when news of his appointment reached him, secured his rear by renewing the treaty of neutrality with Parthia, and took the field against Mithradates in Pontus. At the same time, Tigranes' son, Tigranes the Younger, who had failed in an attempt to overthrow his father, took refuge with Phraates. He soon convinced the Parthian king to attack Armenia. This seems to have had the unintended consequence of splitting the Armenian-Pontic alliance, by compelling Tigranes to divert his forces to meet the Parthian challenge while the Romans invaded Pontus and overwhelmed the Pontic army at Nicopolis.

Although Tigranes soon managed to stop the Parthian advance into Armenia, he would not renew his alliance with Mithradates. Tigranes saw little purpose in continuing the war with Rome, a war that Mithradates could not possibly win. Indeed, when the latter sought refuge in Armenia once again, Tigranes refused to admit him. Nonetheless, undaunted by his defeat in Asia Minor and his abandonment by his principal ally, Mithradates retreated along the coast of the Black Sea to his domain in the Crimea, where he raised a new army and began planning an invasion of Italy by marching up the Danube. However, internal squabbles within the kingdom of the Bosphorus put an end to these bold ambitions, and the Mithradatic era was brought to an end when the aging and despondent king took his own life in 63.

After defeating Mithradates at Nicopolis, Pompeius elected not to pursue him around the Black Sea coast, at least not at once. Instead, he decided to make a detour first into Armenia to deal with Tigranes, who in fact was exhausted by the incessant wars and was ready to reach an accommodation with Rome. Pompeius marched into the country virtually unopposed, and Tigranes soon surrendered, ostensibly without prior conditions although this seems rather unlikely.

In any case, pleased with having taken the country without a fight, Pompeius magnanimously restored Tigranes to the throne of a substantially reduced Armenia. Under the terms of the peace presumably dictated by Pompeius, Tigranes had to concede to Rome all the territories he had conquered in Cappadocia, Cilicia, Syria, and Phoenicia, as well as the province of Sophene east of the Euphrates, leaving him only the original heartland of Greater Armenia.

Having thus disposed of the Armenian question, Pompeius returned to his pursuit of Mithradates in the Crimea. As he moved northward in the Caucasus in 65, he also subdued the kingdoms of Iberia and Albania. However, he soon had second thoughts about the wisdom of proceeding farther into a mountainous region that was unfamiliar to the Romans and was occupied by hard-fighting tribesmen. Pompeius concluded that finishing off Mithradates simply wasn't worth the risks involved. Since Mithradates soon accomplished this himself by his suicide, Pompeius' decision turned out to be prescient.

With the campaign against Mithradates at an end, and Armenia reduced to its original heartland, Pompeius set about redrawing the political map of the region to suit Rome's strategic interests. His scheme reflected what geopoliticians would later term an essentially "rimland strategy" that involved the establishment of a continuous chain of Roman provinces along the Asian coast from Pontus on the Black Sea to Syria on the Mediterranean. Between these provinces and the Parthian frontiers there was to be a network of client states that would constitute a buffer zone between Rome and Parthia. The main client states in Asia Minor and in the region east of Cilicia were Galatia, East Galatia, Paphlagonia, Cappadocia, Lesser Armenia, and Commagene, the northernmost of the Syrian provinces. East of the Euphrates, Pompeius confirmed the rule of Abgar II (68–53) over Osrhoene and decided to return control of Corduene, which had previously been seized by Phraates, to Tigranes, and sent a force under Afranius to occupy the disputed territory.

He also, unwisely as it turned out, refused to respond affirmatively to Phraates' request that the Roman-Parthian border be set at the Euphrates. By this somewhat cavalier if not demeaning treatment of the Parthian king, Pompeius set the stage for the troubled relations between Rome and Parthia, and its successor state of Sassanid Persia, that were to dominate regional affairs during the next six centuries. Pompeius had advanced Rome's strategic frontier, although not necessarily its sphere of direct control, to the Euphrates and the Syrian Desert. Nonetheless, as long as Armenia remained friendly to Rome, and Commagene guarded the crossing points on the upper Euphrates, Parthian expansion westward could be effectively contained.

In Syria and Palestine, to which Pompeius directed his attention in 65, matters clearly needed to be sorted out. Antiochus XIII Asiaticus, whose claims to the Syrian throne had been recognized as legitimate by Lucullus and the Senate, although contested by other claimants, had been acknowledged as king in Antioch after the withdrawal of the Armenians. However, it had become evident that Sampsiceramus, emir of the Arabs of Homs, and Azizus, sheikh of a Bedouin tribe that roamed the area, were in actual control of much of northwestern Syria. As a practical matter, Seleucid claims to the territory appeared questionable. The alternatives for Rome seemed to be either to continue to support Antiochus, and hope that the kingdom would survive encroachment from the peoples of the desert and not come apart at the seams because of internal pressures, or to take a more direct hand in assuring its stability. It was primarily a matter of determining what served Rome's interests in Syria best. For Pompeius, there was little question in this regard. He advised Antiochus Asiaticus that he had no intention of restoring sovereignty to a king who had no knowledge of how to govern or ability to maintain the territorial integrity of his kingdom. In effect, Pompeius brought the Seleucid dynasty to an abrupt end when he decided to establish a satrapy in Syria that would henceforth rule the country as a Roman province.

In Palestine, political affairs were equally confused. Under Alexander Janneus (103–76), Judaea had reached the zenith of its power, expanding its control to virtually all of ancient Israel once again. At his death, Judaea's borders included the strategically important coastal region (except for Ashkelon) from Mount Carmel in the north as far south as Rhinocorura (El Arish), on the Egyptian frontier. East of the Jordan, it encompassed a belt of territory reaching from Panias in the north to the Nabatean kingdom of Petra, southeast of the Dead Sea. Judaea was once more in effective control of the African-Asian land bridge and the important north-south trade routes that passed through Palestine.

With the withdrawal of the Armenians from Phoenicia, the potential for further Judaean northward expansion seemed assured. However, Janneus' demise brought on a succession crisis involving his sons Hyrcanus and Aristobulus. This, coupled with an internal religious and social conflict, threatened to escalate into a full-fledged civil war. The resulting destabilization of the country provided an opportunity for the Nabatean king Aretas III not only to retake the territories wrested from Petra by Alexander Janneus, but also to invade Judaea and lay siege to Jerusalem.

Pompeius sent Aulus Gabinius and Marcus Scaurus to Palestine to help mediate the crisis. They intervened in the dispute over the succession and, apparently swayed by appropriate bribes from the nationalist party, decided in favor of Aristobulus. They also induced Aretas to raise his siege of Jerusalem and withdraw. Aretas, however, was also in control of Damascus, and Pompeius wished to make it clear to all that Rome had entered the region and would no longer tolerate the incessant raiding and territorial encroachments that characterized the traditional politics of the area. To emphasize this point, Pompeius launched a punitive expedition against Petra in 63, but had to interrupt it because of a new revolt that broke out in Palestine. Ultimately Aretas reached an accommodation with the Roman governor of Syria that guaranteed all Nabatean possessions, including Damascus, for a cash payment.

When Pompeius arrived in Damascus and reviewed the current state of affairs in the region, he reversed the decisions of his mediators in the Palestine crisis. He did not want a resurgent Judaea upsetting the regional balance of power that he was so carefully orchestrating. He would not accept Aristobulus, the choice of the Judaean nationalists, as king in Jerusalem. He insisted that the country revert to internal rule by its high priests, the form of government originally recognized by Rome in its treaty with the Hasmoneans in 161. Hyrcanus was to rule the country as high priest and ethnarch, but not as its king. The country could have internal autonomy, but the governing high priest would not be permitted independent control of the country's external affairs. Furthermore, Pompeius demanded that Judaean claims to all the territories conquered by Alexander Janneus be renounced. With the Roman legions camped at the gates of the capital, Aristobulus was forced to capitulate, although some of his fanatical supporters in the army held the Temple Mount in Jerusalem against the Romans for some three months before surrendering.

Farther south, in Egypt, the Romans had long avoided direct rule, even though it would have been a simple matter to annex the country. Instead, the Senate preferred to exercise its control through a succession of weak indigenous rulers. The reasons for this seem to have been twofold. Egypt was a wealthy territory and its royal house contributed large sums to the Roman treasury in return for its security and nominal autonomy. But perhaps more important was the consideration suggested by Theodor Mommsen. "Egypt, by its peculiar position and its financial organization, placed in the hands of any governor commanding it a pecuniary and naval power and generally an independent authority, which were absolutely incompatible with the suspicious and feeble government of the oligarchy: in this point of view it was judicious to forgo the direct possession of the country of the Nile."[4] Accordingly, by allowing Egypt to remain the only nominally independent state of the Hellenic east, the Senate avoided the creation of a competing power center within the Roman Empire.

NOTES

1. E. Badian, *Roman Imperialism in the Late Republic*, p. 56.

2. Appian of Alexandria, *Appian's Roman History*, Vol. 2, *The Mithraditic Wars*, XII.II.11.

3. Flavius Josephus, *Antiquities of the Jews*, XIII.xvi.4.

4. Theodor Mommsen, *The History of Rome*, Vol. 4, pp. 319–320.

11

The Roman–Parthian Conflict

The Roman reconfiguration of the political structure in the region was essentially defensive in character, making it clear that the Senate had little interest in prosecuting an expansionist war against Parthia. However, the republican system of government was beginning to break down as Rome's aristocrats competed for power. In 55, the triumvirate of Caesar, Pompeius, and Crassus dominated the political scene in Rome. The latter two were co-consuls that year, with Crassus designated to become governor of Syria after his term as consul was concluded. Somewhat older than the other two leaders, Crassus had not participated in a military campaign since the suppression of the slave revolt of Spartacus sixteen years earlier. Now approaching the end of his public career, Crassus apparently intended to exploit the opportunity to launch a conflict with Parthia that he expected to shower him with military glory as well as a good deal of booty.

Relations with Parthia had already been soured by Pompeius' somewhat disrespectful treatment of Phraates with regard to formally establishing the Roman-Parthian frontier at the Euphrates. The situation became worse in 55 when Gabinius, the proconsul of Syria, sought to intervene in Parthian affairs by involving himself in the succession crisis that accompanied the enthronement of Orodes II (57–37). Gabinius had given his support to a brother of the new Parthian ruler who was contesting the succession. Relations with Parthia were to become explosive with the arrival of Crassus in Syria to replace Gabinius as proconsul in the spring of 54.

Crassus was in command of seven legions with a total of more than 40,000 troops, and he soon began making probing forays across the Euphrates into Parthian-held territory. He consolidated his foothold as he progressed with the establishment of Roman garrisons in a number of the towns through which he passed in northern Mesopotamia. The populaces of some of the major centers of the former Seleucid Empire, such as Seleucia and Babylon, were disenchanted with Parthian rule and would have welcomed their liberation by the Romans. However, instead of taking immediate advantage of this situation and continuing to penetrate into the heart of Parthian occupied territory, Crassus chose to withdraw back to Syria for the winter and to resume the campaign the following spring. This gave the Parthians the respite they needed to mobilize their forces and to prepare their defense against the coming assault.

Having completely lost the element of surprise, the only thing that Crassus had not signaled to the Parthians was his line of approach. Basically, he had two practical choices. One was to retrace his steps across northern Mesopotamia, marching his forces along the route already secured in part by the garrisons he had established earlier. The other was to work his way north and then east through the hill country of Armenia, from which he would later swoop down into the heart of Mesopotamia. From a tactical standpoint, the Armenian route was the more advantageous for the Roman legions, which were primarily infantry, while the northern Mesopotamian route clearly favored the Parthians, whose most effective forces were cavalry and mounted archers.

The fact that he had already deployed some of his forces in northern Mesopotamia became the basis of Crassus' choice of invasion route for the conquest of Parthia. His plan was to march directly into Mesopotamia with his full army along the route already guarded by the Roman outposts and to head for Seleucia in the heart of the country. His choice of approach to Parthia effectively cost him the support of Artavasdes II (55–33), king of Armenia, who had agreed to participate in the campaign on the supposition that the invasion of Parthia would take place through the hill country of Armenia where the Parthian cavalry would be ineffective. In fact, Orodes fully expected the Roman invasion to be mounted through Armenia and had led the bulk of the Parthian army there to block the Roman advance, effectively tying up the Armenian forces who were no longer available to support Crassus farther south. At the same time, Orodes left behind a cavalry force of some 10,000 horses and camels, to which he assigned the task of protecting the approaches to Parthian territory across northern Mesopotamia. Cut off from his Roman allies, and left alone to confront the powerful Parthian force moving into the Armenian hill country, it was not long before Artavasdes reached an accommodation with Orodes that was sealed by the marriage of his daughter to Pacorus, the Parthian crown prince.

When Crassus finally launched his invasion across Mesopotamia in the spring of 53 he came up against and engaged the far smaller but powerful Parthian mounted forces near Carrhae (Harran). Despite the substantial advantage in numbers enjoyed by the Romans, the Parthian cavalry decimated the Roman legions, which lost about three-fourths of their men in the battle. Crassus' grand scheme had turned into a debacle, costing Rome all of the gains east of the Euphrates achieved by Lucullus and Pompeius. He was subsequently captured by the Parthians while attempting to retreat to Syria through the Armenian hills, and was executed.

The Parthians did not take immediate advantage of the opportunity to follow the remnants of the Roman legions across the Euphrates into Syria because such a decision would have had to be made by the king, and he was away in Armenia at the time. This delay provided Cassius, who took over as governor of Syria upon the death of Crassus, with the time he needed to reorganize the defense of the province with the surviving forces until reinforcements could arrive. By the time that the Parthians decided to move, the Roman forces in Syria were in a much better position to cope with the challenge. This is not to suggest that they were in a position to take the offensive against the Parthians; they were not. The Senate was preoccupied with the increasingly turbulent domestic political developments that were transforming the very nature of the Roman republic, and had little interest in what was taking place far to the east in Asia. Consequently, few reinforcements were to be forthcoming and Cassius had to devise a strategy centered on the defense of Antioch that would permit him, at best, to stop the Parthian advance.

A sizable force of Parthians under Pacorus struck across the Euphrates in 51 and easily overran the district between it and Antioch. However, they were unable to draw the Roman forces under Cassius out of the city into open battle. Unprepared to attempt a siege, and unwilling to advance either farther north or south with a substantial intact Roman force in Antioch behind them, the Parthians soon withdrew back to Mesopotamia, subjected to harassing attacks along their route of march. They returned to Syria the following year, and were again frustrated by the refusal of the Romans to leave Antioch. Although Cassius was able to prevent the loss of Syria in this way, the need to shy away from a possibly decisive battle with the Parthians turned the Roman-Parthian confrontation into a stalemate. Fortunately for the Romans, for reasons that are not entirely clear, the Parthians desisted from launching a major thrust into Syria for another decade.

In the meanwhile, momentous developments were taking place in Rome. The last tie that still bound Caesar and Pompeius, that of family, came to an end with the death of Pompeius' wife Julia, the daughter of Caesar. Their competition for power soon escalated into a major civil war as Caesar crossed the River Rubicon, which divided Cisalpine Gaul from Roman Italy and represented the limit of Caesar's authorized jurisdiction, and marched on Rome in January 49 with a force of some 5,000 men. Pompeius and his aristocratic followers in the Senate were forced to flee the country, crossing the Adriatic into Macedonia, as Caesar made himself master of Italy. Instead of immediately pursuing Pompeius, Caesar chose first to invade Spain, which was his antagonist's main base of support. As he put it: "I go to meet an army without a leader, and I shall return to meet a leader without an army."[1] After subduing Spain in about forty days, Caesar then proceeded to Greece where he ultimately defeated Pompeius decisively in the plains of Pharsalia in 48. Pompeius fled the battlefield and sailed for Egypt, with Caesar in hot pursuit. Upon his arrival in Egypt the counselors of Ptolemy XIII had him assassinated.

Caesar arrived in Alexandria at the head of a small force of about 3,000 men only to learn that his quarry had already been disposed of. Encouraged by the relatively small size of the contingent accompanying Caesar, the Egyptian commander Achillas mounted an attack on the Romans with a large army supported by the mobs of Alexandria. Caesar was forced to burn his ships to prevent their capture, and soon found himself blockaded in a section of the city. His situation was desperate. However, just at this critical point, the army of Mithradates of Pergamum, augmented by a relief force recruited from the principalities of Syria arrived on the scene. Perhaps most important among the client-rulers who came to Caesar's rescue was Antipater, acting on behalf of Hyrcanus, and his force of 3,000 Judaeans. It was Antipater who materially helped Mithradates to pass by Pelusium without incident, as he had done once before for Gabinius, thereby facilitating the junction of the relief forces with those of Caesar, turning the tide of battle in the latter's favor. Caesar was quite grateful to Antipater and his nominal master Hyrcanus, and compensated them both for their help in his hour of need, consciously overlooking the fact that they had initially supported Pompeius in the civil war.

While Caesar was preoccupied with finishing off Pompeius, leaving a veritable power vacuum in Asia Minor, which had been denuded of significant Roman forces as a consequence of the civil war, Pharnaces, the son of Mithradates Eupator, attempted to restore an independent kingdom of Pontus. In 48 Pharnaces moved his army eastward along the Black Sea littoral from his base in the Crimea. He took Colchis and marched into Lesser Armenia and Cappadocia. Moving westward into Anatolia he confronted and severely mauled the small Roman army organized in Asia Minor by Domitius Calvinus, who had been dispatched to the region by Caesar to oversee its security. Once having reasserted Mithradatic control of Pontus with relative ease, all of Asia Minor seemed ripe for conquest. The following spring, Pharnaces struck into neighboring Bithynia, unaware that a Roman army under Caesar was already on the march through Syria to check his ambitions. Caesar subsequently defeated Pharnaces decisively and drove him back to the Crimea, which he held for just a short while as Caesar encouraged his own loyal ally, Mithradates of Pergamum, to seize the territory.

The subsequent murder of Caesar in 44 set in motion a succession struggle between the principal conspirators, Brutus and Cassius, and the pro-

Caesarian triumvirate of Octavian, Antonius, and Lepidus. This struggle was quickly transformed into a major civil war as the contestants for power left Rome to mobilize their forces for the impending struggle. Brutus went to Macedonia, while Cassius, who had been nominated by Caesar to serve as proconsul of Syria for the year 43, went to Antioch to assume control of the province.

The political situation in Syria at the time was particularly unstable. Caecilius Bassus, a former supporter of Pompeius, had revolted in 46 against the proconsul Sextus Caesar. The latter was assassinated by his own mutinous troops who joined forces with the rebels, who were bolstered by a large number of Parthian archers who had intervened on behalf of Bassus. Following the murder of Caesar in 44, the Caesarian general Antistius Vetus, who was soon replaced by L. Statius Murcus, placed Bassus and his forces under siege in Apamea. To further complicate matters, in the summer of 44 Antonius assigned the post of procurator of Syria to Dolabella, who soon arrived in the province to take up his post. To preempt Dolabella from exercising influence on the Roman commanders on behalf of the Caesarians, Cassius quickly won over Statius and forced both Antistius and Bassus out of Syria, over which he now asserted his own control.

Cassius was in dire need of funds to prepare for the inevitable confrontation with the Caesarians, and he therefore abrogated the privileges that had been granted to Judaea by Caesar. He then levied on the small client state an onerous tribute of 700 silver talents, an exorbitant sum for a country that had been looted repeatedly by itinerant Roman generals. To make matters worse, Cassius wanted the money quickly and Antipater simply could not raise the required sums within the given deadline. In retaliation for this failure to produce the demanded revenue, Cassius seized the populations of several Judaean towns and sold them into slavery, thereby ensuring the lasting hostility of the indigenous population toward the Romans.

In the meanwhile, Dolabella succeeded in establishing a foothold at Laodicea (Latakia) on the Syrian coast south of Antioch, from where he threatened Cassius' control over the province. Cassius marched north from Judaea to meet the challenge and captured Laodicea in June 43 as Dolabella had himself killed by his guards. Soon thereafter, Cassius received an urgent message from Brutus to join him in Macedonia to confront the combined forces of Antonius and Octavian, and he left Syria at the beginning of 42.

The subsequent defeat of Cassius and Brutus in October 42, in the plains of Philippi in Macedonia, marked the end of the Roman republican party. It also brought the entire Roman world into the hands of Octavian and Antonius, Lepidus being reduced to a minor role although he still remained a nominal triumvir. They divided the empire between them, Octavian taking control of the west while Antonius became the master of all of Rome's holdings in the east.

Despite Antonius' assumption of power in the Roman east, the general political situation in Syria and Palestine remained quite volatile. Just prior to the disastrous battle of Philippi, Cassius had sent Quintus Labienus as his representative to the Parthian king Orodes II to solicit his assistance against Octavian and Antonius. Although the Parthians did not intervene in time to be of any help to Cassius, they did undertake an invasion of Syria in 41, during which they sought to bring over to their side the numerous Roman garrisons in the country that were hostile to Antonius. Labienus was apparently so convinced that Syria could be wrested away from Rome that he had defected to the Parthians. Orodes' son Pacorus, who led the Parthian invasion of Syria a decade earlier, now joined forces with the renegade Labienus and crossed the Euphrates in a two-pronged assault. Labienus struck into Asia Minor, and Pacorus marched into Syria.

The Parthian advance encountered only feeble military opposition. Many of the inhabitants of the areas under Parthian attack were sufficiently disenchanted with the Roman overlords to welcome the invaders. This was particularly true in Judaea, which had suffered greatly under the iron fist of Cassius. There, Pacorus overthrew Hyrcanus, the high priest and nominal ruler of the country, and placed Antigonus II, son of the Judaean prince Aristobulus who had been deposed by Pompeius, on the throne as king in Jerusalem. Farther north, Commagene, the eastern gateway to Asia Minor, went over to and joined forces with the invading armies, while farther west, Labienus succeeded in seizing control of the Cilician Gates, effectively cutting off Syria from any direct land connection with Roman Asia Minor.

Antonius, who had relocated his headquarters to Alexandria so that he could be with his paramour Cleopatra, the queen of Egypt, was slow to respond to the Parthian challenge in Syria. After some delay, he went to Tyre, the only city in Syria that had managed to hold out against the Parthians, from where he hoped to mount a counteroffensive. Upon his arrival, however, he learned that his political standing in Rome had been placed in jeopardy by the Perusine War that was raging between his estranged wife Fulvia in league with Lucius Antonius, and Octavian. Although Antonius disapproved of the conflict, which Fulvia had started and was losing, his loyalists were being driven out of Italy, giving Octavian an increasing preeminence in Rome that Antonius viewed as extremely dangerous to his interests. As a result, Antonius abandoned his campaign against the Parthians and proceeded to Italy to take up the matter with Octavian. For a while it appeared that a new civil war was imminent, but it was averted at the time because of the opposition of the other military commanders to such a conflict. They saw little sense in butchering each other over an argument that could easily be settled through serious negotiation. Under pressure from them, Antonius and Octavian agreed to negotiate their differences. An agreement concluded at Brundisium (Brindisi) in the early autumn of 40 confirmed Antonius' position as Roman commander over Macedonia, Greece, and the eastern provinces. To cement the alliance between the two leaders, Antonius, whose wife Fulvia had just died, agreed to marry Octavian's sister Octavia. Both the marriage and the peace agreement seemed destined to be short-lived, given the fundamental conflict of interests that existed between Octavian and Antonius. Nevertheless, as long as Antonius remained in Rome there was a semblance of stability in the empire.

Following his temporary reconciliation with Octavian, Antonius returned to the east, taking up residence in Athens and dispatching a fresh army under Publius Ventidius Bassus against the Parthians. The latter, whose forces consisted primarily of cavalry, lost much of their tactical advantages once away from the plains where they could maneuver freely. By 39, the Parthians were in retreat, effectively driven out of Syria and Palestine by Ventidius and his legions. After repelling a Parthian counterattack in Syria in 38 during which Pacorus was killed, the Parthians abandoned the campaign. The following year, Jerusalem fell to the Romans. The Parthian client-king Antigonus was killed and Herod, the son of Antipater and a protégé of Antonius, was installed as king of Judaea by the Roman army.

After the defeat of the Parthian forces under Pacorus, Ventidius took the field against Antiochus of Commagene, who had been an ally of Pacorus, and laid siege to the capital at Samosata. However, it soon was apparent that Ventidius' reputation had become so enhanced as a result of his victory over the Parthians that it aroused the jealousy of Antonius, who began to view him as a possible rival. Antonius therefore left his headquarters at Athens and proceeded to Commagene where he relieved Ventidius of his command and personally took over the siege of Samosata.

In the meantime, in Parthia, possibly because of his distress at the loss of his heir apparent Pacorus, Orodes abdicated the throne and turned it over to Phraates IV (38–2). The latter, to secure his position, promptly killed his father and all his brothers, thereby eliminating all potential claimants to the crown. In the process, he also turned against the nobility, leading one of them, Monaeses, to appeal to Antonius to march on Parthia in the expectation that the Romans would be welcomed there by the Parthian people who were ready to rebel against the tyrannical Phraates. Intrigued by the idea of an easy victory, but eager to avoid the mistake made earlier by Crassus in attempting to attack Parthia across the plains of Mesopotamia, Antonius first marched into Armenia, which was still a nominal ally of Parthia. Artavasdes of Armenia quickly capitulated and was co-opted into assisting Antonius by providing a substantial cavalry escort for the Roman forces, an army of about 100,000 men, that crossed the Euphrates into Media Atropatene in 36.

Once again Rome was to suffer a serious setback as a result of the cocky overconfidence of its military leaders. To facilitate his rapid advance Antonius had split his forces, assigning two legions to guard the slower-moving baggage train while he raced on with the main body of his army to Praaspa, the capital of Media Atropatene. Once there, it became obvious to Antonius that he would have to lay siege to the city, but the required siege equipment was far behind him in the slow-moving baggage train. While awaiting its arrival, Antonius kept himself busy with the erection of great mounds of earth to replace the usual siege towers. However, he had seriously underestimated Phraates. The Parthian king took full tactical advantage of the division of the Roman forces and Antonius' immobilizing preoccupation with the siege of Praaspa. Avoiding a direct confrontation with Antonius, Phraates attacked his baggage train instead, applying overwhelming force. The stratagem proved to be exceptionally successful. Some 10,000 Roman troops were killed in the battle and the remainder of the accompanying legions taken prisoner. All of Antonius' supplies, including the siege equipment he was awaiting, were seized or destroyed. As this was transpiring, perhaps intuitively sensing an impending disaster, Artavasdes, whose participation in the conflict on the side of Rome was halfhearted at best, defected from his forced alliance with Antonius and withdrew his troops back to Armenia. Antonius now found himself in deep trouble with his army effectively cut off, far from its support base in Syria, and without supplies. The Parthians remained determined to avoid a pitched battle and instead mounted a campaign of attrition against the Roman forces. By the time Antonius completed his retreat through Armenia, which made no attempt to impede his passage, to Syria that winter, he had lost more than a third of his entire army without having fought a major engagement.

Apparently anxious to show some positive results from his expensive misadventure, Antonius contrived to take Artavasdes and most of his family prisoner. He had them shipped off to experience the tender mercies of Cleopatra in Egypt while he seized control of Armenia in the spring of 35, making it a Roman province for the next two years. He marched into Media again the following year, but was prevented from consolidating his advanced position by the combined actions of the Parthians and Armenians, the latter now taking a far more aggressive stance against the Romans because of Antonius' betrayal of Artavasdes. However, before he could undertake any further steps to impose his control over the region, Antonius became completely preoccupied with the renewal of the power struggle for the domination of Rome. He was to be defeated decisively in that struggle by Octavian at the battle of Actium in 31. Immediately upon Antonius' withdrawal of his legions from Armenia, Artaxias (Artashes), the son of Artavasdes, regained control of the country, massacring the Roman garrison that was left behind.

Under Octavian, who soon had himself transformed into Emperor Augustus (27 B.C.E.–14 C.E.), Rome adopted a very different attitude toward Parthia from that which had shaped its policy since the time of Sulla. He concluded, as a practical matter, that Parthia simply did not pose a serious threat to Rome or Roman interests anywhere west of the Euphrates for the foreseeable future. Parthia itself was plagued with far too much internal dissension, palace intrigues, rebellions, and succession crises to be an effective aggressor beyond its existing territorial bounds. A dynastic feud had broken out between the king Phraates IV and the pretender Tiridates that had kept the Parthians preoccupied, effectively preventing them from taking advantage of the turmoil in the Roman ranks preceding the battle of Actium. Tiridates was ultimately defeated but managed to escape across the Euphrates to Roman-held territory in Syria. This gave Augustus an important bargaining chip that he exploited with skill, reaching an agreement with Phraates in 23 that delineated their common frontiers.

Notwithstanding the expansionist ambitions of some of his advisers, Augustus had decided to pursue a more conservative policy with regard to Parthia. He was mindful of the fact that the Parthians had demonstrated repeatedly that they could be especially formidable when it came to mobilizing their resources for defense. In other words, Augustus recognized the practical utility of drawing a mutually acceptable frontier between Rome and Parthia at the Euphrates, something that Pompeius had refused to do. As George Rawlinson put it, "Augustus left it as a principle of policy to his successors that the Roman territory had reached its proper limits, and could not with any advantage be extended further. This principle, followed with the utmost strictness by Tiberius, was accepted as a rule by all the earlier Caesars, and only regarded by them as admitting of rare and slight exceptions."[2]

Augustus thus became committed to a Parthian policy that was intended to stabilize the Euphrates frontier. However, his ability to pursue this foreign policy was in large measure dependent on the strength of the Roman position in Syria. As a result, the province of Syria, which now incorporated strategically important Cilicia, was henceforth accorded the status of being considered the most important province in the empire. The four legions that were normally stationed in northern Syria could readily be deployed eastward to the Euphrates or northward to Armenia or Anatolia. To the south, the vital land bridge of Palestine that linked Egypt (which was made a Roman province after 30) to Syria was entrusted to local client-rulers, such as Herod the Great (37–4), who generally proved to be reliable allies of Rome.

When Herod died, his enlarged kingdom was divided among his three sons. Philip ruled the districts of the northeast such as Batanea and Gaulonitis for the next thirty-seven years; Herod Antipas ruled in Galilee and Peraea until 39; while Judaea and Idumea were assigned to Archelaus. The latter was so incompetent that the people petitioned Rome to abolish the monarchy. Rome agreed, and in the year 6 Archelaus was banished. Judaea was transformed into a Roman province, but out of consideration for the sensibilities of the people who attached special religious significance to the city that housed the Temple, the imperial procurator that governed it was headquartered at Caesarea rather than in Jerusalem.

After the death of Cleopatra of Egypt, following the defeat of Antonius, Augustus annexed the country and made it the central granary of the Roman Empire. The defense of Egypt was made relatively easy by its geographical situation. Protected by the sea to the north and the desert on both sides of the Nile Valley, it was only vulnerable along the Nile itself from Ethiopia to the south. The first Roman prefect of Egypt, Cornelius Gallus, therefore moved the southern frontier of Egypt to the First Cataract and reached agreement with the Ethiopians to leave the area between it and the Second Cataract as a neutral buffer zone, an agreement that was generally observed by both sides.

The only significant deviation from Augustus' general policy of nonaggression in the east was made with regard to Arabia, which had a special commercial role in the ancient world. Herodotus, for example, noted that "Arabia is the last of the inhabited lands towards the south, and it is the only country which produces frankincense, myrrh, cassia, cinnamon, and laudanum . . . which is afterwards carried from Arabia into other countries. . . . Concerning the spices of Arabia let no more be said. The whole country is scented with them, and exhales an odour marvelously sweet."[3] In fact, in the time of Augustus, Arabia was the principal source of myrrh and frankincense, both highly valued in Roman life and ritual. In addition, from its center at Arabia Eudaemon (Aden), the kingdom of the Himyarites (successors of the Sabaeans as the dominant state of the peninsula after 115 B.C.E.) in South Arabia was also in effective control of the spice route between Southeast Asia, India, and Europe. From Aden goods were transshipped up the Red Sea to Egypt or the African coast, or to Leuke Kome on the Arabian coast from where they would be carried along the caravan routes to Egypt, Syria, and the Mediterranean littoral.

The primary motivation for Augustus' aggressive policy in Arabia was therefore economic. As one recent writer has observed:

Augustus expressed repeated concern about the Empire's balance of payments; rich Romans had begun to consume vast amounts of exotics—silk from China, spices from the Indies, incense from Arabia—all of which had to be paid for in coin, usually gold, since the mysterious foreign producers of these goods would accept nothing else. Though the Roman Empire had access to large supplies of gold (in Spain particularly) these could not be expected to last for ever [sic]. Something had to be done, and Augustus set about doing it in the directest possible way. In the matter of silk he was powerless: practically nothing was known about this substance except that it came from the "Silk-land" far to the east, and nobody knew how big this land was or precisely how to get there. A campaign against the "Silk-land," moreover, was almost certain to involve war with the Parthians in Iran, which Augustus was anxious to avoid. The trade in spices and incense, however, offered greater scope for direct action. Both were reputed to come from Arabia, which was not very far from Egypt. . . . It seemed worthwhile to send out a small expedition that might make an extremely valuable conquest.[4]

Accordingly, Augustus sent Aelius Gallus and an expedition of some 10,000 men against the Himyarites in 26 B.C.E. While it would have been possible to mount a completely seaborne attack, Gallus elected to sail down the Red Sea only as far as Leuke Kome, and from there to march to South Arabia through the desert. The expedition seemed destined for disaster from the start. A number of the ships were wrecked en route, and the army landed in a state of exhaustion and was plagued with disease. It was led into the desert by Arab guides who made their living from the caravan trade and who therefore had little interest in the successful outcome of the Roman expedition, which would surely result in the diversion of much of the spice and incense trade to maritime carriage. Not surprisingly, the Roman force wandered around the desert somewhat aimlessly without ever getting to its assigned destination. After about a year and a half, Gallus gave up and finally led his force back to Egypt. Nonetheless, the Himyarites were sufficiently impressed with the military capabilities of Rome to have surrendered their monopolistic control of the spice trade route as well as passage through the Bab al-Mandeb Straits, a factor that precipitated their rapid economic decline.

NOTES

1. Suetonius, *The Lives of the Twelve Caesars*, p. 21.
2. George Rawlinson, *The Story of Parthia*, pp. 221–222.
3. Herodotus, *The Persian Wars*, III.106–113.
4. Nigel H.H. Sitwell, *The World the Romans Knew*, pp. 87–88.

12

The Struggle over the Euphrates Frontier

The history of the Middle East during the century following Augustus' establishment of the Principate in Rome was dominated by the focus of both Rome and Parthia on control of the buffer states along the frontier separating the two empires. Of particular strategic importance in this regard was Armenia, which provided an alternate northern route across or around the Euphrates between Parthia and Syria or Asia Minor. Accordingly, both empires sought to include Armenia within their spheres of interest.

Armenia, with Parthian support, had been under the unchallenged rule of Artaxias II (34–20) since the withdrawal of the Roman legions under Antonius from the country. A decade later, however, a group of Armenian nobles sought to replace Artaxias on the throne with his younger brother Tigranes, who had been held prisoner by the Romans since 34 when he was sent to Egypt by Antonius along with his father Artavasdes. This development provided Augustus with the opportunity to replace Parthian influence in Armenia with Roman, and he dispatched his stepson Tiberius to place Tigranes on the Armenian throne in response to the request to intervene in the crisis. Although Artaxias was killed before the Roman force arrived, Tigranes II received his crown from Tiberius, who also placed a Roman client-prince, Ariobarzanes, on the throne of Media Atropatene (Azerbaijan). For the next decade and a half, Roman influence was dominant in the region of the upper Euphrates and the gateways into Parthia.

The situation along the Roman-Parthian frontier became destabilized once again with the death of Tigranes about 6 B.C.E., as both powers sought to intervene in their interests in the question of the Armenian succession. Notwithstanding the attempt of Augustus to influence matters by dispatching his adopted son Gaius Caesar with a Roman force to Armenia in

1 B.C.E. to assure the succession of a Roman-sponsored candidate, the succession crisis continued to fester.

Gaius Caesar and the Parthian king Phraataces (2 B.C.E.-4 C.E.) finally worked out a rough compromise in the year 1 C.E. under the threat of an impending war between the two powers at a time when Parthia itself was undergoing a succession crisis. According to the agreement, Parthia undertook to withdraw its forces from Armenia and to recognize a de facto Roman protectorate over the country. Nonetheless, international intrigue over control and influence in Armenia continued unabated for the next several decades. Although Rome nominated the kings of Armenia, they were occasionally ousted and replaced by others considered more acceptable to Parthia. A major crisis developed when Rome placed Vonones, a son of Phraates IV—who had held the throne of Parthia for a short time with Roman support until displaced by Artabanus III (12–38)—on the throne of Armenia. This was clearly unacceptable to Artabanus, and the Romans ultimately backed down, replacing Vonones with another more acceptable candidate, Zeno. Germanicus Caesar, the legate of Syria, and Artabanus subsequently renewed the Roman-Parthian agreement in the year 18.

Another crisis in Roman-Parthian relations developed over Armenia in 35 after Artabanus placed his son Arsaces on the vacant Armenian throne. The emperor Tiberius took umbrage at this affront to Rome's authority in the country and decided to attempt to secure the overthrow of Artabanus by lending his support to a rival claimant to the Parthian throne. The rather complex plot that was devised was to be carried out by Vitellius, who had been appointed governor of Syria. To facilitate matters, Vitellius first planned to set up a rival king to Arsaces in Armenia. For this purpose, he bribed Pharasamanes, the king of Iberia in the Caucasus, to place his brother Mithradates on the Armenian throne. Arsaces was subsequently murdered and Pharasamanes took the capital without a struggle. This triggered a war with Artabanus in 36. At this point, the Iberians permitted the horde of the Alans, which had been encroaching on their frontier, to move through the Caucasus passes unopposed and to sweep down into Parthian territory. Before Artabanus could decisively engage the invading Alans, Vitellius took to the field with his legions, ostensibly to invade Mesopotamia. This confronted Artabanus with the likelihood of having to fight a two-front war, something that he simply could not afford to risk. Accordingly, he was forced to withdraw from Armenia in order to defend Parthia itself. At the same time, Vitellius organized a campaign of subversion within Parthia that soon forced Artabanus to withdraw east of the Caspian to reorganize his forces. With Artabanus on the run, Vitellius encouraged Tiridates III, a grandson of Phraates IV, to seize the throne of Parthia. Tiridates' Roman-sponsored usurpation was welcomed and quickly recognized as legitimate by the Greek cities of Mesopotamia.

In the meantime, Artabanus, bolstered by contingents of Dahae and Sakae tribesmen, began to move westward with the aim of challenging Tiridates at Seleucia. Tiridates was not much of a soldier and he accepted the advice of some of his counselors who urged him to withdraw across the Tigris into Mesopotamia to await the arrival of Roman and Armenian reinforcements. However, the strategic retreat soon took on the aspects of a rout as Tiridates' forces began to disintegrate and desert. With Tiridates fleeing for his life, Artabanus quickly reassumed control of Parthia. Although the plot to eliminate Artabanus had failed, he was evidently quite shaken and chastened by the experience. It was not long before he reached an understanding with Vitellius that appears to have included a renunciation of Parthian claims to a sphere of influence in Armenia.

A new crisis between Rome and Parthia was triggered in 51, when the throne of Armenia was usurped by Rhadamistus, the son of Pharasmanes of Iberia, from his pro-Roman uncle Mithradates. Notwithstanding the blow this represented to Rome's position in Armenia, the Roman governor of Syria, Ummidius Quadratus, who was responsible for Armenian affairs, took no action other than to insist that Pharasmanes order his son to withdraw. This apparent loss of serious Roman interest in Armenia was seen by the new Parthian king Vologases I (51–80) as presenting an opportunity to oust Rhadamistus and install his own brother Tiridates as king of the country. Vologases intervened in Armenia in 51 for this purpose, but was soon distracted by a crisis in Adiabene that occupied him for the next couple of years. However, he returned to Armenia in 54 and easily overthrew Rhadamistus, who had failed to develop a base of support in the country, and placed Tiridates on the throne in his place. In Rome, this was perceived as an unacceptable violation of the Roman-Parthian arrangement with regard to Armenia, and the new emperor Nero (54–68) prepared for war.

Nonetheless, war did not break out immediately. The prospect of a major war between Rome and Parthia, given the record of indecisive outcomes that characterized their previous conflicts, was not something that could be taken lightly by either side. If it were possible to solve the crisis through diplomacy, that clearly was the preferred course, and an effort was made to resolve the problem peacefully. The negotiations dragged on for three years because Vologases had become distracted by an internal rebellion, led by his son Vardanes, and was anxious to avoid simultaneous hostilities against Rome. Vologases had been insisting not only that Tiridates should retain the throne of Armenia, but also that the country should henceforth be considered a vassal of Parthia rather than Rome. The Romans rejected this position, insisting that Rome could not possibly relinquish any territory it had acquired. Rome was prepared to continue to negotiate but matters soon came to a head as Tiridates commenced attacks on Armenian supporters of Roman suzerainty. This provided the immediate *casus belli* as Roman troops crossed the frontier in 57 to come to their aid.

The Roman intervention in Armenia, led by Domitius Corbulo, coming at a time when Vologases was preoccupied by a major insurrection in Hyrcania, gave the Romans an advantage that they would not otherwise have enjoyed. Under the circumstances, it was not long before Tiridates gave up all hope of prevailing against the Romans without Vologases' full involvement on his side, and fled for safety to Parthia. Corbulo then placed Tigranes, a descendant of Herod the Great and Archelaus, the former king of Cappadocia, on the throne of Armenia and withdrew back to Syria.

Rome's interest in the region went beyond the matter of imperial glory for its own sake. At issue were significant economic interests as well. In the middle of the first century, the Kushans, a group belonging to the confederation of the Yueh-chi or Tokhari, under their king Kujula Kadphises, came south out of Central Asia and occupied Bactria, apparently seized Merv from the Parthians, and established the Kushan frontier at Hyrcania. Thus, when Hyrcania, with the Kushans on its northern and eastern flanks, attempted to break away from Parthia and assert its independence in 58, this provided Rome with the opportunity, by means of an alliance with Hyrcania, to establish an important trade route to China and India. Goods from the east were now able to pass down the Oxus, cross the Caspian Sea, and connect with the Black Sea through the Cyrus River, without the need to cross Parthian territory at any point.

Wima Kadphises, the heir to the Kushan throne, also took full advantage of Parthia's preoccupation with Rome to capture Herat, Sistan, and Arachosia, as well as the region of the mouth of the Indus, thereby sandwiching Parthia between powerful enemies on its eastern and western flanks. Although the Kushans actually showed little interest in further territorial expansion at Parthia's expense—the enormous wealth of India was of much greater interest to them than the arid deserts of eastern Parthia—they were in a position to severely damage Parthia's economic position. Like the Parthians, the Kushans derived much of their income from serving as middlemen and conduits for international trade. By the beginning of the second century, the Kushans were in effective control of the three main routes connecting with the "Silk Road" through Central Asia to China. By their position in the north they dominated the Black Sea-Caspian Sea route, as well as the road that passed through Merv, Hecatompylus, and Ecbatana, across the Euphrates and on to the Mediterranean, the only route that passed through Parthian territory. The third primary trade route was the maritime route between India and the Red Sea. Goods passed from China through Chinese Turkestan, across the Pamirs and the Hindu Kush until they reached the Indus near modern Peshawar, where they were transported downriver and then on ships to the Red Sea and Egypt. With the discovery of the monsoons, this maritime route became heavily used. This adversely affected the economic well-being of Parthia, which was increasingly being cut out of a significant share of its former revenues from international trade.

The situation changed significantly by 62, when Vologases finally succeeded in restoring his control of Hyrcania, obviating the significance of the links with the country established by Rome. Vologases was now once again in a position to give his full attention to the Armenian question, although it is not clear that he was prepared to go to war again in order to obtain a throne for his brother. At this time, however, the Roman puppet king of Armenia, Tigranes, began making attacks on nearby Adiabene, threatening to bring the dependency into the Roman sphere of interest, which would then extend as far east as the Tigris. This prospect provoked Vologases into action. Now that hostilities with Parthia in Armenia had resumed, Corbulo became concerned about a possible Parthian attack on Syria, and was reluctant to leave the country undefended. He therefore appealed to Nero to send a separate army to assist Armenia. Such a force was dispatched under Caesennius Paetus in 62, but was soon defeated by the Parthians.

Vologases now placed Tiridates (63–100) back on the throne of Armenia, but also suggested a political compromise to resolve the seemingly endless conflict with Rome over the country. He proposed that both Rome and Parthia agree to reestablish the Euphrates as the frontier between them. While he continued to insist that Tiridates be acknowledged as king of Armenia, he proposed, as a means of satisfying the public requirements of Roman honor, that Tiridates should receive his crown from the hands of Nero in Rome. This suggestion was acceptable to Nero, who had little interest in attempting to extend Roman control any farther eastward. Nero subsequently formally invested Tiridates, with great pomp, as king of Armenia in Rome in 66. Following this, the relations between Rome and Parthia remained relatively stable and peaceful for another fifty years.

It was at this time that a major but essentially hopeless revolt against Rome broke out in Judaea, primarily because of the political incompetence of its Roman governors. Herod Agrippa II (50–71), the nominal king, tried to prevent it by pointing out, among other things, that the Roman-Parthian peace had radically changed the situation from that which existed in earlier times when the Parthians intervened in Palestine against the Romans. He argued that the Jews had no allies and could not even expect help from their co-religionists in the east. "Unless any of you extend his hopes as far as beyond the Euphrates, and suppose that those of your own nation that dwell in Adiabene will come to your assistance (but certainly these will not embarrass themselves with an unjustifiable war, nor if they should follow such ill advice, will the Parthians permit them so to do); for it is their concern to maintain the truce that is between them and the Romans, and they will be supposed to break the covenants between them, if any under their government march against the Romans."[1]

The future emperor Vespasian (70–79) was placed in charge of the expedition of three legions against Judaea. His strategy was to reduce the districts of the country one at a time before attempting a final assault on Jerusalem. In 67 he took Galilee, and the following year Samaria and Idumea. Vespasian then returned to Rome, soon to become emperor in the wake of the death of Nero and the end of the Claudian line. He left the final assault on Jerusalem to his son and future emperor Titus (79–81). Jerusalem was finally taken after fierce resistance in 70, bringing an end to the Jewish state. Judaea was henceforth a Roman province governed by a senatorial legate at Jerusalem.

The peace between Rome and Parthia was plagued with problems that repeatedly placed it in jeopardy. In 72, Caesennius Paetus, who had earlier been defeated by the Parthians in Armenia, reported to Vespasian that he had uncovered a plot between Vologases and Antiochus, the king of the Roman dependency of Commagene, to transfer the allegiance of the latter country from Rome to Parthia. However, when Paetus subsequently marched into Commagene to assert Rome's supremacy there, Vologases made no move to render assistance to Antiochus. Then, in 75, Parthia came under severe attack from the Alans, who burst through the Caucasian passes once again and in alliance with Hyrcania invaded Media Atropatene and then Armenia. Vologases appealed to Vespasian for help, but he declined to get involved beyond helping Mithradates of Iberia to fortify his capital at Metskheta. Vologases became very bitter toward Rome whose failure to render assistance at a critical moment apparently cost Parthia continued control of Hyrcania. With the succession of Pacorus II (78–108) to the throne of Parthia, the coolness of Roman-Parthian relations progressively deteriorated to barely concealed hostility, which under the aggressive Roman emperor Trajan (98–117) was bound to result in open conflict once again.

Upon the death of Tiridates, king of Armenia, in 100, Pacorus took advantage of Trajan's preoccupation with the Dacian War on Rome's Danubian frontier in Europe and placed his own son Exedares on the Armenian throne. This was a clear violation of the Roman-Parthian agreement that had been negotiated between Vologases and Nero, but Pacorus appears to have assumed that Rome would not pay too much attention to this breach since it was concerned with more serious matters at the time. However, with the end of the Dacian War in 113, Trajan decided that the moment was ripe to resolve the "eastern question" once and for all time by the decisive defeat of Parthia and the annexation of Armenia. It seems quite evident that Trajan harbored dreams of being another Alexander the Great and conquering the world. His justification for a move against Parthia was the vindication of Roman honor with regard to Armenia. He claimed that both Pacorus and his successor, Osroes (109–128), had insulted Rome by treating Armenia as though it were a Parthian province without due respect for Roman interests there. On the contrary, he insisted it was Rome alone that had ultimate authority there. Osroes attempted to placate him by suggesting that they return to the old agreement and that Trajan crown Parthamasiris, the younger brother and successor of Exedares, as king of Armenia.

It appears that Osroes was convinced that Trajan had agreed to his proposal. Trajan had proceeded to the Armenian frontier with an army and awaited Parthamasiris, who was encouraged to present himself to Trajan as a supplicant asking for a crown. He laid his crown at Trajan's feet, expecting the emperor to then place it on his head once again. This, Trajan would not do. He blithely informed the young prince that he had just forfeited the crown of Armenia. Justifiably outraged, Parthamasiris reportedly told Trajan that "he had neither been defeated nor made prisoner by the Romans, but had come of his own free will to hold a conference with the chief of the Roman State, in full assurance that he would suffer no wrong at his hands, but would be invested by him with the Armenian sovereignty, just as Tiridates had been invested by Nero. He demanded to be set at liberty, together with his retinue."[2] Trajan responded by informing him that he had no intention of giving sovereignty over Armenia to anyone. Armenia belonged to Rome and would be ruled by a Roman governor. Parthamasiris then attempted to leave but Trajan had him killed. Greater and Lesser Armenia were subsequently united and placed under direct rule as a Roman province.

Now that he had disposed of the Armenian question, Trajan directed his attention to Parthia. The time was deemed propitious for a Roman move because Osroes was fully preoccupied with internal struggles and would be hard put to organize an effective defense of his territories, and even less likely to mount a counterattack. However, the takeover of Armenia, by pushing the frontier in the north from the Euphrates to the Tigris, made it necessary for Rome to conquer Mesopotamia as well, since otherwise the Armenian salient could be cut off by the Parthians from the south. Trajan therefore marched south, captured Nisibis, and accepted the submission of Abgar VII of Osrhoene, who was awaiting the outcome of events farther north. He then conquered the northern plain of Mesopotamia in 115 and annexed it to Rome as well. The following year Trajan crossed the Tigris and completed the conquest of Adiabene, which straddled the river, transforming it into the Roman province of Assyria. From there he moved on to the Parthian capital, Ctesiphon, which fell after only nominal resistance. Next he followed the course of the Tigris southward until he reached the Persian Gulf. Trajan had, in a short period of time established Roman domination over the trade routes of Mesopotamia and Babylonia, and through the occupation of Armenia he had placed the Roman forces in a position to control the flank of any future Parthian attack against Syria. This advantageous position, however, was not to be maintained for long. Osroes kept falling back, trading space for time, nursing his resources while Trajan's forces were stretching thin their lines of communication to their operational and supply bases.

By 116, Osroes had sufficiently recovered from dealing with his internal problems to begin to contest the Roman invasion. He was aided in this by a series of insurgencies against Roman rule that had broken out at the time in the eastern Mediterranean region. A series of missteps and broken promises led the Jewish communities of Cyrenaica, Egypt, and Cyprus to rise in open revolt. Similar outbreaks soon took place in Palestine, Syria, and northern Mesopotamia as well. Simultaneously, Parthian forces began attacking key Roman positions as the anti-Roman rebellions began spreading throughout the newly conquered territories, behind the Roman lines. The Roman garrisons at Seleucia, Nisibis, and Edessa had been attacked and evicted by the local populaces. Moreover, Trajan's line of retreat was interdicted in several places, raising the distinct possibility that the Roman army might be cut off and trapped beyond the Euphrates. Assyria was soon lost and serious trouble began brewing in Babylonia. Trajan responded by trying to regain control of the key centers at all costs. This effort was only partially successful and Trajan decided that it was time to withdraw from Mesopotamia and proceed to Syria, where he set up his headquarters at Antioch after having sustained very heavy losses in the course of the retreat. Then, in 117, before he could reorganize the effort to consolidate Roman control over the Parthian provinces, Trajan died.

Hadrian (117–138), who succeeded him, promptly reversed Trajan's policy, which he considered overly adventurous and a potential long-term liability for the empire. He decided that it was in Rome's best interests to reestablish the Euphrates as the limit of its direct control. In effect, Hadrian sought a return to the *status quo ante*, and willingly surrendered the territories of Armenia, Mesopotamia, and Adiabene, that were conquered by Trajan, back to their previous rulers and client-kings. Once again, at least for another half century, Rome was to avoid active intervention east of the Euphrates.

At the same time, however, it became more important than ever to assure absolute Roman control of its provinces west of the Euphrates. Particularly troubling in this regard was Palestine. Hadrian had reason to be concerned about the fact that there was an understandably strong pro-Parthian sentiment among the Jews of Palestine. After all, it was the Romans who had destroyed the Jewish state and the Temple in Jerusalem, the center of its religious cult. Were there to be a successful revolt in Palestine, it would effectively split the Roman flank, separating Syria from Egypt, and provide a wedge that the Parthians might attempt to exploit to Rome's strategic disadvantage. Thus, when a revolt under Simon Bar-Kokhba broke out in Palestine early in 132, Hadrian moved to suppress it with all the power at his immediate disposal. Bar-Kokhba, however, who was a competent general in his own right, was able to transform the struggle from a popular rebellion into a full-scale war that lasted until mid-135 and cost Rome an entire legion in its early phase. When the revolt was finally suppressed, Hadrian took steps to wipe out every vestige of nationalist sentiment in the country.

At this same time, relations between Rome and Parthia experienced a downturn once again. Pharasmanes, king of the Roman protectorate of Iberia, allied himself with the Alans and launched an invasion of Armenia, Cappadocia (a Roman province), and Media Atropatene in 133, ravaging these lands. Media Atropatene, however, was a dependency of Parthia, and Vologases II (105–147) complained to Hadrian about the damage that was being done to Parthian interests by a state that was supposed to be under Roman control. But, with a full-scale war going on in Palestine, Hadrian was disinclined to commit any forces for the purpose of helping Parthia. As far as he was concerned, Roman Cappadocia's governor, Arrian, could adequately defend the province, and Vologases would have to deal with the problem in Parthian territory by himself as best he could. The immediate crisis was resolved when Vologases bought off the Alans, causing them to withdraw. Nonetheless, he was again justifiably peeved when he learned, after the Alanic War had come to an end, that Hadrian had called Pharasmanes to Rome where he was treated with honor and loaded with gifts. Presumably, the Alanic War served Rome's purpose by ensuring the improbability of any Parthian intervention in support of the Jewish revolt in Palestine, if indeed such were even being considered by Vologases at the time.

The latter's successor, Vologases III (148–192), was unwilling to accept the continued exclusion of Parthia from maintaining a sphere of influence in strategically important Armenia, and he was intent on reasserting Parthian claims there. Nonetheless, he was dissuaded from taking any immediate action in this regard by Antoninus Pius (138–161) who pursued a peace policy toward Parthia. For as long as Antoninus sat on the throne in Rome, the peace held. However, as soon as Marcus Aurelius (161–180) succeeded him, war erupted between Rome and Parthia once again.

Vologases attacked Armenia in 161, wiping out a Roman legion in the process, and then captured Edessa in 163, placing a Parthian vassal, Wa'el, on its throne. From there he invaded Syria. Lucius Verus (161–169), who shared the throne with Marcus Aurelius, led the Roman forces in response to the Parthian challenge. The Parthians were soon driven out of Syria once again, and in 163 Verus' troops marched into Armenia and reinstalled the Roman protégé, Sohaemus, on the throne. The following year, a column under Avidius Cassius moved down the Euphrates and captured Dura Europos, which now marked Rome's southern frontier in Mesopotamia. The Roman advance, however, was stopped by the outbreak of an epidemic that forced it to withdraw temporarily, while Sohaemus was expelled from Armenia once again by the Parthians. In the course of a new Roman offensive across the northern Mesopotamian plain in 165, Edessa was retaken and the former ruler of Osrhoene, Ma'nu VIII (139–163 and 165–177), was reseated on its throne. It appeared that the forward Roman position in Mesopotamia originally set by Trajan had been reestablished. The net result of Aurelius' activist policy was that Rome's eastern frontier remained relatively peaceful for another three decades.

The death of Marcus Aurelius in 180 set in motion a series of internal upheavals in Rome that were to have significant repercussions in the east. As events unfolded, it was shortly after the succession of Vologases IV (191–208) to the throne of Parthia that the Roman emperor Commodus (180–192) was assassinated. He was succeeded by Pertinax, who ruled Rome for only a brief period before he too was murdered in 193. In turn, Pertinax was followed by Didius Julianus who literally bought the office that same year, triggering revolts in Britain, Pannonia, and Syria, with the Roman legions in each of these countries proclaiming their respective leaders, Clodius Albinus, Septimus Severus, and Pescennius Niger, as emperor of the Romans. Septimus Severus (193–211), who was subsequently acknowledged as emperor in Rome, headed for Syria to contest the claim of Pescennius Niger, who as governor of Syria, held the second most prestigious position in the empire. Pescennius Niger appealed to Armenia and Parthia for help in the coming struggle for the throne, but was turned down by the first, whose king, Vologases (Valarsh), declared his neutrality. The Parthian king, Vologases IV, on the other hand, offered his support, but only when he would be able to mobilize a special army for the purpose. He wanted to retain Pescennius Niger's goodwill in the event that the latter succeeded in taking the throne, but was not really ready to do battle for him. However, Vologases had no objection to the participation of any of his vassals in the conflict on the side of Pescennius.

Reflecting this understanding with Vologases, Pescennius Niger was able to confront Septimus Severus in 193 with the support of troops furnished by the rulers of Osrhoene, Adiabene, and Hatra. These Parthian vassal states sought to exploit their alliance with Pescennius Niger to take advantage of the insurrections against Roman rule that were taking place in Mesopotamia and elsewhere in the region to serve their own political interests. For example, Abgar VIII (177–212) of Osrhoene laid siege to the Roman garrison at Nisibis, but later claimed to Septimus Severus that he did so because the city was supporting Pescennius Niger. As a practical matter, however, the support of these Parthian vassals was insufficient to tip the balance in his favor and Pescennius Niger was defeated and eventually killed near Issus as his army met destruction there in a decisive battle.

Once having disposed of the challenge to his rule from Pescennius Niger, Septimus devoted his attention to restoring order on the eastern frontier. He set out from Syria in 195 and promptly received the submission of Abgar of Osrhoene, giving Rome control of the southern approaches to Armenia once again. From there, Septimus moved against the northern Mesopotamian plain, subjugating Adiabene as well as some other Parthian vassal states. In 196, however, Septimus was forced to call off his eastern campaign in order to be in a position to meet the challenge to his rule that was raised by Clodius Albinus in Gaul. Vologases IV took advantage of Septimus' withdrawal to invade Mesopotamia, where he seized the imperial headquarters at Nisibis and once more asserted Parthian supremacy in Armenia. The following year Septimus returned with three fresh legions, received the voluntary subjugation of Armenia and Osrhoene, and drove the Parthians out of Mesopotamia. He then marched down the Euphrates and sacked Ctesiphon, as Vologases withdrew farther eastward into Persia beyond Rome's reach. Septimus now found himself in the same position that Trajan had been in eighty years earlier. His sway reached from the Mediterranean to the Zagros, and from the Armenian highlands to the Persian Gulf. However, he recognized that he simply did not have the resources to control the southern sections of the former Parthian Empire, and therefore resolved to evacuate them. Indeed, he was virtually out of supplies and had little choice but to withdraw from these distant points before the effectiveness of the army was placed in jeopardy. On his return march he tried twice to conquer Hatra but failed after a prolonged siege, nearly causing a mutiny among his troops. Luckily for Septimus, Vologases failed to take advantage of the situation and what could have proven to be a major military disaster was averted.

Septimus' successor Caracalla (211–217), another self-styled Alexander, also sought to extend the imperial frontiers in Asia. In 212 he began his march eastward. Osrhoene was reduced to a Roman colony in 214, thereby moving the frontier with Parthia well beyond the Euphrates. Then, when the king of Armenia presented himself before Caracalla at the latter's invitation, he and his family were arrested. This politically obtuse act precipitated a revolt in Armenia that quickly got out of hand and resulted in the defeat of the Roman army that was sent there in 215 to suppress it. Nonetheless, Parthia appeared to be more vulnerable to defeat than ever before, as it became seriously weakened by an internal power struggle that effectively split the country, with different kings ruling the north and the south. Caracalla was determined to exploit this perceived weakness.

Caracalla crossed the Tigris in 216 and marched into Adiabene with the intention of continuing on to the Parthian capital at Ctesiphon, but was assassinated at the instigation of his successor Macrinus (217–218) before he could reach the city. At the same time, Artabanus V (213–224), who ruled northern Parthia, outflanked the Roman army and attacked its rear in northern Mesopotamia. The Roman and Parthian armies met in a final major but inconclusive battle at Nisibis in 217. Notwithstanding the Roman claims of victory, the actual peace settlement that was reached required Rome to pay a substantial indemnity to Parthia. However, the Romans were able to retain their hold on northern Mesopotamia, placing them in position to renew the war almost at will. Indeed, although the Romans evidently did not realize it at the time, this last war left Parthia exhausted. Without a substantial period of rest within which it would be allowed to recuperate, it was extremely vulnerable.

NOTES

1. Flavius Josephus, *Wars of the Jews*, II.xvi.4.
2. Quoted by Rawlinson, *The Story of Parthia*, p. 304.

13

The Roman–Persian Stalemate

The incessant wars with Rome, as well as the recurring internal divisions and succession crises coupled with the economic stranglehold being applied by the Kushans to the east, had critically weakened the cohesion of the already loosely constructed Parthian state. In about 220, a revolt against Parthian rule broke out in Persis, in southern Iran, under the leadership of the Sassanid family, the hereditary Zoroastrian priests of Istakhr (Persepolis). Under Artaxerxes or Ardashir (222–240), Sassanid control was quickly extended eastward to Kerman. Buoyed by his initial success, and the lack of a serious Parthian response, Ardashir next turned to the west. Vologases V (207–223), who ruled the Parthian south including Babylonia, appears to have disappeared from the scene after 223, presumably an early victim of Sassanid expansion. Next on the Sassanid agenda was Media, the very heart of the empire. Artabanus belatedly grasped the danger he faced in the Persian uprising and fought desperately but unsuccessfully to stop Ardashir; he was overthrown in 227. Thus, in about five decisive years, the Parthian state was brought to an end after almost five centuries of existence.

The ascendancy of the Sassanids under Ardashir was challenged by a coalition of forces supported by Rome, which had no interest in seeing a powerful Persian dynasty replace the Parthians with whom it had such long experience. The coalition was nominally led by Chosroes I (217–252) of Armenia, himself an Arsacid who had been placed on the throne by the defeated Parthian king Artabanus. Chosroes had attempted to intervene in the conflict with the Persians on behalf of his Parthian overlord, but arrived too late to be of any help. He now assumed the role of patron of the Arsacids and undertook to lead the struggle against the Persian usurper, organizing a coalition of outside forces for the purpose. As described by the Armenian historian Agathangelos:

At the start of the next year [following the defeat of Artabanus] Khosrov king of Armenia began to raise forces and assemble an army. He gathered the armies of the Albanians and the Georgians, opened the gates of the Alans [the Darialan, the pass through the Caucasus on the Aragvi River] and the stronghold of the Chor [the Derbent pass]; he brought through the army of the Huns [Kushans] in order to attack Persian territory and invade Asorestan [Mesopotamia] as far as the gates of Ctesiphon. He ravaged the whole country, ruining the populous cities and prosperous towns. He left all the inhabited land devastated and plundered. He attempted to eradicate, destroy completely, extirpate, and overthrow the Persian kingdom and aimed at abolishing its civilization.[1]

Ardashir smashed the coalition in a series of battles, as well as by bribing some of its members to abandon what seemed to be a hopeless cause. In 228, after two years of struggle, the Romans, Kushans, and Scythians withdrew their forces, leaving Armenia to continue the conflict by itself. Although Ardashir, in alliance with the ruler of Kirkuk and Shahrat, the king of Adiabene, was now free to attack Armenia in force, he was unable to achieve a decisive victory, in part because Rome was unwilling to see strategically important Armenia fall into his hands. With continued Roman support, Chosroes managed to maintain the independence of his country.

In 230, in an apparent retaliation for Roman involvement in the Armenian-led coalition against him, Ardashir invaded the Roman province of Mesopotamia, which offered only token resistance and was quickly overrun. He was now in a position to threaten an attack on Syria. Instead of moving aggressively to thwart the Persian challenge, Severus Alexander (222–235) attempted to resolve the crisis through diplomacy. According to Herodian, he dispatched ambassadors to Ardashir with a rather arrogant and patronizing message. It suggested that the Persian ruler "must remain in his own territory without stirring up trouble; he must not incite a war because he was carried away by foolish optimism; everyone should be content with their lot; for he would not find a war against the Romans the same proposition as one against neighbours and barbarians like himself."[2]

While his forces were consolidating their grip on Mesopotamia, Ardashir responded to Severus Alexander by dispatching an embassy of his own that included 400 handsomely dressed youths who were intended to demonstrate the great wealth and power of the new Persian dynasty. The message they bore was an ultimatum that "by order of the great king the Romans and their ruler must abandon Syria and the whole of Asia opposite Europe, allowing Persian rule to extend as far as Ionia and Caria and the peoples contained within the Aegean-Pontus seaboard. For these were the traditional possessions of Persians."[3] Severus Alexander was so infuriated by this response that he made the envoys prisoners of war, sending them to live in Phrygia as agricultural workers. It was now clear that Ardashir harbored the ambition to be another Cyrus the Great, and that he could only be stopped by force.

Severus Alexander left Rome for the east and began mobilizing an army from the various provinces he passed through en route, arriving in Antioch in the fall of 231 with a substantial force that was augmented by the legions already positioned in Syria and Egypt. The Romans struck in the spring of 232 with a three-pronged attack. One column marched north toward friendly Armenia, from which it was to swerve southward and attack Media. A second column moved south down the Euphrates Valley toward Babylon, from where it was to swing eastward for an attack on central Persia. The main body, under the personal command of the emperor, was to advance across the northern Mesopotamian plain for a direct assault into the heart of the enemy's territory.

For reasons that remain unclear, the column under the command of the emperor failed to advance in a timely fashion and therefore allowed the Persians to concentrate their forces on the other two. It appears that the northern column met with considerable tactical success and was able to lay waste a good part of Media. The southern column, however, found itself facing the main body of the Persian army under Ardashir's personal command. The Roman forces were quickly overwhelmed and annihilated. The news of the defeat so demoralized the emperor that he ordered a general retreat, his army suffering heavy attrition on the return march because of disease, bad weather, and continual harassment by the Persians.

Ardashir, however, did not attempt to press his advantage and follow Severus Alexander into Syria. Although the recent contest had turned into a debacle for Rome, Ardashir was surely impressed by the fact that the Romans were able to attack on three fronts simultaneously and to wreak havoc in Media. He recognized that forcing the Romans out of Asia was probably a rather naive objective and that he would have to settle for more realistic goals. One of these had to be a satisfactory resolution of the Armenian problem. Rome's successes in Media were a direct consequence of its ability to move its forces through a friendly Armenia. As long as Armenia was not brought under Sassanid control, Persia would be vulnerable to attack from the north.

Since Chosroes had allied himself with the Romans, the withdrawal of the latter now left Armenia alone once again to face the Persians. As before, however, the outcome of the ensuing military confrontation was indecisive. The Persian army consisted primarily of cavalry, which simply could not be employed effectively in the mountainous terrain of Armenia. Unable to resolve the problem by force of arms alone, Ardashir resorted to more unorthodox means and contrived to have Chosroes assassinated. Since Chosroes had no heir who could undertake the responsibility for a coordinated defense of the country, it fell to the provincial satraps who had difficulty in working together. The Persians were therefore easily able to defeat them. Armenia was now absorbed into the new Sassanid Empire, and with the western frontier with Rome effectively reestablished at the Euphrates, Ardashir was able to devote most of the rest of his reign to the consolidation of Persian power over the empire.

One of the more historically significant steps that Ardashir took was to establish Zoroastrianism as the state religion, not only of Persia but of the entire Sassanid Empire as well. He recognized the value of an official religion as a force for national cohesion and state power, and undertook to eliminate or suppress all competing religious movements. This introduced an ideological component in international relations that had been absent from the region since the aggressive Hellenism of the Seleucid king Antiochus IV, which had precipitated a successful war of liberation in Palestine almost 400 years earlier. The addition of religion as a factor in the regional geopolitical equation would soon prove to be a particularly destabilizing factor, making prudent political accommodations difficult, setting a pattern of parochial state behavior that would characterize international relations in the Middle East throughout most of its subsequent history.

Ardashir saw it as his mission to subordinate the wide diversity of religious beliefs and practices prevailing in western Asia to a common political purpose, and he became determined to impose absolute uniformity of religion as a means of welding the empire together. He is reported to have left a testament to his heir that articulated his views in this regard in unmistakable terms. "Never forget that, as a king, you are at once the protector of religion and of your country. Consider the altar and the throne as inseparable; they must always sustain each other. A sovereign without religion is a tyrant; and a people who have none may be deemed the most monstrous of all societies. Religion may exist without a state; but a state cannot exist without religion; and it is by holy laws that a political association can alone be bound."[4] This was the essence of Ardashir's political legacy to the Sassanids.

The immediate focus of Ardashir's son and successor, Shapur I (241–272), was on his eastern frontiers where the growing power of the Kushans posed an unacceptable threat to the security and economic well-being of the empire. Of particular concern was the Kushan grip on the key transcontinental trade routes. In a major military campaign that he initiated shortly after his accession to the throne, Shapur invaded and occupied the Indus Valley, crossed the Hindu Kush to conquer Bactria, and reached as far as Tashkent and Samarkand. The ruling dynasty of the Kushans was deposed and replaced by a line of princes that were forced to acknowledge Persian suzerainty. Buoyed by these successes, he resolved to try his hand at expansion westward against the Romans; in effect, he sought to fulfill the ambitions reluctantly abandoned by his father.

The moment seemed especially ripe for a war against Rome. After the assassination of Severus Alexander in 235, Rome seemed to be in complete political disarray, with no less than six emperors mounting the throne within a period of three years. The last of these, Gordian III (238–244), was but fifteen years of age and presumably incapable of inspiring much confidence in his leadership among the Roman legions. Anxious to take advantage of the situation, Shapur sent his forces across the Middle Tigris into Mesopotamia in 241. Nisibis, Harran (Carrhae), and Edessa fell in relatively rapid succession. The Persian army then crossed the Euphrates into Syria and captured Antioch. In the meanwhile, Gordian had left Rome and marched overland to Thrace with an army nominally under his command but actually under the control of his father-in-law, Timesitheus, and crossed the Bosphorus into Asia.

The Roman counterattack from the north caught the Persians by surprise and smashed Shapur's forces. Antioch, Harran, and Nisibis were recovered, as the Persian army was defeated decisively near Ras al-Ain, giving Rome control of all northern Mesopotamia once again. Osrhoene was restored as a Roman client-kingdom and Abgar X was placed on its throne. As the Roman army moved into position to threaten Ctesiphon, Shapur was forced to abandon most of the territories he had conquered and to withdraw across the Tigris. However, before the Romans could march on the city, Timesitheus died of illness and Gordian was promptly murdered by Philip the Arab (244–249), who usurped the imperial throne. Philip urgently needed to return to Rome to assert his control there, and he was therefore quite anxious to bring a prompt end to the campaign by coming to terms with Shapur. The precise terms of the peace treaty that was agreed to in 244 are not known, but they apparently involved the Roman retention of Mesopotamia in exchange for the payment of a large sum to Persia as well as the abandonment of Roman claims to Armenia.

The peace with Rome lasted for some fifteen years, primarily because Shapur once again had his hands full on his northeast frontier where Bactria was struggling to free itself from the Sassanid yoke. In the meantime, Shapur carefully observed developments in Rome, which seemed to be in an unremitting state of decline. Since Philip seized the throne there had been another five emperors, four of whom met violent deaths between 249–254. Moreover, Rome was under assault by the Alemanni, Goths, and Franks, who placed the continued viability of the empire in question. Once again the time seemed ripe to challenge Rome in Asia and, in 258, Shapur launched a series of campaigns of conquest in the west. He invaded Mesopotamia, took Nisibis and Harran, and then succeeded in inflicting a major defeat on the Romans near Edessa in 260, capturing the emperor Valerian (253–260) along with thousands of Roman troops who were sent into exile in Persia. Shapur followed up with an invasion of Syria, where he captured Antioch, and then, recalling the earlier defeat he had suffered from a Ro-

man attack from Anatolia, he swung north and took Cilicia and Cappadocia, giving him control of the critical Taurus passes. With Roman
dominance in the region shattered, he stood poised to conquer all of Anatolia. However, Shapur made no move to do so and soon withdrew south of
the Taurus for practical reasons. He simply was not in a position to occupy
the relatively remote regions. Moreover, his principal aim had not been to
expand his empire westward, but rather to prevent the emergence of a
power on his western flank that might threaten his sphere of control.

The inherent character of the Sassanid Empire, like that of the Parthian
and Seleucid Empires that preceded it, prevented it from exercising the degree of control necessary to integrate conquered territories into a coherent
structure. The strength of the empire depended on the personality of the
king. If he were forceful, his writ would extend far and wide. If he were
weak, revolts could be expected everywhere. The army, which was for the
most part made up of temporary levies, was organized for periodic raiding
rather than for permanent mobilization. Accordingly, the army could not
be kept in the field for extended periods of time and still maintain its cohesion as a disciplined fighting force. This meant that the Romans were able to
reestablish their grip on a territory once the Persian forces withdrew. This
created a situation in which a balance of power emerged between Persia
and Rome that might swing one way or the other, depending on the circumstances prevailing at any particular point in time.

Odenathus, the ruler of semiautonomous Palmyra, originally a major
caravan stop on the overland trade route from northern Syria through Petra
to South Arabia that had developed into a thriving commercial center,
sought to take advantage of the stalemated Roman-Persian conflict to assert his independence from the Sassanids. In the process, he earned the
gratitude of the Romans by harassing the Persian forces as they withdrew
to the Euphrates with the loot of Syria, and in fact caused the Persians to
lose a good part of the booty they had accumulated.

At the same time, Gallienus (260–268), who mounted the throne after the
defeat of Valerian, made no effort to regain the lost Roman provinces in
Mesopotamia. He was fully preoccupied with the challenge to his rule by
the two leading Roman generals, Macrianus, who was largely responsible
for deliberately causing Valerian's defeat, and Callistus. The two commanders were conspiring to seize the imperial throne on behalf of one of
Macrianus' sons. Throughout this crisis, Odenathus remained loyal to Gallienus and was rewarded for his faithfulness by the latter in 262 with appointment as *dux orientis*, the equivalent of a vice-emperor for the East.

Gathering a large force of desert tribesmen, bolstered by the remnants of
the Roman army, Odenathus crossed the Euphrates into Mesopotamia in
263 and succeeded in re-conquering Harran and Nisibis from the Persians.
He laid siege to Ctesiphon, but was forced to abandon his attempt to take
the city when Persian reinforcements arrived. It thus developed that while

Mesopotamia was nominally restored to Rome, it actually became part of a new Palmyrene Empire under the rule of Odenathus. Rome was quite prepared to accept the new arrangements since it served its purpose to have a powerful but friendly buffer between it and the Persians.

Under Odenathus, Palmyra underwent a rapid expansion that soon brought Syria and Arabia within its compass. When Odenathus was assassinated about 267, his wife Zenobia succeeded him and continued his expansionist policy. She sent an army, possibly as large as 70,000 men, to occupy Egypt over the vigorous opposition of the Roman governor Probus, professing to act under the joint-rule arrangements established by Gallienus. Her son, Wahab-allath, or Athenodorus, ruled the newly acquired territory as king of Egypt. When the new Roman emperor, Aurelian (270–275), mounted the throne, Wahab-allath issued coins at Alexandria that depicted both himself and Aurelian. By the following year, however, he was issuing coins that bore only his own picture. This and other symbolic acts carried out in Palmyra in 271 made it clear that Zenobia was in effect declaring Palmyra's complete independence from Rome.

Aurelian determined that it was time to take action to protect Rome's interests and he began to prepare for war. He decided to try for a decisive solution to the problem by attacking Palmyra itself. In 272, he crossed Cappadocia, wiped out the Palmyrene garrisons there, and then invaded Syria through Cilicia. Persia sent some troops to Zenobia's aid, preferring to see Palmyra remain intact as a useful buffer state. Nonetheless, Aurelian decisively defeated the Palmyrenes as well as the Persian relief column at Emesa. Zenobia was captured and sent to Rome, and Roman control over Syria and Mesopotamia was restored once more. When a revolt subsequently broke out in Palmyra in August 272, which resulted in the massacre of the Roman garrison there, Aurelian had the city completely destroyed and its population annihilated.

Overt Persian support of Zenobia, even though it did not prove to be of any great significance in affecting the outcome of the conflict, nonetheless left a score to be settled. By 275, with the idle Roman legions getting restive, Aurelian decided it was an appropriate moment to clear the account with Persia. He suddenly declared war and began marching toward Asia. He passed through Illyria and Macedonia, amassing troops along his way to Thrace, and was almost within reach of the Bosphorus when he was assassinated in the spring of 275 near Byzantium. His death brought to an end the prospect of an immediate Roman-Persian War, and it was to take another seven years before hostilities between the antagonists were renewed. Once again, it was not as a consequence of a desire for peace that war was averted for the moment, but rather because of Rome's internal and Persia's external problems at the time.

The two emperors that followed Aurelian, Tacitus (275) and Probus (276–282), were simply not in a position to initiate hostilities against Persia, although Probus probably would have taken steps in this direction had he survived a bit longer. Instead, this was to become the project of his successor, Carus (282–283), who made the prosecution of such a war his highest priority. As a practical matter, it was an opportune moment for Rome. The Persians, under Bahram II (276–293), were especially vulnerable on their western frontiers at that time because their armies were already actively engaged in hostilities on the eastern flank of the empire. They simply were not capable of conducting large-scale campaigns on two fronts simultaneously, and were unable to disengage in the east quickly enough to meet the Roman challenge in the west.

Taking advantage of the situation, Carus crossed into Mesopotamia where he encountered little opposition and soon overran the country as far eastward as the Tigris, easily taking the major centers of Seleucia and Ctesiphon. He was poised to strike into the heartland of Persia when he suddenly and mysteriously died from unknown causes, perhaps disease, perhaps assassination. In either case, his death brought the campaign to an abrupt end. The troops had little desire to march farther east into regions where no Roman army had ever been before, and Carus' son and ostensible successor, Numerian, did not have the stature to compel their obedience. Once again, it appears that Persia was saved from impending disaster, as the issue of the succession to the imperial throne became the paramount Roman concern over the next two years.

Matters took a serious turn for the worse for the Sassanids with the accession of Diocletian (285–305) to the Roman throne. When Diocletian decided to resume the assault on the Persian Empire in 286, Bahram was preoccupied once more with the coincidental outbreak of a serious revolt in the eastern part of his realm. The king's brother, the viceroy of Sistan, had attempted to seize the throne in collusion with the ruler of the Kushans, who was apparently promised independence from Persian suzerainty if the plot succeeded. To compound Bahram's problems, Diocletian also decided to place Tiridates III (287–313), the refugee son of Chosroes the former king of Armenia, back on the throne as a Roman vassal. He was welcomed by the Armenians, who were quite disenchanted with Persian rule, and promptly initiated a war of liberation that drove the Persians out of Armenia within a year. Unable to prosecute a war on both fronts simultaneously, Bahram was forced to reach an accommodation with Rome that cost him northern Mesopotamia and Armenia, but which left him free to dispose of the internal challenge to his rule.

Rome's fortunes in the east continued to improve under Diocletian after Tiridates provoked a new war between Rome and Persia, in large measure because he persisted in raiding Persian territory. Although Diocletian did nothing to restrain the Armenian king, the political climate in Rome was such that he could not afford to tolerate a Persian attack on his vassal, something that might have been interpreted as a sign of weakness by his domestic enemies. Thus, when the Persian ruler Narsah (294–301) took punitive measures against Tiridates in 296, the latter abandoned Armenia to the Persians and sought Rome's protection. Diocletian declared war.

Initially, the conflict went poorly for Rome. Narsah invaded Mesopotamia and was threatening to cross the Euphrates into Syria. The Roman army under Diocletian's son-in-law Galerius was severely mauled by the superior Persian cavalry and Galerius himself barely escaped from the disaster with his life. Galerius mounted a new offensive in the spring of 297, but this time through Armenia where the Persian cavalry was effectively neutralized. Narsah unwisely accepted the Roman challenge on terrain where he was at a tactical disadvantage and was defeated decisively, the royal household being captured as he retreated. Under the circumstances, he had little choice but to quit Armenia and sue for peace. Diocletian, however, decided not to make the mistake of attempting to exploit the existing opportunity to move Rome's frontiers beyond the Tigris, something that would have made them too difficult to maintain. Instead, he opted for Persia's formal acceptance of the new reality that the Roman frontier, which for centuries had been at the Euphrates, was henceforth to be located at the Tigris.

Under the peace terms that Diocletian offered, and that Narsah readily accepted since they could easily have been considerably harsher, the Tigris was indeed recognized as the general line separating the two empires. Persia ceded five provinces to Rome that included all of Corduene (Kurdistan) and the region of the upper Tigris as far as Lake Van. In addition, the Armenian border was extended southward into Media, probably incorporating Media Atropatene (Azerbaijan). Armenia became a Roman protectorate and the king of Iberia (approximating modern Georgia) became a Roman vassal. This development was of particular strategic significance since it bolstered the Caucasus frontier against invasion from the barbarian north. To help assure the security of Rome's new forward position in Mesopotamia, Nisibis was made a central headquarters from which Rome was able to dominate Armenia to the north as well as control the flank of any Persian move across the Tigris in the direction of the Euphrates.

NOTES

1. Agathangelos, *History of the Armenians*, no. 19, p. 37.
2. Herodian, VI.2.4.
3. Ibid., VI.4.5.
4. John Malcolm, *The History of Persia*, Vol. 1, p. 95.

14

The Era of Shapur II

The Roman-Persian peace held for about forty years, as Persia became increasingly enmeshed in problems within its own imperial frontiers. The short reign of Narsah's successor Hormizd II (301–309) was generally uneventful. However, with the accession of the latter's infant son Shapur II (309–379) to the throne, the Sassanids were faced with significant erosion of their authority over the southern reaches of the empire. Taking advantage of the intrinsic weakness of the regency that ruled the empire, the Arab tribes of the south began a pattern of depredations that lasted for some sixteen years and threatened to tear the kingdom apart, although they made no attempt to consolidate control over the territories they raided. The tribes of Beni-Ayar and Abdul Kais of Bahrain, which at the time encompassed the Arabian districts of Hasa and Qatif on the western shores of the Persian Gulf, subjected Babylonia and Khuzistan to a long series of devastating raids. Farther north, a Mesopotamian sheikh, Tayir, attacked and captured Ctesiphon.

About 325, having attained the age of sixteen, Shapur took direct control of Persia's affairs, and matters took an almost immediate turn for the better. During the next dozen years, he reversed the security situation by taking the offensive and bringing the struggle to the lands of the marauding Arab tribes with great brutality. At the same time, Shapur reacted very strongly to the inroads that Christianity was making in the region.

The adoption of Christianity as the state religion of Armenia in 301 under Tiridates III, and its spread throughout the eastern Roman Empire, particularly under Constantine the Great (324–337), had a profound effect on the general political climate in the region. With Christianity accorded the status of an official religion of the Roman Empire, Constantine saw himself as protector of Christians throughout the world. One consequence of this was that closer ties now developed between Armenia and Rome, at the same time that a section of the Armenian nobility maintained a close connection to Persia. Armenia, which had for more than three centuries been the flashpoint for conflict between Rome and Parthia-Persia, was now torn in two along religious-cultural lines corresponding to its pro-Roman and pro-Persian factions. With Christianity rapidly becoming the dominant religion of the Roman Empire, the Christians under Persian rule automatically became suspected of treason, and the remainder of Shapur's long reign was characterized by bloody persecutions.

When Constantine attempted to intervene with Shapur on behalf of the Christians residing within the Sassanid domains, Shapur began to threaten the resumption of hostilities. However, he was not really in any hurry to do so. He recognized Constantine as a formidable enemy who had undisputed command of the resources of the Roman Empire, and as one who was without serious political rivals who might be exploited to undermine his position at home. The death of Constantine altered the regional political balance dramatically.

The Roman Empire was now divided among Constantine's sons into three separate kingdoms, with Thrace, Asia Minor, Syria, Mesopotamia, and Egypt coming under the rule of Constantius (337–361), who did not have the powerful Roman armies of Europe at his disposal. This gave Shapur the opportunity he had long awaited. Having secured his eastern flank by smashing the kingdom of the Kushans and annexing their territories, Shapur went to war in the west, determined to wipe out the gains that the Romans had achieved since the death of his namesake several decades earlier.

The flash point, once again, was Armenia. With the death of Tiridates III in 313, Armenia was no longer able to stave off the Persians. Shapur had already wrested Media Atropatene back from Chosroes II (c. 315–324). He now began to apply pressure on the Romans by throwing his open support to the pagan elements in Armenia, who had been subjected to severe persecution by Tiridates as he tried to force their conversion to Christianity. They soon rebelled against Tiranus (c 325–337), who was overthrown and handed over to Shapur, and began making incursions into Roman territory. Farther south, Shapur employed Arab marauders to raid Mesopotamia and Syria. Then, in 338, he took to the field in force, with the patent aim of driving the Romans back to the Euphrates. However, to do this he first had to take Nisibis. Otherwise, he would run the danger of being cut off from the north if he attempted to move as far westward as the Euphrates. Shapur laid siege to Nisibis for two months, but failed to take the city. In effect, he had been fought to a stalemate. Nevertheless, hostilities continued indecisively for the next several years, with the Persian forces commanding the field but unable to penetrate the fortified Roman positions.

In the meantime, Shapur's attempts to rule Armenia directly failed miserably, provoking rebellions against him even by those who had previously supported him. Accordingly, in 341, he decided to change his Armenian policy and restore Tiranus' son Arsaces (341–363) to the throne as a Sassanid vassal. This stabilized the situation in Armenia and facilitated the extension of Shapur's influence as far as the Caucasus. Having settled affairs in Armenia, he turned once more to the conquest of Mesopotamia and in 346 laid siege to Nisibis, but once again failed to take the strategically essential stronghold.

Undaunted, Shapur returned to Mesopotamia a third time in 348 and succeeded in inflicting a major defeat on Constantius at the battle of Singara. But for reasons that are unclear, he failed to exploit his advantage in any significant way. It was not until the summer of 350 that he attempted to take Nisibis for the third time. Once again, the city withstood the siege for some three months before Shapur was forced to withdraw, after sustaining losses estimated to be as great as 20,000 men, because of a new threat that arose on his Transcaspian frontier.

A horde of the Massagetae, at this time probably consisting mostly of Turko-Mongol elements, invaded the Caspian regions of Hyrcania and Parthia. This compelled Shapur to shift his attention away from his campaign against the Romans in the west. For Constantius, this could not have happened at a more opportune moment since he too had a new threat to deal with in the west where the generals Magnentius and Vetranio had usurped the thrones assigned to his brothers under the succession arrangements. Under the circumstances, a tacit truce between Rome and Persia that lasted for some eight years went into effect. During the respite, Constantius was able to make himself sole master of the Roman world.

While Shapur was preoccupied with events in the east, Arsaces, whom he had placed on the throne of Armenia to rule the country on his behalf, evidently became disenchanted with the arrangement and sought to align himself with Constantius. Arsaces' overture soon resulted in his marriage to a member of the Roman nobility and a subsequent treaty between Byzantium and Armenia. This not only constituted an Armenian betrayal of Persia, but also led in effect to a strengthening of the Roman position in an area where the Persian Empire had always proven militarily vulnerable.

It was not to be expected that Shapur would stand still for this change in the status quo for very long. At the same time, however, two senior Roman officials took the initiative in attempting to translate the informal truce with Persia into a formal peace agreement. They approached Tamsapur, the satrap of Adiabene, and requested that he serve as their intermediary. The latter conveyed their message to Shapur who was apparently led to believe that Constantius was suing for peace. According to Ammianus Marcellinus, Shapur's terms were contained in a highly patronizing letter that read, in part, as follows:

I will be content to receive Mesopotamia and Armenia, which was fraudulently ex-
torted from my grandfather. We Persians have never admitted the principle, which
you proclaim with such effrontery, that success in war is always glorious, whether it
be the fruit of courage or trickery. In conclusion, if you will take the advice of one
who speaks for your good, sacrifice a small tract of territory, one always in dispute,
and causing continual bloodshed, in order that you may rule the remainder se-
curely. Physicians, remember, often cut and burn, and even amputate portions of
the body, that the patient may have the healthy use of what is left to him . . . I warn
you, that, if my ambassador returns in vain, I will take the field against you, so soon
as the winter is past, with all my forces, confiding in my good fortune and in the fair-
ness of the conditions which I have now offered.[1]

Although Constantius was somewhat dismayed at the tone of Shapur's
message, he did not disavow the idea of a peace treaty. He would have preferred one that would have permitted him to focus all his attention on the
growing threat to the empire from the Germanic tribes. However, he could
not accept Shapur's territorial demands, which he considered outrageous.
For his part, Shapur was as good as his word. In 359, he crossed the Tigris in
force and confronted the Roman army that had advanced to the river. The
Romans, however, did not engage the Persians and began to withdraw. But,
as they retreated, the Romans applied a "scorched earth" policy that turned
the area between the Tigris and Euphrates into a desert wasteland. Constantius left Constantinople and crossed into Anatolia, stopping in Cappadocia to assure the loyalty of the king of Armenia, and then proceeded to
Edessa where he mobilized the forces coming from the different reaches of
the empire to take on the Persians.

In the meantime, Shapur decided not to waste his time and resources on
yet another siege of Nisibis. He concluded that it would be better to bypass
it and invade Syria from the north. Unable to cross the Euphrates directly
because of the swollen waters, he headed north to Amida (Diyarbekir)
where he defeated the Roman forces and laid siege to the fortified city,
which fell after seventy-three days. However, with Constantius now en-
sconced with substantial forces in Edessa, it appeared that the conflict was
once again heading for a stalemate, and Shapur returned to the Tigris
where he camped for the winter.

In 361 Constantius found himself in an awkward position. Shapur kept
threatening to cross the Tigris again, forcing the emperor to keep his forces
in position to block their advance, while at the same time his cousin Julian
was threatening his position in the west. Once again, instead of exploiting
his advantage, Shapur appears to have been distracted, probably by another threat emerging in the east, and he withdrew his army from the Tigris.
This freed Constantius to march west to deal with the rebellion that was being fomented by Julian. However, he became seriously ill while en route to
Constantinople and died in Cilicia toward the end of the year, allowing Jul-

ian the Apostate (361–363), a far abler military leader, to succeed to the imperial Byzantine throne.

In a last vain attempt to restore the glory of Roman arms, Julian decided to invade Persia. Crossing the Euphrates with most of his army in 363, he apparently thought to repeat Trajan's march on Ctesiphon. His general strategy was to divide his forces in two at Harran. While he proceeded down the Euphrates Valley with one army, his generals Procopius and Sebastian were to join forces with the Armenian army of Arsaces and march south through Media and Adiabene along the east bank of the Tigris. Both Roman armies were then to converge on Ctesiphon simultaneously from two directions.

The army under Procopius and Sebastian proceeded across northern Mesopotamia toward Armenia and, as planned, was joined by an Armenian force sent by Arsaces. The joint forces invaded Media and ravaged one of the more fruitful districts, also according to the agreed-upon scheme. Then, quite suddenly, the Armenian forces withdrew and began marching back to Armenia. It seems that the Armenian commander, Zuraeus, had second thoughts about the wisdom of joining forces with the anti-Christian Julian. He ostensibly decided to quit the joint operation on his own authority, although there is a lingering suspicion that Zuraeus actually acted on Arsaces' instructions.

When Julian heard what had occurred he warned Arsaces that unless he did something about the situation immediately he would pay heavily for this treachery later. To placate Julian, Arsaces had Zuraeus executed along with his entire family. However, never particularly enthusiastic about participating directly in the war, presumably because of his uncertainty as to which side would emerge victorious, Arsaces did not send any new troops to join up with the Roman army. Instead, he sat back and watched events unfold, thereby lending support to the notion that Zuraeus' defection was Arsaces' idea in the first place. Without the anticipated Armenian reinforcements, the viability of the planned assault along the Tigris by Procopius and Sebastian was now in question. The generals, however, were unable to agree on an alternative course of action. While one favored continuing the campaign in accordance with the original plan even without Armenian support, the other was adamantly opposed to taking the risk of a march to the south without adequate forces, and insisted on returning to Mesopotamia. As a consequence, the northern army effectively became immobilized.

In the meanwhile, Julian marched virtually unopposed as far as the outskirts of Ctesiphon where he encountered stiff resistance for the first time, his own northern army nowhere in sight. He defeated the Persian forces that had been assembled hastily to defend the city, and was now in a position to lay siege and conquer Ctesiphon as Trajan and Septimus Severus had done in earlier times. It was at this point, however, that Julian had to deal realistically with the objectives of the expedition he had undertaken. His situation was quite different from that of the emperors who had previously conquered Ctesiphon. They had taken the city after decisively defeating the largest army that the Parthians were able to mobilize. He, on the other hand, had not yet engaged the main body of the Persian army, and had apparently lost his own northern army. Accordingly, it would be very risky to engage in a protracted siege when he could be attacked by the main Persian forces, which might easily cut his main lines of communication to the west, effectively trapping him on the east bank of the Tigris. But, without taking Ctesiphon, it made little military sense to attempt to drive farther into Persia toward Persepolis. In effect, Julian had placed himself in an untenable position. He could not stay where he was, since the summer had already arrived and there was great risk that his troops might contract malaria. Moreover, his supplies were nearly exhausted, and there was considerable doubt as to whether his army could live off the land for a protracted period. The only real alternative that he had to attacking Ctesiphon was to retreat. After weighing the alternatives, Julian decided to terminate the campaign and withdraw.

It would appear that Shapur's decision to delay deployment of his main army against Julian's forces turned out to be the decisive factor in bringing about the Roman decision to retreat. The withdrawal itself was to prove a very difficult process. With its supplies exhausted, the Roman army could not retrace its steps across Mesopotamia since it had stripped the land during its earlier advance to the Tigris. Accordingly, Julian decided that the retreat would follow the course of the Tigris along its east bank through the rich province of Corduene about 250 miles to the north. However, as the Romans marched north, they found themselves being harassed in the rear by the Persian army that now appeared behind them, and by Persian units that were busy turning the land in the path of their march into a desert. In brief, the Roman withdrawal quickly turned into a debacle, with Julian himself being killed during a Persian attack. The army elected Jovian (363–364) emperor in his place.

Jovian immediately came under great pressure from his troops to do something to salvage the situation. When the army reached Dura, it was decided to attempt to cross the Tigris. A unit of some 500 Gauls and Sarmatians swam the river at night, surprised the Persian units on the western bank, and established a secure foothold there. Jovian then began to prepare to move the entire army across, scavenging for wood and animal skins with which to build rafts for those who could not swim. Shapur knew that it would not be possible for him similarly to move his own army across the river. His forces consisted primarily of cavalry, and he had not brought the necessary boats with him in anticipation of such a contingency. Moreover, it seemed certain that by the time he might finish building a suitable bridge the Romans would have been able to elude his grasp. To make the most of the situation, he appears to have decided to offer to negotiate peace terms with Jovian. He knew that the emperor would be very amenable to this since he was by no means certain of what lay between his forces, even assuming that the Persians allowed them to cross the Tigris intact, and the Euphrates which was still about 200 miles away. Shapur is reported by the Persian historians to have sent the following message to Jovian:

I have reassembled my numerous army. I am resolved to revenge my subjects, who have been plundered, made captives, and slain. It is for this that I have bared my arm, and girded my loins. If you consent to pay the price of the blood which has been shed, to deliver up the booty which has been plundered, and to restore the city of Nisibis, which is in Irak, and belongs to our empire, though now in your possession, I will sheathe the sword of war; but should you refuse these terms, the hoofs of my horse, which are as hard as steel, shall efface the name of the Romans from the earth; and my glorious cimeter, that destroys like fire, shall exterminate the people of your empire.[2]

The actual terms that Shapur subsequently offered, and from which he would not deviate, included the return of the five provinces north of the Tigris that Narsah had been forced to concede to Galerius and the surrender of Nisibis and two other fortresses in eastern Mesopotamia. He also demanded a rupture of relations between Rome and Armenia. With regard to the latter, Rome was to commit itself not to render any aid whatsoever to Arsaces for any conflict that the latter might have with Persia. Jovian ultimately accepted these terms, and a thirty-year peace agreement was concluded. In essence, the peace treaty reestablished the Roman-Persian frontier at the Euphrates once again.

THE REEMERGENCE OF THE ARMENIAN QUESTION

Once Jovian repudiated the Roman protectorate over Armenia, giving Shapur a free hand there, the latter turned his attention once more to a resolution of the long-standing Armenian problem. Unwilling to engage in another difficult full-scale military campaign in the Armenian highlands, Shapur resorted to subversion and harassment as his principal instruments of policy. He made overtures to some of the provincial satraps while raiding the territories of the others. In this way, one by one, the satraps were induced to transfer their allegiance to the Persians. It soon became apparent to Arsaces that it was essential for him to make his peace with Shapur if Armenia was to continue as a viable political entity. Arsaces was ultimately lured to Shapur's headquarters on a promise of safe conduct. There he was promptly blinded and imprisoned, and then took his own life. This did not resolve the problem, however, since a rebellion against the Persians soon broke out under a nationalist party led by Arsaces' widow and his son Para, who was subsequently murdered. This revolt was eventually suppressed, and it seemed as though Persian control was about to be firmly imposed over Armenia.

In the meantime, however, Jovian had been replaced as emperor of the Romans by the brothers Valentinian (364–375) and Valens (364–378), the Eastern Empire falling to the latter. Valens was quite disinclined to adhere strictly to the terms of the treaty signed by his predecessor at Dura. It seemed unconscionable for him to allow an expansion of Persia's sphere of influence at Roman expense. As a result, Roman-Persian relations soon deteriorated once again, the immediate cause this time being developments that took place in Iberia.

Immediately after he disposed of Arsaces, Shapur moved to extend his influence to the neighboring Christian country of Iberia. Its king, Sauromaces, who had been crowned by Rome, was too partial to Roman interests to suit the Persian monarch. Accordingly, Shapur forced him out of the country and set up his own proxy, Aspacures, as its ruler. Since the Dura treaty did not deal specifically with Iberia, Valens felt no constraint on lending Roman support to the deposed Sauromaces.

Toward the end of 370, Valens dispatched Terentius to Iberia from Lazica, a Roman controlled territory on the southeast shore of the Black Sea, along with a dozen legions to reinstall Sauromaces on the Iberian throne. Terentius proceeded south through Iberia with relative ease as far as the Cyrus (Kur) River, where he met Aspacures. The latter proposed a compromise whereby Iberia would be partitioned, with Sauromaces ruling the region north of the Cyrus, while Aspacures would retain the crown of the territory south of the river. Terentius accepted the proposal and two separate kingdoms were established.

To Shapur, this intervention by Valens constituted a clear violation of the spirit, if not the letter, of the Dura treaty. As far as he was concerned, the pact implicitly linked the futures of Iberia and Armenia. He was also outraged that another Roman army was sitting on the Armenian frontier, ready to intervene at any moment. Shapur's protests to Rome fell on deaf ears and he prepared for war. For its part, in anticipation of a Persian attack, Rome sent a powerful army to the east with instructions not to initiate hostilities, but to allow Persia to break the treaty first.

Shapur's forces crossed the frontier in the spring of 371, and the ensuing war dragged on inconclusively for several years, interspersed by periods of negotiations. A new peace agreement was finally reached in 376 under which both powers appear to have agreed to a "hands off" policy with respect to both Iberia and Armenia. In practical terms, this represented a victory for Rome, since both Christian countries were far more likely to lean in its direction for support than to Persia.

Once the Romans came to the conclusion that Para, the son of Arsaces and claimant to the Armenian throne, could no longer be trusted to serve their interests they had him murdered. Then they contrived to place the crown on Varaztad, while the real power in the country was entrusted to the hands of Moushegh, a member of a powerful family of nobles, who ruled as *sparapet* or generalissimo. Matters soon got out of hand once again as Varaztad suspected Moushegh of planning to overthrow him. He had Moushegh done away with, precipitating a revolt against him by the slain minister's brother Manuel that succeeded in overthrowing the king and forcing him to flee the country. Manuel installed the two sons of the slain Para, Arsaces and Valarsaces, as nominal co-rulers while he took his slain brother's place as de facto ruler of Armenia.

However, since Manuel had overthrown a Roman proxy, he was forced to seek a political alliance with the Persians as an offset to the Romans who were none too pleased at what he had done. Manuel appealed to Ardashir II (379–383) for protection from Rome, in exchange for which he offered to pay tribute and acknowledge Persian hegemony in Armenia. Ardashir was only too pleased to accept the offer and sent a satrap with 10,000 troops to help Manuel run the country. However, it was not long before Manuel became convinced that the Persian satrap was going to do away with him, and he decided to preempt such a development. He attacked the resident Persian force with his entire army and annihilated it, thereby precipitating a new war between Persia and Armenia. As was the case in the past, the Persian armies had great difficulty in fighting their way into Armenia, and Manuel was able to repel the repeated Persian attempts at invasion without finding it necessary to appeal to Rome for assistance.

The situation changed dramatically when Manuel died about 383, the same year that Shapur III (383–388) ascended the throne of Persia. The contending factions within Armenia could not agree on a common course and each appealed for help to their respective patrons, Rome and Persia. In this way, Armenia once again became the flash point for a new Roman-Persian war. This time, however, neither power was anxious to renew their competition for control of Armenia on the battlefield. Persia had a serious need for peace with Rome as it faced the growing menace of the Huns who were sweeping across the Caucasus in intermittent waves. And Rome, for its part, was engaged in a life-or-death struggle with the Goths, and was still recovering from the blow received at their hands at Adrianople in 378. Accordingly, a compromise was reached in 384 between Shapur and Theodosius I (379–395) under which Armenia was partitioned, with some four-fifths of the country coming under Persian suzerainty, and the remainder being designated a Roman protectorate. This solution to the Armenian question led to peace, and even cooperation, between the two powers for the next thirty-six years. Thus, when the Huns invaded Armenia in 395 and then extended their depredations to Cappadocia and northern Syria, posing a threat to Antioch, both states saw it to be in their mutual interest to cooperate in defending the Caucasian passes.

NOTES

1. Ammianus Marcellinus, XVII.5. Quoted by George Rawlinson, *The Seventh Great Oriental Monarchy*, Vol. 1, pp. 171–172.

2. John Malcolm, *The History of Persia*, Vol. 1, p. 87.

15

The Struggle for Persia's Frontiers

Notwithstanding the fact that the peace agreement between Rome and Persia was generally observed, the Euphrates frontier and Armenia remained regions of continual tension, aggravated by the fact that they had become religious frontiers as well. Yezdegird I (399–420) initially pursued a policy of religious toleration within the Persian Empire, issuing a decree in 409 that permitted the Christians to rebuild their churches and to practice their religion openly. It also established what later became known under the Turks as the *millet* system, whereby the Christians and other subject religious communities were accorded a special status that permitted them to deal with the Persian authorities through a communal leader that was formally appointed for the purpose by the government. However, Yezdegird's policy of religious toleration soon began to create internal problems for him with the official Persian religious establishment. Under considerable domestic pressure, the king made a dramatic reversal of policy that triggered an intense persecution of the Christians during the last five years of his reign.

The persecutions were continued by his successor Bahram V (420–439), and became so intense that a large number of Christians fled across the frontier to seek Roman protection. Bahram demanded of Theodosius II (408–450) that these Persian subjects be deported back to Persian territory. When the Byzantine (Roman) emperor refused to turn over the refugees, Bahram prepared for war. Anticipating that this would happen, the Byzantines took to the field before the Persians were fully ready for hostilities. The Byzantine commander, Ardaburius, marched his army through Armenia into the Persian province of Arzanene where he defeated the troops sent by Bahram to block his passage, and proceeded to plunder the area. But the battle there was not decisive, and the war continued for another two years before it was apparent to both sides that it was going to end in another stalemate. Thus, when Theodosius suggested that they come to terms, Bahram was only too ready to agree. It appears that the Persians were being pressed once again by marauders coming across their eastern frontiers, and they were eager to reach some accommodation with Byzantium that would make it possible to avoid the necessity of conducting military operations on more than one front at a time. In addition, the political situation in Persian-controlled Armenia was becoming chaotic and urgently required Bahram's attention.

The terms of the Byzantine-Persian agreement of 422 simply called for a cessation of the persecutions on the part of the Persians, and acceptance of the fact that the refugees would not be returned by the Romans. Nonetheless, the problem of living as a Christian under Persian rule remained an explosive issue that kept passions inflamed on both sides of the frontier. The Christians were perceived as natural allies, if not agents, of Byzantium, and were frequently treated as traitors by the Persians. During Bahram's reign, a more fundamental way of dealing with the sensitive issue of religion was found. With his support, a synod was convened in 424, the Council of Dad-Ishu, which made the Eastern Church independent of the Western Church and Byzantium. This formal separation brought an end to the accusations of treason against the Christians. Then, in 428, the territory of Armenia that was within the Persian sphere of control was transformed into a Persian province, Persarmenia, while the area under Roman control fared likewise.

CHRONIC INSTABILITY ON PERSIA'S FRONTIERS

The conflict with Rome was settled none too early. In addition to the repeated incursions of Huns from across the Caucasus to the north, Persia was also confronted with a challenge from a new power in the east. The Chionite-Ephthalites (White Huns), who had settled in the lands of the Kushans, were now crossing the Hindu Kush and posing a serious threat to the security of Persia's eastern frontiers.

In 425, a horde of White Huns poured across the Oxus and overran Merv, crossed the Elburz Mountains into Khorasan, and raided westward as far as Rai (Tehran). It seemed as though the shock of the invasion had driven Bahram out of his senses, for instead of marching to confront the enemy he went off to Azerbaijan to hunt, leaving the government in the hands of his brother Narsah. The latter, feeling helpless, sent an embassy to the khan of the Ephthalites proposing that Persia acknowledge his suzerainty and pay tribute in return for his withdrawal. The proposal was accepted and the invaders kept their position, awaiting the delivery of the tribute. In the meantime, Bahram took the small handpicked force of some 7,000 men that accompanied him, gathered additional forces from Azerbaijan and Armenia, and proceeded along the Caspian Sea to Hyrcania and then to Nishapur, reaching the vicinity of Merv undetected. He then launched a surprise night attack on the White Huns that completely disoriented them. The Ephthalite khan was killed and the White Huns were forced to abandon their equipment and booty and flee for safety across the Oxus. Bahram then sent a force after them and defeated them once again on their home territory.

Although the peace with Byzantium seemed to be holding, actions by Roman frontier officials became increasingly provocative. Thus, when in addition to other frontier encroachments a large Roman force was observed in the vicinity of Nisibis, it was considered by Yezdegird II (440–457) to be an unacceptable alteration of the military balance in the region. Shortly after he mounted the throne, he declared war and invaded Roman-held territory. Theodosius, however, was anxious to maintain the peace and quickly sought to arrange a truce. Surprisingly, Yezdegird proved quite amenable and a new agreement was soon negotiated. The resulting peace treaty of 442 attempted to deal with the problems that precipitated the conflict by forbidding the construction of new fortifications by either side in the vicinity of the Byzantine-Persian border. It also reconfirmed the provision of the treaty of 363 that required the Romans to contribute a fixed sum to keep the defenses of the Caspian Gates in good repair.

It is not clear why the Persian king suddenly had such a change of heart after having initiated the war. However, it is not at all unlikely that the primary factor may have been a resurgence of the threat on the increasingly volatile eastern frontier. Indeed, Yezdegird soon became engaged in a long defensive war against the encroaching tribes of Transoxiana that involved annual campaigns against them between 443 and 451. To better conduct this protracted conflict, Yezdegird left the capital in the hands of his vizier and moved his own residence to Nishapur, from which he would be better able to oversee military operations. He invaded Transoxiana in 451 and was able to inflict an apparently decisive defeat on the Ephthalites that permitted him to consider the war as won. This left him free to pursue a project that he had long contemplated, one which he was unable to devote his full attention to until now.

Political activists in the Persian capital had long been applying pressure on Yezdegird to do something further about Armenia. Irrespective of the treaty between Byzantium and Persia, Roman influence had been making additional inroads in Persarmenia, capitalizing on the fact that both nations were formally Christian. Moreover, few among the Persian elite believed that the current partition of Armenia was final. They were quite concerned that, in the event of another flare-up, the Armenians under Persian rule would probably side with the Romans. Therefore, they argued persuasively, as long as Armenia was Christian and Persia was Zoroastrian, there could never really be a commonality of interest between the two that could be relied upon at a time of crisis, particularly if it involved a conflict with Byzantium. As a result, Yezdegird decided to attempt to bring about the conversion of the Armenians to Zoroastrianism. His initial efforts to accomplish this relied on gentle persuasion. When this approach failed dismally, he undertook the vigorous persecution and suppression of the Armenian religious leaders. This placed Theodosius under considerable pressure to do something on behalf of his co-religionists across the Armenian frontier. As described by the Armenian historian Elish:

While the blessed Theodosius was questioning the whole Senate, anxious to find a peaceable solution to the matter and greatly concerned lest the churches of the East be ravaged by the imperious heathen, at that very time the end of his life suddenly befell him. This put a serious obstruction in the way of procuring help.

In his stead the emperor Marcianus [sic] [450–457] came to the throne. The king was influenced by his evil counselors . . . so he was unwilling to heed the united pact of the Armenians, who with all their strength were opposing the wickedness of the heathens. But this ignoble man thought it better to preserve the pact with the heathen for the sake of terrestrial peace, than to join in war for the Christian covenant. Therefore he quickly dispatched . . . [an] ambassador to the Persian king and contracted a firm pact with him that he would not support the Armenian forces with troops, arms, or any form of assistance.[1]

What this description fails to mention is that at the time, Attila the Hun was at the peak of his power and stood ready to overrun the Western Roman Empire, which would surely be quickly followed by an assault on Byzantium. Under these circumstances, Marcian was in no position to go to war with Persia over the Armenians, whether co-religionists or not. Abandoned by the Byzantines, the Armenians mounted a major rebellion in 451 that took the Persians five years to suppress. The uprising was quelled with great severity, with the leading members of the great families and clergy taken to Persia where they were subsequently killed. Zoroastrianism, the official state religion of Persia, was now forcibly imposed on the Armenians. Only a few managed to flee to safety in Roman territory, or to find refuge in the mountains of Kurdistan.

On Persia's eastern frontier, the situation remained relatively stable for several years until the reign of Firuz or Peroz (459–484). The Ephthalites had ceased making their customary offerings to the Persian king, which Firuz correctly saw as default on their obligation to pay tribute. To assert his rights as suzerain, he invaded their territory in about 464. The campaign, however, was inconclusive. Unable to resolve the issue on the battlefield, Firuz decided to make peace and exact his tribute in another manner. To seal the peace agreement, he proposed that the Ephthalites bind themselves to the Sassanids through marriage. It was arranged that the Ephthalite khan, Khush-Newaz ("The High-Minded"), would wed one of Firuz's daughters. However, instead of a daughter, Firuz sent a slave girl to the khan, whom the latter married as agreed. This tasteless practical joke was to be paid for in Persian blood and humiliation.

When Khush-Newaz discovered the deception, he decided to retaliate in kind. He wrote to Firuz that he had need of some experienced Persian military officers to assist him in a conflict with a neighboring tribe. Seeing this request as an opportunity to extend his influence into the Ephthalite army, Firuz sent a military assistance mission of 300 officers to the khan. Khush-Newaz had some of them killed, and the rest mutilated and sent back to Persia. This was taken as the equivalent of a declaration of war, and Firuz invaded Ephthalite territory once again. Khush-Newaz soon lured Firuz into a trap, along with his entire army. However, the Ephthalite khan saw little purpose in completely destroying the Persian forces. His ambitions apparently did not include anything as grandiose as the conquest of the Persian Empire. He also was not interested in triggering a long war of attrition with Persia, which would surely develop if he wiped out the trapped army. Accordingly, Khush-Newaz was prepared to be magnanimous if Firuz would meet his terms. These were that Firuz take an oath that Persia would maintain perpetual peace with the Ephthalites, and that the Persian king humiliate himself personally by rendering homage to the Ephthalite khan. Firuz had no good alternative to accepting these rather generous terms. Failure to comply would have meant both his death and the senseless slaughter of his army. By agreeing, Firuz was permitted to extricate himself and his army intact from what would otherwise have been an unmitigated disaster.

The continuing pressures on Persia in the east and the north, a direct consequence of the vast tribal movements that were taking place at the time in Central Asia, presented Byzantium with some opportunities to manipulate Persia's problems to its advantage. It was clear that Byzantium needed Persia as a buffer against the Huns, whose incursions across the Caucasus threatened the eastern frontiers of the Byzantine Empire. On the other hand, it wanted to put an end to the Persian practice of attacking and looting the rich provinces of Mesopotamia, which was now being done regularly as a means of bolstering the declining Persian economy as trade with the east was being interrupted more and more frequently. Accordingly, the Byzantine emperor Zeno (474–491) made it his policy to do what was necessary to prevent Persia from suffering too serious a defeat. At the same time he also took steps to foment conflicts with the Huns so as to keep Persia preoccupied on its northern and eastern frontiers, and away from the Byzantine-Persian frontier.

This Byzantine policy of draining the strength of Persia became particularly acute during the reign of Firuz, and helps account for the series of setbacks that Persia experienced under his rule. The Sassanid Empire was simply not capable of sustaining serious military operations on two fronts simultaneously, and since it could not ignore events on one front to deal with the other, it suffered defeats on both. Beyond the matter of resources, both human and material, it was also a question of culture. The king was the leader, and generally speaking, his presence was necessary to stimulate a maximum effort by his troops. Of course, he could not be in two places at once.

In 481, Firuz suffered defeat at the hands of the Kushans, who occupied a tract of land between Astarabad and Derbent, along the Caspian. This immediately set the stage for a revolt in Iberia, which overthrew its Zoroastrian king, Vazken, and placed a Christian, Vakhtang, on the throne in his place. When the Persian governor of Armenia, Ader-Veshnasp, tried to intervene in Iberia with all the troops he could assemble, leaving a power vacuum in Armenia, the Armenians rose in revolt as well. Before long, the long-suppressed Christians seized the capital and made themselves masters of all Persarmenia, establishing a new national government there. When the Persian governor tried to return with a relatively small force to restore control, he was defeated and killed at the Araxes River. The following year Firuz tried to recapture his northern position by sending one army into Armenia and another into Iberia. The Armenians succeeded in defeating the Persian force sent against them, and then turned to assist the Iberians who were in desperate straits.

In the meanwhile, the king of Iberia, Vakhtang, bought peace from the Persians by betraying his Armenian allies. The new Armenian king, Sahag, was killed and his *sparparet*, Vahan, was forced into hiding. However, before the Persian commander could finish off the Armenian forces, he was suddenly recalled by Firuz and dispatched to the Caspian where fighting had broken out again with the Kushans. Upon the Persian withdrawal, Vahan easily reassumed control of Armenia.

Firuz sent another army into Armenia in 483, which after some initial successes became bogged down in an inconclusive struggle against Vahan. But instead of putting more forces into Armenia to turn the tide in Persia's favor, and against the advice of his counselors, Firuz picked just this moment to attempt to wipe out the stain of the humiliation he had suffered by his defeat at the hands of the Ephthalites. There was, however, more than personal pride at issue. With Ephthalite power growing steadily on his eastern flank, Firuz undoubtedly saw Persia as increasingly being squeezed in a geostrategic vise that threatened the long-term viability of the empire. In any case, the venture turned into a debacle, as Firuz was simply outclassed as a general by Khush-Newaz. The Persians were defeated and Firuz himself was killed. It was left to his brother and successor Vologases (483–487) to reach a new accommodation with Khush-Newaz. The terms that were agreed upon had the unprecedented effect of making the Ephthalites the virtual suzerains over Persia, with the latter forced to pay heavy annual tribute to the Ephthalite ruler.

With his eastern frontier stabilized once again, Vologases turned to re-solve the outstanding problem of Armenia. He appointed Nikhor, an astute statesman, as governor of the province. Nikhor, in turn, reached an agree-ment with Vahan on the conditions under which Armenia would be satis-fied to terminate its struggle and accept its former status as a Persian dependency. Vahan's demands were essentially twofold. First, he de-manded religious freedom and a cessation of all attempts at conversion of the Armenians to Zoroastrianism. Second, he insisted that Armenia be ad-ministered directly by the Persian king, and not through a Persian satrap. Presumably, direct access to the king would avoid many of the problems previously encountered. Vologases approved the terms and formally ap-pointed Vahan as the Sassanid governor of Armenia, making him the de facto ruler of the country. Under Vahan's rule, Christianity once again be-came the official state religion and, for the first time, Armenia and Iberia be-came stable and peaceful components of the Sassanid Empire.

While Firuz was still king of Persia, his son Qavad had made an aborted attempt to seize the throne and subsequently took refuge with the Ephthal-ites, with whom he remained for some three years. When his successor, Vo-logases, discontinued the payments of tribute to the Ephthalites shortly before his death, Khush-Newaz apparently made a pact with Qavad, under which the Persian prince committed himself to a faithful continuation of Persia's tribute payments if he were to mount the throne. In return, Khush-Newaz gave him an army with which to seize the throne from his uncle. The anticipated civil war was averted, however, by the timely demise of Vo-logases, and Qavad (487–531) became ruler of Persia.

Qavad's obligation to meet the Ephthalite demands for tribute, at the same time that the northern frontier had to be held against the influx of ma-rauding tribes such as the Khazars, was beginning to bankrupt the Persian treasury. According to the treaty of 442 between Theodosius II and Yezde-gird II, Byzantium was obligated to pay an annual sum toward the mainte-nance of the Derbent garrison. However, the Byzantines had long since defaulted on such payments. Desperate for some financial relief, Qavad ap-pealed to the new emperor, Anastasius (491–518), to make good on the commitment to help secure the Caucasian passes. But his appeal was ig-nored since the Byzantines preferred to see Persia in a weakened position, squeezed between themselves and the Ephthalites and threatened from the north. Eventually, Qavad saw no practical alternative for replenishing his treasury other than raiding and looting the Roman provinces of northern Mesopotamia. Qavad did just that in 502, invading Roman Armenia, tak-ing Theodosiopolis by treachery and then, turning south, sacking Amida (Diyarbekir) after an eighty-day siege. By the time that the Byzantine army arrived to relieve Amida, Qavad had already withdrawn to Nisibis with his train loaded with plunder.

As the war progressed, it seemed that Persia was gaining the upper hand. During 503, however, Qavad was forced to withdraw most of his army and proceed to Khorasan to block an invasion by the Ephthalites, leaving the campaign in the west in the hands of subordinates. No sooner had Qavad left than the tide of battle turned in favor of the Byzantines. Qavad soon came under heavy pressure to come to terms with Anastasius quickly in order to be free to defend eastern Persia from the Ephthalites. A seven-year truce was concluded in 505 that was to restore the conditions that existed before the outbreak of the conflict. Anastasius subsequently violated the fortifications provision of the 442 treaty by building a fortress at Dara, near Nisibis and the Tigris crossing, to bolster the defenses on the Byzantine frontier.

At the time, Qavad was too preoccupied to take any action in response to this blatant violation of the treaty. However, once the war with the Ephthalites was successfully concluded about 513, he had his ambassadors raise the matter directly with the Byzantines. Anastasius could not deny the validity of the complaint and apparently was compelled to assuage Qavad's anger, at least temporarily, with a substantial cash payment as compensation. However, Byzantine violations of the terms of the treaty continued apace under Justin I (518–527), who took full advantage of the fact that Qavad was prevented from reacting forcefully because he was beset by a seemingly endless series of internal crises.

No sooner had Qavad finally resolved his internal problems in 523, than he was confronted by a rebellion in Iberia as a result of his ill-conceived attempt to force the Iberian king Gurgenes to convert from Christianity to Zoroastrianism. Gurgenes rose in revolt and sought support from Byzantium, declaring himself a Byzantine vassal. Justin, however, was reluctant to get directly involved in the remote region and attempted instead to precipitate an invasion by the Huns, that is, the Tatars of the Crimea, to offset the Persians. This effort collapsed without result and a small Byzantine force was ultimately sent to Iberia, setting the stage for a renewal of the Byzantine-Persian conflict.

Qavad now sent a large army into Iberia that brought the country back under Persian control. Gurgenes was forced to seek refuge in Lazica (Mingrelia), where the Romans offered him protection. The Persian forces, in hot pursuit of Gurgenes, penetrated into Lazica and took over some forts that commanded the passes between it and Iberia. Justin retaliated in 526 by an invasion of Persarmenia and Mesopotamia. The initial effort was inconclusive and the Byzantine forces were placed under the command of Byzantium's most prominent general, Belisarius, who set up his headquarters at Dara as the fighting subsided.

NOTE

1. Elishe, *History of Vardan and the Armenian War*, p. 124.

16

End of the Sassanid Empire

Justinian (527–565), who replaced Justin as Byzantine emperor during this period of heightened tensions with Persia, continued his predecessor's policy of strengthening the fortifications along the Persian frontier, ordering the improvement of the fortifications at a number of sites as well as the construction of a new fort near Nisibis. This blatant disregard of the 442 treaty, which specifically prohibited such actions, provoked an attack in 528 by a Persian army, under the prince Xerxes, that saw the defeat of the great Byzantine general Belisarius, who was forced to flee for his safety. The setback was only temporary, however, and Belisarius soon returned with a larger Byzantine army that subsequently inflicted a significant defeat on the Persians. Nonetheless, the struggle remained inconclusive and was ultimately brought to an end in the spring of 532, after Qavad had died and was succeeded by Chosroes (Khusrau) I or Nushirwan (531–579).

The treaty that brought the conflict to a close was supposed to provide for an "Endless Peace." Under its terms, Byzantium was to pay to Persia the sum of 11,000 pounds of gold to finance the defense of the Caucasian passes, which was to be carried out by Persia. Second, Dara was to be permitted to remain a fortified post, but was not to serve as Byzantine military headquarters in Mesopotamia. Third, Byzantium was to return a district and castle recently captured from the Persians, while the latter were to return the forts taken by them in Lazica. Finally, the pact contained a mutual security and assistance provision under which Byzantium and Persia were obligated to come to each other's aid with men and money whenever such became necessary as a result of third-party conflicts.

While it would appear that Persia gained the most from the treaty, it was actually of far greater significance to Justinian. He urgently needed peace on his eastern frontiers in order to be able to proceed with the re-conquest of North Africa and Italy. For Justinian, the treaty was a matter of political expediency, and it is not at all clear that he ever intended to honor it as the definitive and permanent disposition of the Byzantine frontiers in Asia. The Endless Peace thus lasted no more than eight years. During that interval of peace in the east, Justinian made highly significant conquests in Africa and Europe, raising fears in Persia that he would next turn to Asia and attempt to re-conquer those provinces that had at one time been Roman. Chosroes therefore sought a pretext for breaking the treaty, and soon found it in the conflict that erupted between the Arabs of Hira and those of Ghassan.

The independent Ghassanid tribes had long been harassing the Byzantine provinces on the western periphery of the Arabian Desert. Justinian sought to alleviate this problem by creating a Ghassanid state under a supreme phylarch nominated by the emperor. This state would also serve as a counter to the Lakhmids of Hira (the clients of Persia) on the eastern rim of the desert. Accordingly, Harith (c. 528–570), a sheikh of the Ghassanids, was appointed phylarch, given the title of king, and made a Roman patrician. Across the desert, the sheikh of the Lakhmids, Mundhir (c. 508–554), also bore a similar royal title.

A squabble had developed between these two Arab states over which had sovereignty over a tract of wasteland south of Palmyra. Justinian sent two arbitrators to attempt to resolve the matter. Chosroes, however, now alleged that one of the arbitrators had made overtures to Mundhir, attempting to subvert his loyalty to Persia. He also claimed to be in possession of information that clearly proved that Justinian had encouraged the Ephthalites to attack Persia. At the same time, in 539, an embassy arrived from Witigis, king of the Ostrogoths, that pleaded with Chosroes to attack Justinian to help relieve the pressure the Ostrogoths were under in Italy from the Roman army under Belisarius. Finally, a similar plea came from Armenia, which was now groaning under intrusive Byzantine rule. Believing the time to be ripe, Chosroes initiated a war with Justinian in the spring of 540 that was to last five years.

In the past, most wars between Rome or Byzantium and Persia had been fought in Armenia, where the Persians were always tactically at a disadvantage. This time, however, Chosroes was determined to conduct the war in a manner that would best capitalize on the tactical superiority of the Persian cavalry in open country. As a result, the war raged not only in the mountains of Armenia but across the plains of Mesopotamia and Syria as well, exacting a heavy toll of casualties on both sides. During the course of the campaign, the Persians raided Antioch, completely razing the ancient city in the process. In addition, Edessa was placed under siege in 544 and forced to pay a tribute of 500 pounds of gold. The subsequent settlement of 545 called for a five-year truce as well as the payment by the Byzantines of an indemnity of 2,000 pounds of gold. It was at this time that Chosroes fi-

nally felt sufficiently strong to risk discontinuing his own payments of tribute to the Ephthalites, who were now coming under heavy pressure from
encroachments by the Turks of Central Asia. Curiously, the truce agreement did not resolve the question of Byzantine and Persian rights in the
small kingdom of Lazica, near the Black Sea, where the war went on for another eleven years until 556.

Lazica, known in earlier times as Colchis, was located on the southeastern coast of the Black Sea and commanded access to the mountain passes
through the Caucasus. It was therefore a strategically valuable chunk of territory that also happened to be a Christian client state of the Persian Empire. As such, it served as a useful buffer zone between the Persians and
Byzantines in the region. A conflict broke out there when the Byzantine
commander of the coastal fortress of Petra imposed a monopoly on trade
that caused the Lazi to appeal to their Persian suzerain for help. The question of Persian rights in the country was of particular concern to the Byzantines because Lazica offered the Persians a point of potential access to the
Black Sea and therefore to the Byzantine heartland.

Justinian, who had little interest in prosecuting a war in the region, effectively purchased additional five-year truces in 551 and 557, and established
the practice of paying tribute for security on the Byzantine-Persian frontier.
In 562, a peace treaty was finally negotiated on terms very favorable to Persia. The treaty was to last for a fifty-year period, with the Byzantine government undertaking to compensate the Persians at the rate of 30,000 gold
pieces annually in exchange for which Lazica was to be returned to Roman
control. In accordance with another provision of the agreement, Persia undertook to prevent the Huns, Alans, and other barbarians from traversing
the central passes of the Caucasus for the purpose of attacking Byzantine
territory.

With the Byzantine frontier relatively peaceful, Chosroes was in a position to restore a good deal of Persian power in the broader region. In 554, he
formed an alliance with Mokan Khan, the leader of the western Turks, and
together they attacked and effectively eliminated the Ephthalites as a political force. The Ephthalite territories were partitioned between the victors,
permitting the extension of the eastern frontier of Persia to the Oxus once
again. To the north, the Hun threat was blunted, while to the south Chosroes reached as far as the Yemen, which he annexed.

In the Yemen, which had long been within the Byzantine sphere of influence, Byzantine interests had become threatened when the last of the Himyarite kings, Yusuf dhu-Nuwas (c. 517–525), who had converted to Judaism
before his elevation, succeeded to the throne. Although the treatment of
Jews under the Sassanids left much to be desired, dhu-Nuwas, who was in
close touch with the Jewish sages of Tiberias in Byzantine-controlled Palestine, considered the situation of his co-religionists to be far more favorable
under the Zoroastrian Persians than under the Christian Byzantines. Ac-

cordingly, both the Jews and pagans of Arabia tended to favor Persia, while the Christians identified with Byzantium. Dhu-Nuwas apparently saw the indigenous Christians of the Yemen as being in league with the hated Ethiopians, across the Bab al-Mandeb Strait, who were also Christians. As a result, he employed an iron fist in dealing with the Christians of South Arabia, and is considered to be responsible for their massacre at Najran in October 523.

An appeal for intervention on behalf of the Christians was made to Justin who, as Byzantine emperor at the time, was regarded as the protector of Christians everywhere in the broader region. He in turn requested that the Negus of Ethiopia, Kaleb Ella Asbaha, who was the Christian ruler closest to the scene, undertake the intervention in the Yemen in his behalf. For Justin, this represented an opportunity to use the Ethiopians to help bring the South Arabian tribes further within the Byzantine sphere of influence, and to exploit them in the ongoing conflict with the Sassanids. The Negus responded favorably to the emperor's request and sent a sizable army under Abraha to the Yemen.

After experiencing successive defeats at the hands of the Ethiopians in 523 and 525, dhu-Nuwas being killed during the latter campaign, the Himyarite kingdom was overthrown and with it the independence of the Yemen. The Ethiopian commander, Abraha, made himself master of the country. He established his own dynasty there, leaving the throne to his son Yaksum, who was succeeded by his brother Masruq. It appears that it was their intention to convert the people of the land to Christianity and thereby to create a commercial center in the south that would rival the pagan pilgrimage center that had existed at Mecca in the Hejaz since remote antiquity. This would enable them to reap some of the substantial economic benefits long enjoyed by the latter. In addition, the successful conversion of the Yemen to Christianity promised also to serve as an additional barrier to the spread of Persian influence in the Red Sea region.

Justinian quite naturally saw this development as a boon to Byzantine interests and developed warm relations with both Ethiopia and its South Arabian offshoot. With Ethiopia's cooperation, direct access to the sea-lanes of the Indian Ocean provided an important opportunity for Byzantium to open an alternate and independent route to the Far East, undercutting Persian dominance of the maritime trade, and strengthening its own commercial position. The extensive Persian trade with the Far East, particularly in gems, spices, and silk, for which there was great demand in Europe, had created an unfavorable balance of trade for Byzantium. At the same time, the growing prosperity of Roman Syria was largely a result of its involvement in the business of finishing imported raw silk into yard goods. It wasn't until later in the century that the increasing demand for silk was accommodated through the officially encouraged smuggling of Asian silkworm eggs into the empire. This eventually permitted the development of a domestic silk industry that could satisfy the growing demands of the European market.

For Persia, however, the emergence of a Christian state in the Arabian Peninsula allied to Byzantium posed a serious security threat to its southern flank. Chosroes therefore exploited the opportunity provided by the peace treaty of 562 to mount a substantial attack on South Arabia that was designed to eliminate Ethiopian control of the Yemen. By doing this, he would be able to extend the Persian sphere of influence as far as the Arabian Sea and confront Byzantium along the entire length of its sphere of influence in the east. Aided by Saif, a scion of the Himyarites who had taken refuge at the Persian court, Chosroes dispatched an expeditionary force from the Persian Gulf that made its way by boat to Aden where it was joined by the Himyarites, who had long chafed under Ethiopian religious persecution. The war that ensued resulted in the Ethiopians being driven completely out of Asia. Saif mounted the throne of the Yemen and the country became a vassal state of Persia.

Persia's unanticipated resurgence as the paramount power in the region, reflected in its territorial expansion under Chosroes, became a matter of grave concern in Byzantium, which now expected renewed aggression to be directed at its territories in Asia. Justin II (565–578) was therefore receptive to the offer of an anti-Persian alliance proposed by an embassy sent to Constantinople in 568 by Dizabul, the khan of the Turks. It seems that Dizabul had earlier sought to reach an accommodation with Chosroes that the latter rejected because of a distrust of Turkish intentions. A Turkish-Byzantine treaty was concluded the following year, and Dizabul launched an expedition into Persia, although Byzantium played no role in it beyond sending an ambassador, Zemarchus, along as an observer. For the moment, at least, Justin was not prepared to challenge Persia directly. After some initial successes, the Turkish expedition turned into a debacle and Dizabul was forced to retreat back into Turkestan.

Another Turkish diplomatic mission arrived in Constantinople in 571 to urge Justin to abandon the peace treaty with Persia and join in a simultaneous attack on its eastern and western flanks that would surely destroy the Sassanid state. Other factors made such a move appear timely. Chosroes' successes in the Yemen had made the Ethiopians ready to join in a war against Persia, and Persian misgovernment in Armenia had provoked disorders and rebellion in that traditional flash point.

Justin decided to act, and in 572 he unilaterally renounced the decade-old peace treaty, refusing to make the stipulated annual payment of tribute. This was, in effect, the equivalent of an open declaration of war and Chosroes, notwithstanding his advanced age, took personal command of his armies in the field. The conflict was fought primarily in northern Mesopotamia, although the Persians also made incursions into Syria, reaching as far as Antioch before being repulsed. Justin's putative allies, the

Turks and Ethiopians, do not appear to have gotten involved in the conflict to any noticeable extent. During this struggle, Chosroes captured the fortress of Dara in 573, after a long siege. By eliminating this strongpoint, he significantly reduced his vulnerability to being outflanked while engaged in Armenia to the north.

Justin, shaken by this setback, asked for a year's truce which Chosroes, in need of revenue, granted in return for the payment of a substantial indemnity. The former used the period to gather a large army of some 150,000 men, which he deployed on the eastern frontier. Nevertheless, concerned about the possibility of suffering another defeat, in 575 Justin sought the extension of the truce into a general armistice that would bring an end to all hostilities, but would not constitute a long-term commitment to peace. Chosroes, on the other hand, wanted a formal long-term peace agreement, but nonetheless insisted that an armistice should not apply to Armenia, which had to be pacified once again. The Byzantines refused to meet the Persian terms and the conflict resumed for a brief period after the expiration of the renewed truce. Beaten by the Persians once again, the Byzantines were forced to agree to a three-year truce that did not apply to Armenia.

Freed from the threat of an immediate Byzantine intervention, Chosroes marched into Armenia and crushed the revolt there. Then, unexpectedly, and in clear violation of the truce, the Persians marched into Roman Armenia and threatened Cappadocia. The Byzantines blocked the Persian advance and retaliated by invading and plundering Persian Armenia in 576. This triggered a number of inconclusive campaigns and sporadic raids by both sides in Armenia and northern Mesopotamia that ravaged both regions over the next several years. In 580 and 581, the escalating conflict also reached into Media.

THE FINAL PHASE OF THE SASSANID EMPIRE

With the accessions of Hormizd IV (579–590) and Maurice (582–602) to the Persian and Byzantine thrones respectively, the indecisive war dragged on for another decade. However, under Hormizd's evidently mediocre leadership, Persian power began to wane significantly, as the Byzantine policy of fomenting crises on Persia's several frontiers finally began to bear fruit. Although Persia managed once again to defeat the Huns in the north and the Turks in the east, it was unable to do likewise with the Byzantines to the west. Thus, when Hormizd, buoyed by his defeat of the Turks, decided to invade and ravage Lazica, his forces were defeated in a pitched battle at the Araxes in 589 by the Byzantine army that came to its defense. Hormizd was subsequently deposed by his general, Bahram, and was replaced by his son Chosroes II (590–627). He, in turn, was soon faced by a military *coup d'e-tat* led by Bahram that triggered a civil war, and was compelled to seek assistance from the Byzantine emperor Maurice in order to regain his throne.

For some in Byzantium, the state of affairs in Persia seemed to offer an unparalleled opportunity. They urged that the civil war be allowed, indeed encouraged, to continue, exhausting Persia and making it ripe for a subsequent takeover by the Byzantines. This raised the prospect of a Greater Byzantium that would equal the Macedonian Empire of Alexander. The emperor, on the other hand, leaned toward another group that argued that it was unrealistic to imagine that they could effectively extend and maintain Byzantine rule over such a vast empire, given the difficulties they faced in Europe. Their fear was that if chaos were allowed to reign in Persia, the empire might fall into the hands of some new dynamic power that would forge it into an instrument that could attack the Byzantine empire with greater force and efficacy than the Sassanids were capable of mustering. Viewed from this perspective, it would best serve Byzantine interests to prop up a weak Sassanid regime under Chosroes, rather than risk the emergence of a possibly more powerful and more dangerous alternative.

Maurice decided to pursue the latter course, and with active Byzantine support for his cause, Chosroes was able to suppress the rebellion and regain his throne. However, there was a substantial price to be paid as compensation for Maurice's invaluable assistance. In 591 Chosroes was required to cede Persarmenia and eastern Mesopotamia, including the fortresses of Dara and Martyropolis, to Maurice. Byzantium's frontier was thereby extended to a point where it obtained a commanding strategic position with respect to the security of the Persian heartland.

A renewal of hostilities between Byzantium and Persia came in 603 with the assassination of Maurice, who had appealed to Chosroes for assistance in retaining his throne in the face of a rebellion against him. Although Chosroes, by design or circumstance, was unable to intervene in time to save his erstwhile benefactor, he took advantage of the situation to repudiate his earlier agreements and then ostensibly proceeded to avenge Maurice's murder by seizing most of the Byzantine possessions in the Middle East. It seems that Maurice had made a tragic error in helping Chosroes regain his throne.

The Persians retook Dara in 605, followed by the conquest of western Mesopotamia, including the strongholds of Harran and Edessa, in 607 and Armenia and much of Anatolia in 609. A Persian army also overran Syria and Palestine, capturing and looting Antioch in 612, Damascus in 614, and Jerusalem the following year. These successes in the west against the Byzantines were matched by simultaneous victories against the Ephthalite vassals of the Turks in the east, extending Persian control to frontiers it had not held since the days of the Achaemenids.

The Persian juggernaut appeared to be unstoppable as it continued to roll on through Byzantine territories. With the fall of Gaza in 616, the road to Egypt was open and the Persian commander Shahr-Barz marched into the country, which had not been subject to foreign invasion since the time of Julius Caesar. Fighting their way across the delta, the Persians took Babylon (Old Cairo) and then captured Alexandria in 619. Egypt capitulated and the Persian army proceeded up the Nile as far as the Ethiopian frontier. The loss of Egypt, still the principal granary of the empire, was an unmitigated disaster for Byzantium. Shortages of grain raised the threat of a famine in Constantinople, and the government was compelled to cancel the free dole of grain that had been allotted to the residents of the capital since the days of Constantine. While the campaign in Egypt was still under way, another Persian army set out from Cappadocia across Anatolia and laid siege to Chalcedon, directly across the Bosphorus from Constantinople, taking the city in 617. The capital itself now appeared to be in danger, threatening the stability of what remained of the Byzantine Empire.

Faced simultaneously with a serious challenge in the Balkans from the Avars, who had already overrun Thrace, Heraclius (610–641) was unable to concentrate the necessary forces in Asia and was compelled to seek a negotiated settlement of the conflict with the Persians. However, his overture was rejected. There was little reason for the Persians to be accommodating after experiencing decades of Byzantine intrigue with Persia's northern and eastern neighbors designed to sap their strength. Chosroes would now accept nothing less than unconditional surrender. He taunted Heraclius with the following response: "Chosroes, greatest of gods, and master of the whole earth, to Heraclius, his vile and insensate slave. Have I not destroyed the Greeks? You say you trust in your God: why, then, has he not delivered out of my hand Caesarea, Jerusalem, and Alexandria? Shall I not also destroy Constantinople? But I will pardon all your sins if you will come to me with your wife and children; I will give you lands, vines, and olive groves, and will look upon you with a kindly aspect."[1]

This reassertion of Persian power, however, was not to last very long. By 622, the Byzantine security position in Europe, primarily as a result of its payment of tribute to the Avars, had improved to the point where Heraclius was able to mount a series of major counterattacks that soon drove the Persians out of Anatolia. He eliminated the threat to Constantinople by landing an army in Cilicia and advancing on Cappadocia from the south, thereby threatening to trap the Persian army at Chalcedon. As a result, Shahr-Barz was compelled to withdraw eastward across Anatolia to a more tenable position. In three campaigns between 622–628, the Byzantines conquered Armenia and penetrated into Azerbaijan, threatening the Persian heartland. These campaigns were undertaken with the help of reinforcements from the Christian tribes of the Caucasus, and an alliance that Heraclius had negotiated with the Khagan of the Khazars who loaned him a force of some 40,000 men.

However, the Persians rallied in 626, as Constantinople was once again faced with the threat of a simultaneous Avar invasion from the north, and pushed through Anatolia to the Bosphorus once more. For a while it seemed that the combined land and sea siege of Constantinople by the Avars, in league with the Slavs, Bulgars, and Gepids, coupled with the threat from across the strait by the Persians, might spell the end for Byzantium. However, the subsequent defeat of the Slav fleet by the Byzantines also triggered the lifting of the siege by the combined land forces, which retreated in disorder from Constantinople.

The collapse of the threat from the Avars also effectively signaled the end of a serious Persian threat to the heart of the empire. The Byzantines were now free to devote their undivided attention to Asia. Heraclius set out from Lazica with a large army, marched through Armenia and Azaerbaijan practically unopposed, and then descended into the heart of the enemy's territory, inflicting a significant although not decisive defeat on the Persian army in a major battle fought near Nineveh in December 627.

Chosroes was still capable of regrouping his forces and emerging victorious from the struggle with Byzantium, but squandered the opportunity by indulging in personal revenge against the commanders who had suffered setbacks in the conflict. He even went so far as to order the execution of Shahr-Barz, who was so informed by the Byzantines. The reign of terror that Chosroes unleashed soon precipitated a palace revolt in which he was taken prisoner and executed. His immediate successor Shiroz, or Qavad II (628–629), promptly sued for peace, a proposal that Heraclius openly welcomed.

Heraclius desperately needed a period of peace because the Persian Wars had taken an enormous toll and their continuation threatened the viability of the Byzantine state. As Edward Gibbon observed: "The loss of two hundred thousand soldiers who had fallen by the sword, was of less fatal importance than the decay of arts, agriculture, and population, in this long and destructive war: and although a victorious army had been formed under the standard of Heraclius, the unnatural effort appears to have exhausted rather than exercised their strength."[2]

The general principle underlying the resulting peace agreement was the restoration of the situation as it existed before the war had erupted a quarter of a century earlier. Persia was to relinquish control over Egypt, Palestine, Syria, Anatolia, western Mesopotamia, and any other lands it may have conquered from Byzantium.

When Shiroz died after a reign of only some sixteen months, Shahr-Barz, in collusion with the Byzantines, attempted to usurp the throne, killing the legitimate Sassanid heir. Shahr-Barz, in turn, was deposed about two months after he seized power, leaving a power vacuum in the Persian Empire that created political chaos there. During the next five years, a dozen kings mounted the Persian throne, none of which were capable of imposing order in the empire. The Sassanid state simply disintegrated in a proliferation of petty kingdoms. By the time the Persian house was put in order in 634 with the election of a Sassanid prince, Yezdegird III, who was deemed generally acceptable to the rulers of the country, it was already too late to salvage the Sassanid Empire. It had become too enfeebled to be able to deal adequately with the new and dynamic imperialist challenge that was emerging from Arabia, and which would sound its death knell before the end of the decade.

NOTES

1. Charles W. Oman, *The Byzantine Empire*, pp. 132–133.
2. Edward Gibbon, *The History of the Decline and Fall of the Roman Empire*, Vol. 4, p. 486.

Afterword

Although the geopolitical history of the Middle East is basically seamless, I have chosen to end this book with the end stage of the decline of the Sassanid Empire. The account of its final destruction is an integral part of the story of the conquest of the core and much of the periphery of the Middle East under the banner of Islam, which emerged out of the Arabian Peninsula with extraordinary force at a time when the major regional powers, Byzantium and Persia, were exhausted from centuries of almost continual geopolitical struggle. I hope to provide a geopolitical treatment of the period from the rise of the prophet Muhammad and the Arab empires to the domination of most of the region by the Ottoman Turks in a subsequent volume.

It is my contention that familiarity with the period covered in this book is crucial to an understanding of the contemporary Middle East, because it was during this long period that the seeds of the diverse religions and cultures of the region were sown in the geopolitical soil of the region. As has been shown, the use of religion as an instrument of the state for political purposes has its roots in ancient Greece, and has continued to serve as a force for both national cohesion and regional division ever since.

Geopolitically, we have seen that there are no significant natural frontiers in the Middle East from its eastern reaches into Central Asia to the Mediterranean in the west. As a consequence, the political and military leaders of the states of the region have always been obsessed with the problems of physical security, and have struggled mightily to create buffer zones to provide some strategic depth in which to repel aggressors. Viewed from the perspective of the early history of the region, one can begin to see most clearly that the boundaries of the contemporary states that fill it are all rather arbitrary, often straight lines drawn far more clearly on a map than in the shifting sands.

Although it is now possible to move large military forces through the desert with relative ease, the patterns of population settlement in the Fertile Crescent have not changed much from antiquity to the present day. However, the availability of adequate supplies of potable water for its peoples may be a far more serious problem today than ever before, and the availability of non-conventional weapons of mass destruction in the hands of irresponsible political and military leaders poses unprecedented threats to the security of the peoples and states of the region.

The core region of the ancient Middle East was and for the most part remains a fertile crescent, but it has also been a crescent of conflict and turmoil. Although it continues to be such today, perhaps it may be different tomorrow. Perhaps we can learn from the mistakes of the past. Upon reflection, I believe the attentive reader can readily draw numerous analogies beween contemporary leaders in the Middle East and their ancient counterparts. However, if they are to avoid repeating the mistakes of the past, they must first understand the past. As the philosopher George Santayana once observed, those who do not learn from the past are condemned to repeat it. In some respects, the vast distance in time between the period discussed in this book and the present makes the task of understanding the past in relation to the present easier, and if this study can contribute toward that understanding, the author's efforts will be well rewarded.

Bibliography

The following is a list of references and secondary sources consulted in the preparation of this book. Because this is primarily a work of synthesis from a geopolitical perspective, I have drawn on the scholarly expertise of numerous authors for the bits of information pieced together here to form a geopolitical mosaic. Because the geopolitical perspective is not yet well developed among historians, I am unable to refer the reader to any single one of the works listed below for further elucidation of the premises and theses of this book.

Agathangelos. *History of the Armenians*. Translation and Commentary by Robert Thomson. Albany, N.Y.: State University of New York Press, 1976.

Aldred, Cyril. *The Egyptians*. London: Thames and Hudson, 1984.

Allen, R. E. *The Attalid Kingdom: A Constitutional History*. Oxford: Oxford University Press, 1983.

Ammianus Marcellinus. 3 vols. Translated by John C. Rolfe. Cambridge, Mass.: Harvard University Press, 1935.

Appian of Alexandria. *Appian's Roman History*. Vol. 2. Translated by Horace White. Cambridge, Mass.: Harvard University Press, 1912.

Arrian. *Anabasis Alexandri*. Vol. 1. Translated by E. Iliff Robson. Cambridge, Mass.: Harvard University Press, 1929.

Badian, E. *Roman Imperialism in the Late Republic*. Ithaca, N.Y.: Cornell University Press, 1968.

Baikie, James. *A History of Egypt*. Vol. 1. New York: Macmillan, 1929.

Baramki, Dimitri. *Phoenicia and the Phoenicians*. Beirut: Khayats, 1961.

Barker, John W. *Justinian and the Later Roman Empire*. Madison, Wisc.: University of Wisconsin Press, 1966.

Bengtson, Hermann. *The Greeks and the Persians: From the Sixth to the Fourth Centuries*. London: Weidenfeld and Nicolson, 1969.

Benjamin, Samuel G. W. *The Story of Persia*. New York: G. P. Putnam's Sons, 1896.

Bevan, Edwyn R. *A History of Egypt under the Ptolemaic Dynasty*. London: Methuen, 1927.

———. *The House of Seleucus*. 2 vols. New York: Barnes & Noble, 1966.

Bosworth, A. B. *Conquest and Empire: The Reign of Alexander the Great*. Cambridge: Cambridge University Press, 1988.

Brauer, George C. *The Young Emperors: Rome, A.D. 193–244*. New York: Thomas Y. Crowell, 1967.

Breasted, James H. *A History of Egypt*. New York: Charles Scribner's Sons, 1937.

———. *The Conquest of Civilization*. New York: The Literary Guild of America, 1938.

Bright, John. *A History of Israel*. Philadelphia: Westminster Press, 1959.

Burckhardt, Jacob. *The Age of Constantine the Great*. New York: Pantheon Books, 1949.

Burn, A. R. *Minoans, Philistines, and Greeks: B.C. 1400–900*. New York: Alfred A. Knopf, 1930.

———. *Alexander the Great and the Hellenistic Empire*. London: Hodder and Stoughton, 1947.

———. *Persia and the Greeks: The Defense of the West, c. 546–478 B.C.* London: Duckworth, 1984.

Bury, John B. *A History of Greece*. New York: Random House, n.d.

———. *History of the Later Roman Empire*. Vol. 2. New York: Dover Publications, 1958.

Carter, Elizabeth and Matthew W. Stolper. *Elam: Surveys of Political History and Archeology*. Berkeley, Calif.: University of California Press, 1984.

Chahin, M. *The Kingdom of Armenia*. London: Croom Helm, 1987.

Christensen, Arthur. *L'Iran sous les Sassanides*. Copenhagen: Ejnar Munksgaard, 1944.

Colledge, Malcolm A. R. *The Parthians*. New York: Frederick A. Praeger, 1967.

Conder, C. R. *The Hittites and Their Language*. New York: Dodd, Mead, 1898.

Cook, John M. *The Greeks in Ionia and the East*. New York: Frederick A. Praeger, 1963.

———. *The Persian Empire*. New York: Schocken Books, 1983.

Cormack, George. *Egypt in Asia: A Plain Account of Pre-Biblical Syria and Palestine*. London: Adam and Charles Black, 1908.

Culicon, William. *The Medes and the Persians*. New York: Frederick A. Praeger, 1965.

Curtis, Adrian. *Ugarit (Ras Shamra)*. Cambridge: Lutterworth Press, 1985.

Debevoise, Neilson C. *A Political History of Parthia*. Chicago: University of Chicago Press, 1938.

Demosthenes. Vol. 1. Translated by J. H. Vince. Cambridge, Mass.: Harvard University Press, 1930.

Diodorus of Sicily. Translated by C. Bradford Welles. Cambridge, Mass.: Harvard University Press, 1938.

Dodgeon, Michael H. and Samuel N. C. Lieu, eds. *The Roman Eastern Frontier and the Persian Wars (A.D. 226–363)*. London: Routledge, 1991.

Dougherty, Raymond P. *The Sealand of Ancient Arabia*. New Haven, Conn.: Yale University Press, 1932.

Downey, Glanville. *Ancient Antioch*. Princeton, N.J.: Princeton University Press, 1963.

Duncan, Andrew and Michel Opatowski. *War in the Holy Land: From Meggido to the West Bank*. Gloucestershire, U.K.: Sutton Publishing, 1998.

Durant, Will. *Our Oriental Heritage*. New York: Simon and Schuster, 1954.

Ehtecham, Morteza. *L'Iran sous les Achemenides*. Fribourg: Imprimerie St-Paul (Universite de Lausanne), 1946.

Elishe. *History of Vardan and the Armenian War*. Translation and Commentary by Robert W. Thomson. Cambridge, Mass.: Harvard University Press, 1982.

Ellis, J. R. *Philip II and Macedonian Imperialism*. London: Thames and Hudson, 1976.

Ellis, Walter M. *Ptolemy of Egypt*. London and New York: Routledge, 1994.

Errington, R. Malcolm. *The Dawn of Empire: Rome's Rise to World Power*. Ithaca, N.Y.: Cornell University Press, 1972.

———. *A History of Macedonia*. New York: Barnes & Noble, 1993.

Ferrill, Arthur. *The Fall of the Roman Empire: The Military Explanation*. London: Thames and Hudson, 1986.

Finnegan, Jack. *Archeological History of the Ancient Middle East*. Boulder, Colo.: Westview Press, 1979.

Foord, Edward. *The Byzantine Empire*. London: Adam and Charles Black, 1911.

Frankfort, Henri. *The Birth of Civilization in the Near East*. Garden City, N.Y.: Doubleday, 1956.

Frye, Richard N. *The Heritage of Persia*. Cleveland, Ohio: World Publishing, 1963.

Fuller, J.F.C. *The Generalship of Alexander the Great*. New Brunswick, N.J.: Rutgers University Press, 1960.

Gardiner, Alan. *Egypt of the Pharaohs*. London: Oxford University Press, 1961.

Garstang, John. *The Hittite Empire*. London: Constable, 1929.

Gershevitch, Ilya, ed. *The Cambridge History of Iran*. Vol. 2. Cambridge: Cambridge University Press, 1985.

Ghirshman, R. *Iran: From the Earliest Times to the Islamic Conquest*. Baltimore, Md.: Penguin Books, 1954.

Gibbon, Edward. *The History of the Decline and Fall of the Roman Empire*. 6 vols. New York: Harper & Brothers, 1879.

Grainger, John D. *Seleukos Nikator: Constructing a Hellenistic Kingdom*. London: Routledge, 1990.

Grant, Michael. *The Jews in the Roman World*. New York: Dorset Press, 1984.

Green, Peter. *The Year of Salamis 480–479 B.C.* London: Weidenfeld and Nicolson, 1970.

Grimal, Nicolas. *A History of Ancient Egypt*. Oxford: Blackwell Publishers, 1992.

Grousset, Rene. *The Empire of the Steppes: A History of Central Asia*. New Brunswick, N.J.: Rutgers University Press, 1970.

———. *Histoire de l'Armenie des Origines . . . 1071*. Paris: Payot, 1973.

Gurney, O. R. *The Hittites*. Harmondsworth, U.K.: Penguin Books, 1954.

Hall, H. R. *The Ancient History of the Near East*. 11th ed. London: Methuen, 1950.

Hammond, N.G.L. *The Macedonian State: Origins, Institutions, and History*. Oxford: Clarendon Press, 1989.

Hawkes, Jacquetta. *The First Great Civilizations*. New York: Alfred A. Knopf, 1973.

Herm, Gerhard. *The Phoenicians: The Purple Empire of the Ancient World*. New York: William Morrow, 1975.

Herodian. 2 vols. Translated by C. R. Whittaker. Cambridge, Mass.: Harvard University Press, 1970.

Herodotus. *The Persian Wars.* Translated by George Rawlinson. New York: Random House, 1947.

Herzog, Chaim and Mordechai Gichon. *Battles of the Bible.* New York: Random House, 1978.

Higgins, Martin J. *The Persian War of the Emperor Maurice (582–602).* Washington, D.C.: Catholic University of America, 1939.

Hignett, Charles. *Xerxes' Invasion of Greece.* Oxford: Oxford University Press, 1963.

Hinz, Walther. *The Lost World of Elam.* New York: New York University Press, 1973.

Hirsch, Steven W. *The Friendship of the Barbarians: Xenophon and the Persian Empire.* Hanover, N.H.: University Press of New England, 1985.

Hitti, Philip K. *The Near East in History.* Princeton, N.J.: D. Van Nostrand, 1961.

Huart, Clement. *Ancient Persia and Iranian Civilization.* New York: Barnes & Noble, 1972.

Humphreys, Eileen. *The Royal Road.* London: Scorpion Publishing, 1991.

Isaac, Benjamin. *The Limits of Empire: The Roman Army in the East.* Oxford: Clarendon Press, 1990.

Isocrates. Vol. 1. Translated by George Norlin. Cambridge, Mass.: Harvard University Press, 1928.

Jastrow, Morris. *The Civilization of Babylonia and Assyria.* Philadelphia, Penn.: J. B. Lippincott, 1915.

Jones, A.H.M. *Sparta.* New York: Barnes & Noble, 1993.

Josephus, Flavius. *Complete Works of Flavius Josephus.* Grand Rapids, Mich.: Kregel Publications, 1977.

Jouget, Pierre. *Macedonian Imperialism and the Hellenization of the East.* New York: Alfred A. Knopf, 1932.

Justinus, M. Junianus. *Justini Epitoma Historiarum Philippicarum Pompei Trogi.* Translated by John S. Watson. London: H. G. Bohn, 1853.

Kraeling, Emil G. H. *Aram and Israel.* New York: Columbia University Press, 1918.

Kramer, Samuel N. *The Sumerians: Their History, Culture, and Character.* Chicago: University of Chicago Press, 1963.

Lehmann, Johannes. *The Hittites: People of a Thousand Gods.* New York: Viking Press, 1977.

Livy. Vol. X-XIII. Translated by Evan T. Sage. Cambridge, Mass.: Harvard University Press, 1965.

Luttwak, Edward N. *The Grand Strategy of the Roman Empire.* Baltimore, Md.: Johns Hopkins University Press, 1976.

1 Maccabees. Translation and Commentary by Jonathan A. Goldstein. Garden City, N.Y.: Doubleday, 1976.

McGing, B. C. *The Foreign Policy of Mithridates VI Eupator King of Pontus.* Leiden: E. J. Brill, 1986.

Mackenzie, Compton. *Marathon and Salamis.* Edinburgh: Peter Davies, 1934.

Macqueen, J. G. *The Hittites and Their Contemporaries in Asia Minor.* London: Thames and Hudson, 1986.

Magie, David. *Roman Rule in Asia Minor.* 2 vols. Princeton, N.J.: Princeton University Press, 1950.

Malcolm, John. *The History of Persia*. London: J. Murray, 1815.

Marsden, E. W. *The Campaign of Gaugemela*. Liverpool, U.K.: Liverpool University Press, 1964.

Mommsen, Theodor. *The History of Rome*. Vol. 4. Glencoe, Ill.: The Free Press, n.d.

——— . *The Provinces of the Roman Empire from Caesar to Diocletian*. Vol. 2. Chicago: Ares Publishers, 1974

Moscati, Sabatino. *The Face of the Ancient Orient*. Garden City, N.Y.: Doubleday, 1962.

Moses Khorenats'i. *History of the Armenians*. Cambridge, Mass.: Harvard University Press, 1978.

Newby, P. H. *Warrior Pharaohs: The Rise and Fall of the Egyptian Empire*. London: Faber and Faber, 1980.

Nissen, Hans J. *The Early History of the Ancient Near East 9000–2000 B.C.* Chicago: University of Chicago Press, 1988.

Noth, Martin. *The History of Israel*. 2nd ed. New York: Harper & Brothers, 1960.

Oates, David. *Studies in the Ancient History of Northern Iraq*. London: Oxford University Press, 1968.

Oates, Joan. *Babylon*. London: Thames and Hudson, 1979.

Olmstead, Albert T. *History of the Persian Empire*. Chicago: University of Chicago Press, 1948.

Oman, Charles W. *The Byzantine Empire*. New York: G. P. Putnam's Sons, 1898.

Oppenheim, A. Leo. *Ancient Mesopotamia: Portrait of a Dead Civilization*. Chicago: University of Chicago Press, 1964.

Ostrogorsky, George. *History of the Byzantine State*. New Brunswick, N.J.: Rutgers University Press, 1957.

Parker, Henry M. D. *A History of the Roman World: From A.D 138 to 337*. 2nd ed. London: Methuen, 1958.

Parrot, Andre. *Nineveh and the Old Testament*. New York: Philosophical Library, 1955.

——— . *Babylon and the Old Testament*. New York: Philosophical Library, 1958.

Paton, Lewis B. *The Early History of Syria and Palestine*. New York: Charles Scribner's Sons, 1905.

Peters, F. E. *The Harvest of Hellenism: A History of the Near East from Alexander the Great to the Triumph of Christianity*. New York : Barnes & Noble, 1996.

Pettinato, Giovanni. *Ebla: A New Look at History*. Baltimore, Md.: Johns Hopkins University, 1991.

Piotrovsky, Boris B. *The Ancient Civilization of Urartu*. New York: Cowles Book, 1969.

Potts, D. T. *The Arabian Gulf in Antiquity*. 2 vols. Oxford: Clarendon Press, 1990.

Pritchard, James B., ed. *Ancient Near Eastern Texts Relating to the Old Testament*. Princeton, N.J.: Princeton University Press, 1955.

——— . *The Ancient Near East: An Anthology of Texts and Pictures*. Princeton, N.J.: Princeton University Press, 1965.

——— . *The Ancient Near East*, Vol. II, *A New Anthology of Texts and Pictures*. Princeton, N.J.: Princeton University Press, 1975.

Procopius. Vol. 6 (The Anecdota or Secret History). Translated by H. B. Dewing. Cambridge, Mass.: Harvard University Press, 1914.

Rawlinson, George. *The Seventh Great Oriental Monarchy*. 2 vols. New York: Dodd, Mead, n.d.

———. *The Seven Great Monarchies of the Ancient Eastern World*. Vol. 1. New York: John W. Lovell, 1870.

———. *History of Ancient Egypt*. Vol. 1. New York: Belford, Clarke, 1880.

———. *The Story of Parthia*. New York: G. P. Putnam's Sons, 1893.

Redford, Donald B. *History and Chronology of the Eighteenth Dynasty of Egypt*. Toronto, Canada: University of Toronto Press, 1967.

———. *Akhenaten: The Heretic King*. Princeton, N.J.: Princeton University Press, 1984.

———. *Egypt, Canaan, and Israel in Ancient Times*. Princeton, N.J.: Princeton University Press, 1992.

Rogers, Robert W. *A History of Ancient Persia*. New York: Charles Scribner's Sons, 1929.

Rostovtzeff, M. *A History of the Ancient World*. 2nd ed. 2 vols. Oxford: Clarendon Press, 1930.

Roux, Georges. *Ancient Iraq*. Harmondsworth, U.K.: Penguin Books, 1964.

Ruzica, Stephen. *Politics of a Persian Dynasty: The Hecatomnids in the Fourth Century B.C.* Norman, Okla. and London: University of Oklahoma Press, 1992.

Saggs, H.W.F. *The Greatness That Was Babylon*. New York: Frederick A. Praeger, 1969.

Salmon, Edward T. *A History of the Roman World: From 30 B.C. to A.D. 138*. 3rd ed. London: Methuen, 1957.

Sanford, Eva M. *The Mediterranean World in Ancient Times*. New York: Ronald Press, 1951.

Sayce, A. H. *The Ancient Empires of the East*. New York: Charles Scribner's Sons, 1911.

The Scriptores Historiae Augustae. 3 vols. Translated by David Magie. Cambridge, Mass.: Harvard University Press, 1953.

Scullard, H. H. *From the Gracchi to Nero: A History of Rome from 133 B.C. to A.D. 68*. London: Methuen, 1970.

Sealey, Raphael. *A History of the Greek City States ca. 700–338 B.C.* Berkeley, Calif.: University of California Press, 1976.

Segal, J. B. *Edessa "The Blessed City."* Oxford: Oxford University Press, 1970.

Sharpe, Samuel. *The History of Egypt*. London: Edward Moxon, 1846.

Sherwin-White, A. N. *Roman Foreign Policy in the East: 168 B.C. to A.D. 1*. Norman, Okla.: University of Oklahoma Press, 1984.

Sherwin-White, Susan and Amelie Kuhrt. *From Samarkhand to Sardis: A New Approach to the Seleucid Empire*. Berkeley, Calif.: University of California Press, 1993.

Sitwell, Nigel H. H. *The World the Romans Knew*. London: Hamish Hamilton, 1984.

Stark, Freya. *Rome on the Euphrates: The Story of a Frontier*. New York: Harcourt, Brace and World, 1966.

Steindorff, George and Keith C. Seele. *When Egypt Ruled the East*. 2nd ed. Chicago: University of Chicago Press, 1957.

Stoneman, Richard. *Palmyra and Its Empire: Zenobia's Revolt against Rome*. Ann Arbor, Mich.: University of Michigan Press, 1992.

Suetonius. *The Lives of the Twelve Caesers*. Translated by Joseph Gavorse. New York: Random House, 1959.

Sullivan, Richard D. *Near Eastern Royalty and Rome, 100–30 B.C.* Toronto, Canada: University of Toronto Press, 1990.

Sykes, Percy. *A History of Persia*. 3rd ed. Vol. 1. London: Macmillan, 1930.

Tacitus. *The Complete Works*. New York: Random House, 1942.

Tarn, W. W. *Alexander the Great*. Boston: Beacon Press, 1956.

Teggart, Frederick J. *Rome and China: A Study of Correlations in Historical Events*. Berkeley, Calif.: University of California Press, 1939.

Thucydides. *The Complete Writings of Thucydides: The Peloponnesian War*. Translated by Joseph Gavorse. New York: Random House, 1934.

Van Seters, John. *The Hyksos: A New Investigation*. New Haven, Conn.: Yale University Press, 1966.

Vasiliev, A. A. *History of the Byzantine Empire*. Vol. 1. Madison, Wisc.: University of Wisconsin Press, 1964.

Walbank, F. W. *Philip V of Macedon*. Cambridge: Cambridge University Press, 1940.

Weigall, Arthur. *A History of the Pharaohs*. Vol. 2. New York: E. P. Dutton, 1927.

Whitaker, C. R. *Frontiers of the Roman Empire: A Social and Economic Study*. Baltimore, Md. and London: Johns Hopkins University Press, 1994.

Williams, Stephan and Gerard Friell. *Theodosius: The Empire at Bay*. New Haven, Conn. and London: Yale University Press, 1995.

Winton, Thomas D., ed. *Documents from Old Testament Times*. New York: Harper and Row, 1958.

Wright, William. *The Empire of the Hittites*. London: James Nisbet, 1884.

Xenophon. *The Persian Expedition*. Translated by Rex Warner. Baltimore, Md.: Penguin Books, 1949.

——— . *Hellenica: Books V-VII*. Translated by Carleton L. Brownson. Cambridge, Mass.: Harvard University Press, 1968.

Yarshater, Ehsan, ed. *The Cambridge History of Iran*. Vol. 3 (1). Cambridge: Cambridge University Press, 1983.

Index

About the Author

MARTIN SICKER is an independent consultant who has served as a senior executive in the United States government and has taught political science at American University and George Washington University. He has written widely in the fields of political science and international affairs and is the author of numerous books on Middle East history and politics. His latest publications are *Reshaping Palestine: From Muhammad Ali to the British Mandate, 1831–1922* (Praeger, 1999) and *Pangs of the Messiah: The Troubled Birth of the Jewish State* (Praeger, forthcoming).

ISBN 0-275-96890-1

90000>

EAN

9 780275 968908

HARDCOVER BAR CODE